Covert Radar and Signals Interception

THIS BOOK IS DEDICATED TO THE MEMORY OF
ERIC ACKERMANN, OF WHOM HIS LIFELONG
FRIEND, DR R.V. JONES, WROTE IN A LETTER TO
PETER ACKERMANN IN FEBRUARY 1990:

HE WAS ONE OF THOSE WHO MADE THE WORLD
TICK, SOMETIMES TWO OR EVEN THREE TIMES AS
FAST AS IT HAD TICKED PREVIOUSLY.

COVERT RADAR AND SIGNALS INTERCEPTION

THE SECRET CAREER OF
ERIC ACKERMANN

PETER JACKSON & DAVID HAYSOM

IN ASSOCIATION WITH THE RADIO SOCIETY OF GREAT BRITAIN

Pen & Sword
AVIATION

First published in Great Britain in 2014 and reprinted in this format in 2022
by
Pen & Sword Aviation
an imprint of
Pen & Sword Books Ltd
47 Church Street
Barnsley
South Yorkshire
S70 2AS

ISBN 978 1 39902 051 0

Typeset in Ehrhardt by
Mac Style, Bridlington, East Yorkshire
Printed and bound in the UK by CPI Group (UK) Ltd, Croydon, CRO 4YY

MIX
Paper | Supporting
responsible forestry
FSC
www.fsc.org   FSC® C013604

Pen & Sword Books Ltd incorporates the imprints of Pen & Sword
Archaeology, Atlas, Aviation, Battleground, Discovery, Family History,
History, Maritime, Military, Naval, Politics, Railways, Select,
Social History, Transport, True Crime, and Claymore Press,
Frontline Books, Leo Cooper, Praetorian Press, Remember When, Seaforth
Publishing and Wharncliffe.

For a complete list of Pen & Sword titles please contact
PEN & SWORD BOOKS LIMITED
47 Church Street, Barnsley, South Yorkshire, S70 2AS, England
E-mail: enquiries@pen-and-sword.co.uk
Website: www.pen-and-sword.co.uk

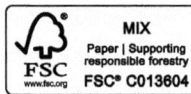

Contents

Illustrations and Maps

There are too many photographs in this book for them to be listed here. They are spread throughout the text and are placed as close as possible to the events they illustrate. Many of them have been from Dorothy Hartnell-Beavis's album of her married life to Eric Ackermann and her kindness is most gratefully acknowledged. Eric's younger son, Nick, sent several photographs of his father and mother in America in the 1970s, showing them in middle age. Those of his time at Obernkirchen from 1946 to 1959 are almost entirely of the airmen who served under his command, and there are only four showing Eric himself. The willingness of those veterans to lend these to us for copying is also very much appreciated. The opportunity has also been taken to include some photographs of RAF Obernkirchen taken many years after it closed. A visit in 2013 showed that the camp has now been completely demolished and there are now hundreds of solar panels covering the site.

The Ackermanns' domestic life in Obernkirchen has been covered by the photographs taken by Herr Rosocha who worked for the Ackermann family as a gardener and general handyman. Other photographs and maps come from printed and archive sources and are reproduced with the kind permission of the copyright owners.

Eric's life was in the shadows and he was very seldom photographed, particularly as his career developed after the war and the fact that there are only four of him in uniform shows his reluctance to have his photograph taken.

The maps make some attempt to show where he was during his RAF service, and there are also some extracts from the *London Gazette* showing his promotions and other important incidents during his twenty years in uniform.

Preface

There are two Royal Air Force mottos which sum up Eric Ackermann: 'Per Ardua ad Astra' (By Endeavour to the Stars), which is the motto of the Royal Air Force, and 'Kein Hindernis zu Hoch' (No Obstacle too High), the motto of No. 646 Signals Unit. His life story is that of a man who exemplified what these mottoes mean. He joined the Royal Air Force as a by-product of his work as a scientist, specializing in radar and later signals intelligence, with other diversions along the way. He was given an honorary commission as a Pilot Officer in 1940 and in his twenty year career as an air force officer he reached the rank of Wing Commander, though always with the give-away letters (CC) – Honorary Commission – after his name in the Air Force List.

Eric's career in the Royal Air Force began by spending his first two years in finding ways of confounding the enemy's radar and thereafter he worked mainly in intelligence and interception. The armed services in every country need to know, through listening to the enemy and then interpreting the results, where he is, what he is doing and what he is planning to do, and this was Eric's work for most of his time in the air force. After leaving the RAF he continued with similar work in the more advanced technologies of the time and this occupied his last twenty-five years. He worked largely behind the scenes and sometimes under conditions of considerable danger. Whatever he was given to do, whether it was potentially, or actually dangerous, or more routine, he always gave it everything he had.

Despite his long and distinguished service in war and peace he remains almost unknown in RAF historical circles, is seldom mentioned in histories of the period, appears erratically in the official records and is only remembered now by the airmen who served with him and some of those German civilians who worked for him in Obernkirchen. The exception to this invisibility is to be found in the papers of Professor R.V. Jones, who, in a way, 'made' Eric Ackermann. These, in Churchill College, Cambridge, have more references to Eric than any other source and the help of the staff there is gratefully acknowledged. Research in the Liddell Hart Centre for Military Archives at King's College, London, produced valuable information and the help of the staff there is also acknowledged. The National Archives at Kew was used extensively and proved to be a splendid source of essential material. The Purbeck Radar Trust was the source for much material about the Telecommunications Research Establishment at Worth Matravers.

More information from personal rather than official sources has come from Eric's family: his first wife Dorothy, his brother Keith, who sadly died in 2011, and Keith's wife Eileen also gave valuable support and encouragement as well as much essential information about his early years in the RAF. His sons, Peter and Nick and Peter's wife Judy have been unstinting in their support for the project and provided us with insights into their remarkable father as well as filling in many gaps in the story. Dorothy died in 2013 at the great age of 93 and her contribution to the story has been crucial, giving the authors information which could never have been discovered otherwise.

Former air force colleagues in North Africa and Germany have shown what it was like to work with Eric Ackermann and their help is gratefully acknowledged: Frank Brigham, Alan Cox, Geoff Eastough, Harry English, Bert Evans, Colin Gammon, Charles Garrad, John Gay, Alan Harris, Brian Lagden, David Lewis, Ted Lines, Geoff Lipscombe, Keith Lofthouse, Ron Matheson, Charlie Olito, Stan Platts, John Pope, Malcolm Stewart, John Vickerman and Mervyn Williams. The help given by members of the Bad Eilsen Association, which includes those who served at Obernkirchen and who are specifically named above, has been much appreciated. Their testimonies pay eloquent tribute to the kind of man he was, both as a commanding officer and a human being. Geoff Lipscombe, the Association's Secretary, was most helpful in encouraging Association members to contribute their memories. Andrew Jackson gave valuable help in formatting the book for publication and in scanning many of the photographs.

David Haysom carried out painstaking interviews with several Obernkirchen residents who had contacted him after he had written articles for the local newspaper. This was a real scoop and to find those who had worked for the family in their home gave us an unrivalled picture of their life there. They are: Frau Hobohm, Herr Rosocha, Dr Stephan Walter, Herr Fritz Walter, Herr Horst Börner and Frau Vera Freise-Folle.

The book has the sub-title '*The Secret Career of Eric Ackermann*'. Eric was a hero – his George Medal proves that – but a hero in the shadows, behind the scenes and out of sight, at least to the majority who were his contemporaries in the RAF. Their testimonies pay eloquent tribute to the kind of man he was, both as a commanding officer and a human being.

The photographs vary in quality but they are all gratefully acknowledged. Dorothy Hartnell-Beavis, Eric's first wife, kindly lent her own collection of photographs of them both in their married life together. Herr Rosocha, who worked for Eric and his family at Obernkirchen, provided some of the few we have of him in Germany (the airmen themselves seldom took photos of their commanding officer); most of the rest have been taken from published works and their permission is also acknowledged. Nick Ackermann provided photographs of Eric and his second wife, Marianna, mainly of their time in America.

A note on names and photographs. Eric Ackermann is referred to in this way or just as Eric, and occasionally by his rank, but never as Ackermann except when quoting from external sources. His first wife is Dorothy, Dorothy Ackermann or Dorothy Hartnell-Beavis, depending on the context, and his second wife is Marianna rather than her first Christian name of Gizella. The quotations and photographs in the book are a mixture, ranging from a telegram sent by Churchill to Stalin in 1944, to the airmen's Christmas Day menus in 1957.

Eric Ackermann deserves much wider recognition. Perhaps this book will go some way towards putting that right.

We wish to thank Laura Hirst and Ken Patterson, our editors at Pen and Sword, for their very hard work in converting our raw material into such a fine book and for guiding us through the shoals of publishing, with which neither of us were familiar.

The authors wish to thank their wives, Helga (Haysom) and Christine (Jackson) for their patience and tolerance during the years when this book was in preparation.

David Haysom, Peter Jackson – November 2013

Chapter One

Family Background and Early Life

S ometime between 1783 and 1786 a young German coach builder named Rudolph Ackermann left his native country and came to England via a brief stay in Paris. He was born in Schneeberg in Saxony in 1764. Rudolf came from a long line of landowners who had their own coat of arms and could trace their history back for seven generations before his birth, to one George Ackermann, who flourished around 1530. Another ancestor, Jakob Ackermann, had the misfortune to be shot by a passing soldier during the Thirty Years' War which devastated Europe and particularly Germany between 1618 and 1648, though he himself was not a combatant, but just happened to be in the wrong place at the wrong time.

After an apprenticeship as a saddle maker in his father's business, Rudolph was encouraged to take up drawing, possibly with an eye to becoming a draughtsman. As he showed considerable talent it was decided that he should train as a carriage designer. His training began in Leipzig, and after a short period there he moved to Hueningen near Basle in Switzerland, where he completed a three year apprenticeship in his new trade. He then joined a firm of leading carriage makers in Paris before deciding, at the age of about twenty, that London would offer him more opportunities.

This was indeed what happened and within a short time he had established valuable contacts which eventually led to his setting up a business at 101 The Strand, though not as a carriage maker but as a printer of fine art prints and books. The business also sold what it produced and it is still trading as Arthur Ackermann Ltd. at its premises in Lowndes Street, London SW1.

He was both an astute businessman and an inventor, and in 1801 he patented a method for waterproofing paper and cloth which he then manufactured at a factory in Chelsea. He was enterprising in other ways too, and was one of the first people to light his premises with gas. He also patented the Ackermann steering geometry, which was a device to link the steering of a wheeled vehicle so that the wheels on the inside and outside could trace the same radii and therefore did not slide on wet

Arthur Ackermann Ltd.'s premises in Lowndes Street. This photograph was taken in 2011.

surfaces. He was of such eminence that his portrait, painted by the French painter François Mousset between 1810 and 1814, hangs in a prominent place in the National Portrait Gallery in London. It is reproduced here by kind permission of the Gallery. Rudolph was also a philanthropist and the money he raised to aid his home city of Leipzig after its devastation by Napoleon in 1813 made him a public figure in both Germany and England.

Rudolph's grandson Arthur (1830–1914) took the firm to new heights, not that it really needed any more acknowledgement by those who counted in London society. By the middle of the nineteenth century it had received the royal warrant as publishers and fine art dealers to, successively, Queen Victoria, Queen Alexandra and Queen Mary. The *London Gazette* states that

Rudolph Ackermann (1764–1830): a portrait painted by François Mousset. © National Portrait Gallery, London

Ackermanns could style itself 'By appointment to Queen Victoria [etc.] with authority to use the Royal Arms', although it adds that the warrant did not carry the right to fly the Royal Standard. By this time Arthur was living in Regent Street and his son Rudolph was at another fashionable address, 113 Park Village East, Regent's Park. Their occupation is given as 'Gentleman', which shows that they were of independent means rather than having to demean themselves by working for a living, although clearly they were not entirely idle. The side seems to have been let down a bit by Rudolph's son, Eric's grandfather, and Eric's father ordered his two sons never to ask about their grandfather nor to mention his name. He, however, was an exception to the honest and industrious lives which others in the family led. Although none of this is strictly relevant to Eric's own life story, it shows his unusual and enterprising ancestry and perhaps explains how he came to be the man he was.

Five generations after Rudolph's birth, his great-great-great-grandson, Eric George was born, and it is not too fanciful to find in him some of Rudolph's qualities and abilities. Eric certainly showed determination and enterprise and inherited his ancestor's talent for engineering and invention. Another similarity is in their strong Christian faith. Rudolph became a regular worshipper at St. Clement Danes Church in the Strand, close to his home and place of business. It has been the RAF church

since 1958 and Eric may well have attended services there during his time in the air force. Rudolph died in 1834 at the age of seventy.

Eric was born on 6 October 1919 in the village of Gurnard near Cowes, on the Isle of Wight. The long-standing family name of Rudolph was not passed on to him, but he did inherit his father's second name of George, as a nod in the direction of all those previous Ackermanns. Eric's father, however, was another Rudolph, who was born in Holborn in 1891 and worked as a railway clerk. He was the last member of the family to bear his famous ancestor's Christian name which had been handed down through so many generations. Eric's mother was Dorothy Webb, and she and Rudolph were married in 1915 in Camberwell. The young couple were both deeply religious people although they belonged to different churches, he to the Plymouth Brethren and Dorothy to the Baptist Church.

In 1915, Rudolph joined the army and was sensibly put into the Railway Operating Division of the Royal Engineers and reached the rank of corporal. His name in the War Office record is given as Randolph G. Ackerman (one 'n'). Randolph was a clerical error, but the single 'n' was not, as Rudolph had decided to erase the final 'n' from his surname to make it seem less German. This was probably a prudent move as anti-German feeling was running high and people were, it is alleged, even given to kicking dachshunds in the street. The Royal Family changed its name from the House of Saxe-Coburg-Gotha to Windsor and the Battenbergs to Mountbatten. The Ackermanns just docked an 'n'.

The Railway Operating Division was formed in 1915, the year when Rudolph enlisted, and its task was to operate railways in all theatres of the war. Its personnel were mostly railway employees and Rudolph was posted to the Western Front where he worked on the railways which moved the British heavy guns to and from their firing positions near the front line. When the war ended he returned to his civilian occupation, but Dorothy remained on the Isle of Wight where she had been living since her husband enlisted in the army. During the war she had been working for the Sopwith Aircraft Company making steam-bent wooden ribs for aircraft wings at a factory in Cowes. One of Sopwith's sub-contractors on the island was the Fairey Aviation Company for which her father worked.

Dorothy returned to the mainland to join Rudolph shortly after Eric's birth, living at No. 35 Shelley Crescent in Southall, and her second son Keith was born there on 3 September 1931. The boys' father had been on Sunday School trips there as a child and was convinced that this was where he wanted to live. Southall at that time was on the edge of the west London green belt and with trams running from Shepherds Bush as far out as Uxbridge, travel from central London to their new home was an easy journey.

Rudolph's work as a railwayman meant that the family could enjoy special rates for train travel, which they used for holidays in Devon and their annual visits to the Isle of Wight. Keith Ackermann, Eric's younger brother, remembers that they had a happy childhood, although his parents were 'very upright and God-fearing'. Their house in Shelley Crescent, which was not really a crescent at all, but a cul-de-sac with a pan at one end, provided Eric with an early opportunity to show his skill at telecommunications. No. 35 was on one side of the pan and Eric ran a telephone line across it to the house of a friend, Jack Hall, who lived on the opposite side.

Although he was a Plymouth Brother, Rudolph was now attending the Methodist Central Hall in Southall which backed onto Southall Technical College. This was ideally placed for Eric, because on Sundays he would disappear from the Young Men's Group, which was where he was supposed to be, and go to the college laboratory. There was an early television receiver there, which Eric took Keith to see in 1938. Also in 1938, Eric went to Germany on a visit organized by the college and Keith remembered that his brother was disgusted by the behaviour of the Hitler youth.

Maybe other interests distracted Eric, but remarkably, despite being coached by his mother, he failed to be selected for a grammar school education and so continued at his all age elementary school until 1934, when he reached the leaving age of fourteen. He then moved to Southall Technical College (now the Southall campus of the Ealing, Hammersmith and West London College) where he stayed for five years. It seems that this 'failure' stayed with Eric all his life, for when his own sons were at the same stage in their education he urged them to work hard to achieve what he had failed to do. For Eric himself, however, it turned out for the better, at least according to his brother Keith who believed that had he attended a grammar school he might not have had the remarkable career which he was to enjoy for the rest of his life.

On leaving school in 1934 and going to Southall Technical College (now the Southall Campus of the Ealing, Hammersmith and West London College), he took the City and Guilds Ordinary and Higher National Certificates in Electrical Engineering which automatically gave him a qualification of the Institution of Electrical Engineers. These achievements were just as valuable as the Higher School Certificates awarded in grammar schools, and as University degrees, at least in their usefulness in building a good career. The fact that Eric later worked with people with strings of higher degrees and other academic qualifications did not hinder his own career prospects, as he brought to his chosen profession a wealth of practical experience, gained in action in wartime.

After five years Eric left Southall College in 1939, having, as Keith recalled 'done extremely well', focussing his studies on 'electro-tec'. He was also working as a laboratory assistant, possibly to help pay his way through college and it was through this that he made his only contribution to a published book. This was in collaboration with his tutor, one E.T.A. Rapson, on a book entitled *'Experimental Radio Engineering'*, first published in 1940. It had considerable success and ran into five editions by the time the final edition was published in 1964. The book's title page says that Mr Rapson was 'assisted by E.G. Ackermann, Student I.E.E., C. and G. Final Laboratory Assistant'. Eric's part in it was slight, being limited to drawings rather than text, but he nevertheless appears on the title page, and is generously shown as the joint author.

In the preface Mr Rapson wrote, 'The author acknowledges the help received from his former assistant, Mr E.G. Ackermann, to whom fell the task of drawing the diagrams and preparing the experimental work'. The 3rd edition, 1944, still describes Eric as 'Student I.E.E., C. and G. Final,' but also as a Junior Scientific Officer at the Air Ministry. National security prevented any reference to his RAF status (he was a flight lieutenant by the time of the 3rd edition), nor to his George Medal. The 4th and 5th editions omit his name from the title page and the updated preface also ignores him, although the preface to the first edition is included in these later editions. Eric must have taken some pride in this and the title page of the first edition is shown at the end of the chapter.

By the time the first edition was published Eric was already working

EXPERIMENTAL
RADIO ENGINEERING

BY

E. T. A. RAPSON
M.SC. (ENG.), LONDON
A.C.G.I., D.I.C., A.M.I.E.E., ASSOC.I.R.E., F.P.S.
WHITWORTH EXHIBITIONER
SENIOR LECTURER IN ELECTRICAL AND RADIO ENGINEERING
SOUTHALL TECHNICAL COLLEGE

ASSISTED BY

E. G. ACKERMANN
STUDENT I.E.E., C. AND G. FINAL
LABORATORY ASSISTANT

LONDON
SIR ISAAC PITMAN & SONS, LTD.
1940

Eric's first venture into print.

for the Telecommunications Research Establishment (TRE), whose staff he joined on 19 February 1940. A staff list shows that his salary in the AIII grade was £200 per year, though another column in the list gives his actual annual pay at £206-11-0d. Another list shows him as working in Dundee for what was then called the Air Ministry Research Establishment.

So, after a contented and mainly uneventful childhood and adolescence, and qualifying as an electrical engineer, Eric may have wondered what the future held for him, particularly as war was imminent. His first wife, Dorothy, remembers that he wanted to join the Royal Air Force, but to his great disappointment he was rejected. He had proved that he was an adventurous and lively young man with excellent technical qualifications in a subject which was just what the RAF needed, but the decision to join the TRE was to change his life totally. There is no evidence that he was headhunted, though he probably was, given what he had to offer his new employer. Very soon though, the man who was to become his mentor and lifelong friend, Dr Reginald Victor Jones, was to appear in his life and to be responsible for the many twists and turns his career was to take over the next twenty years.

Chapter Two

The Telecommunications Research Establishment

The Telecommunications Research Establishment was established at Worth Matravers, four miles from Swanage in Dorset, in May 1940. It had started life in 1936 as the Bawdsey Research Station (BRE) at Bawdsey, near Orford Ness in Suffolk and then continued very briefly as the Air Ministry Research Establishment (AMRE) in Dundee. The BRE and its successor organizations arose from the British government's realization in the mid-1930s that Germany's intentions were far from peaceful, despite constant assurances from Berlin that peace in Europe was the cornerstone of its foreign policy. As far as the BRE, the AMRE and the TRE were concerned, the main impact of this was on the work carried out by what, despite all these initials, was one and the same organization which was re-named almost every time it moved.

Although Britain had made strenuous efforts to rearm from the mid- 1930s onward, even by 1939 it was still woefully short of strength in the Army and the Royal Air Force. The RAF did have 1,982 operational aircraft on its strength in 1938, but most of these were obsolete or obsolescent and no match for the modern Luftwaffe, which was nearly double the strength of the RAF by August 1939. The actual figure was 3,750 first-line aircraft with a further 3,000 to 3,500 being used for training. All of these were newly developed machines with little or none of the out-of-date aircraft types with which the RAF was equipped.

Furthermore, the Luftwaffe's Condor Legion had gained invaluable and brutal experience in the Spanish Civil War, earning particular notoriety in the devastating bombing raid on Guernica in April 1937. The British government's refusal to become involved in that war was probably politically correct, but militarily it set its armed forces, and particularly the RAF, at a disadvantage when full-scale war broke out in Europe a few months after the end of the conflict in April 1939.

Nevertheless, the RAF's strength was to grow rapidly in the first few years to reach 4,287 aircraft by 1942. The old machines had mostly been withdrawn from front-line service to be replaced by the new Hurricane and Spitfire fighters, the Mosquito fighter-bomber and the Lancaster four-engine bomber. Meanwhile, the country had to defend itself against the worst, which had been described by the then Prime Minister, Stanley Baldwin, in a speech in the House of Commons in 1932 in which he said that 'the bomber will always get through'. This was still remembered seven years later and it cannot have been a particularly helpful contribution to the nation's morale. Fortunately, Baldwin proved to be wrong, because by 1939 much progress had been made, both in aircraft production itself and in indirect defence against attack, which Baldwin could not have predicted.

Research into ways of preventing the bomber getting through had been intensifying since 1935, and by the outbreak of war the RAF and its civilian scientists had developed methods of identifying enemy aircraft approaching Britain and also of deflecting them away from their target area. And finally there were the newly acquired Hurricanes and Spitfires which reinforced in the most direct way possible the country's ability to defend itself against aerial attack.

Before taking the story to the point where Eric Ackermann becomes involved, it is important to look at the development of radar and of the jamming systems used against enemy aircraft. In 1935 a new detection system called Radio Detection and Ranging (christened RADAR by the Americans in 1941) was being developed (some say invented, though in fact there had been primitive radar-type systems in other countries a few years earlier) by a scientist named Robert Watson-Watt, who patented his invention in 1935. Sir Henry Tizard (Chairman of the Aeronautical Research Committee throughout the war), writing in 1946, describes the invention of radar in these words:

'When I went to Washington in 1940 I found that radar had been invented in America about the same time as it had been invented in England. We were, however, a very long way ahead in its practical applications to war. The reason for this was that scientists and serving officers had combined before the war to study its practical uses. This is the great lesson of the last war.'

Although Eric did not join the TRE until five months after the war had started, he came to be one of those scientists who continued to practise the lesson which Tizard had so much praised. His own position was unusual, combining the holding of a commission in the RAF with a post as a Scientific Officer in the Air Ministry, and so had a foot in both camps.

It is worth recalling that Neville Chamberlain, the Prime Minister at the time of the Munich Agreement, strongly supported the development of radar and indeed rearmament generally, despite his reputation for indifference. The time gained by Munich was used to improve Britain's ability to defend itself, something in which radar was to play a vital part. Richard Brett-Knowles confirmed this in a letter he wrote to R.V. Jones on 17 August 1989:

'Chamberlain was intimately associated with Lord Swinton [Secretary of State for Air, 1935–38] and [Sir Henry] Tizard [Chairman of the Aeronautical Research Committee throughout the Second World War] in finding an answer to the air threat posed by the late A. Hitler, Esq. This puts a vastly different interpretation on the meetings at Munich.Chamberlain knew the potentiality of our radar, but he also knew our lamentable strength in 1938. I have no doubt that he bought a year in which to rearm at the expense of his own reputation, fooling Hitler rather than the other way round.'

Brett-Knowles, who had spent part of the war working for the TRE as a Junior Scientific Officer and later gave lectures on the history of radar, knew what he was talking about. He also served in the RAF and by 1944 he was a Squadron Leader serving in the Middle East.

In 1936, Robert Watson-Watt became Superintendent of the newly-formed Bawdsey Research Station to continue the further trials and development of the new system whose function was to use radio waves to detect metallic objects. It could operate from the ground, at sea and in the air, using equipment fitted to specially adapted ships and aircraft. The effect on the skyline of southern and eastern England was the appearance of sets of huge masts pointing to and across the English Channel and the North Sea.

Irreverently known to his staff as Lord Kilowatt, though he was never given a peerage, Sir Robert Watson-Watt's importance to the British war effort cannot be overestimated. His work gave Britain a decisive advantage over the Luftwaffe and its associated scientists and planners in ensuring that approaching aircraft were detected early in their flight and also, for our own pilots, the ability it gave them to navigate in fog and darkness. By way of compensation the British Government later awarded him £50,000 for his wartime work. He was not without an appreciation of his own worth and when he was given the temporary rank of Group Captain on a visit to Holland in 1945, he complained that he should be an Air Commodore. He was sharply reminded that that was the rank used by Winston Churchill.

Later in his life, in a trivial incident in Canada, Sir Robert became the biter bit when he was pulled over for speeding, having been spotted by a radar gun. He is reputed to have said to a bemused policeman: 'Had I known what you were going to do with it I would never have invented it!' To mark his experience he wrote the following poem which he called 'Rough Justice'.

'Pity Sir Robert Watson-Watt,
Strange target of this radar plot.
And thus, with others I can mention
The victim of his own invention
His magical all-seeing eye
Enabled cloud-bound planes to fly
But now by some ironic twist
It spots the speeding motorist
And bites, no doubt with legal wit,
The hand that once created it.
Of Frankenstein who lost control
Of monsters man created whole,
With fondest sympathy regard
One more hoist with his petard.
As for you courageous boffins
Who may be nailing up your coffins,

particularly those whose mission
Deals in the realm of nuclear fission.
And learn with us what's Watson-Watt.'

With the approach of war, Bawdsey was felt to be vulnerable to air attack and in September 1939 the Research Station was moved far away to a site at Dundee Teacher Training College with a new name: The Air Ministry Research Establishment.

The concerns over Bawdsey were caused by the appearance of an LZ130 Graf Zeppelin airship which hovered over the station in May, and again in August 1939, for almost a whole day trying to identify its RDF (radio direction finder) transmissions. Despite this surveillance, however, Bawdsey was never attacked. The Germans must have been aware that a change of some kind had been made, if not precisely that it had moved, but presumably considered that it was just not worth bothering to attack the site. Nevertheless, a small outstation was maintained there for some years after the main base had moved.

There had been a suggestion by A.P. Rowe, who had succeeded Watson-Watt as Superintendent of the BRE, that Bawdsey should move to Poling, a CH (Chain Home) radar station in West Sussex, not far from the Fighter Command station at Tangmere, but fortunately Watson-Watt persuaded Rowe against the idea. Poling turned out to be one of the most heavily bombed radar stations during the Battle of Britain. This was not at all like Rowe, who seems to have been the most careful of men.

Dr Bill Penley, founder of the Purbeck Radar Trust, outside the Red and White towers of Bawdsey Manor in 1997. The background has remained virtually unchanged in over sixty years. from '*Pioneers of Radar*' by Colin Latham and Ann Stobbs, by kind permission.

Having persuaded Rowe to drop Poling as the BRE's next home, Watson-Watt recalled a conversation he had had the year before on a visit to Scotland. To recall past times, but also with an ulterior motive, he decided to visit Dundee University College, of which he was an alumnus, and in the course of an apparently casual conversation with the Principal, mentioned that there was a secret installation way down south in England which had to move further northwards. That the discussion was informal, if not actually light-hearted, can be judged by E.G. Bowen's account of it which is quoted by David Zimmerman:

'[Watson-Watt] must have been overcome by nostalgia and remembrance of things past because he mentioned that there is a problem – in the event of war being declared, some members of an important Defence Laboratory might need emergency accommodation.

'"No problem at all", said the Vice-Chancellor [sic: i.e. the Principal] gaily, "we would be only too glad to help in a case like that" – without enquiring too closely into how many staff were involved and how much space was required.'

Unfortunately, the Principal neglected to mention this fact to anyone else, and although Watson-Watt took it at face value, he nevertheless failed to follow it up and confirm by letter, telephone or anything else, his erstwhile host's generous offer. So when the elaborate process of moving began and cars and lorries appeared carrying awkward looking equipment and, followed by groups of scientists and their support staff, they found to their surprise that they were not expected.

The Principal was found and must have been somewhat shamefaced, but being what E.G. Bowen in '*Radar Days*' calls 'an accommodating soul', he offered the new arrivals two rooms, each twenty feet square, which was all he could spare for the several hundred people who had either already arrived or were still on their way by land, sea and air. Much of the blame must attach to Watson-Watt for not forewarning the Principal with the full details of his plans. But nevertheless there they all were and so the newly-named Air Ministry Research Establishment began to settle down to life 350 miles from its former home.

Although this would have been inconvenient to the staff, to say the least, there was the additional problem that an essential requirement for the unit was a large airbase nearby. Dundee's nearest airfield of any kind was at Perth. This was a small civilian establishment twenty-two miles away which was quite unsuitable on the grounds of size if nothing else. It had just one small hangar, a few offices and a single grass runway.

Not only that, but the staff discovered that the electricity and the radio sets, which the citizens of Dundee tiresomely insisted on using, interfered with their equipment, and furthermore, the Air Ministry had refused to compensate the AMRE's civilian staff for the cost of their move. And even worse, the move from Bawdsey interrupted vital research and delayed the introduction of a night defence which it was intended would start operating early in 1940.

David Zimmerman, in '*Britain's Shield: radar and the defeat of the Luftwaffe*', describes this move as 'perhaps as destructive as the most devastating German air attack'. This comment is echoed by E.G. Bowen: 'There had been a monumental blunder, from which the AMRE, as it was called, took more than a year to recover'. Dr Bowen knew what he was talking about, as he was a Senior Scientific Officer at the Bawdsey Research Station and head of the Airborne Radar Group. For good measure, he was later awarded the CBE and became a Fellow of the Royal Society.

So bad were things that one A.C.B. Lovell, a junior scientist at the time, wrote an excoriating letter to a colleague, P.M.S. Blackett, in which he describes the deteriorating morale of the researchers and technicians and the appalling performance of the A1 sets:

'In six tests out of about twelve it has caught fire in the air, due to extremely bad design. The power packs flash over, thin flex leads break off etc. etc.The tester knows exactly how to put things right in future designs, he is never consulted and has given up trying to be helpful in sheer despair.It is designed by men sitting in secluded offices here, who to be frank, have no social sense and no vestige of organizing ability. By the peculiar [Air Ministry] system they have attained positions for which they are in no way fitted. The situation is really unbelievable. Here they are shouting for hundreds of aircraft to be fitted. The fitters are working seven days per week, and occasionally fifteen hour days. In their own words "the apparatus is tripe even for a television receiver."'

The writer and the recipient of this missive were not insignificant junior staff with a grievance. A.C.B. Lovell became Sir Bernard Lovell and one of our most distinguished radio astronomers, and P.M.S. Blackett (later Sir Patrick and later still Lord Blackett) won the Nobel Prize for physics in 1948.

Eric Ackermann arrived all unknowing into this maelstrom of discontent in Dundee in February 1940, having been seen off by his fiancée, Dorothy Radcliffe, at Kings Cross Station to travel north on the Aberdonian night train. He must have wondered what he had got into. In fact in December 1939, two months before Eric arrived, the Air Ministry had already decided that the AMRE should move once again. The disadvantages of Dundee had proved to far outweigh its very few advantages. The new location could hardly have been further away, four hundred miles to the south at Worth Matravers, on the Dorset coast near Swanage.

It took a while to organize everything down south and it was not until five months later, on 6 May 1940, that the AMRE – about to be given yet another new name, the Telecommunications Research Establishment – became operational on this windy cliff-top site overlooking the English Channel.

Dundee had proved to be too remote from the heart of things in the south of England, and its rapidly changing weather conditions made it doubly unsuitable for both ground and air operations, as well as being uncomfortably cold in the winter. The weather in the south was warmer, despite the wind off the sea, and more settled, and Worth Matravers had the additional advantage of being relatively near a fully operational RAF station at Boscombe Down, near Amesbury in Wiltshire. Radar was already in place at Worth where there was a CH station. Another basic requirement which Dundee had lacked was a good

Dundee Teacher Training College, where Eric worked from February to May 1940. Reproduced from '*Pioneers of Radar*'.

electricity supply and Worth had that as well. Dundee could only offer a DC system, with consequent limitations on the station's operations, whereas Worth had both AC and DC, as well as being spared radio interference from the local populace.

It was not only for the quality of its electricity that Worth was an improvement on Dundee. Unless you were from Scotland or the north of England it was a better location for the staff as well. The seaside resort of Swanage was a pleasant place to live, despite being within easy range of enemy bombers. In fact Swanage had more air raid warnings (964) than London (which had 920), though raids on the scale of those suffered in London were few and 'only' twenty people were killed.

The move required complex planning, with much of it involving the staff in frequent reconnaissance forays to Dorset. Files held at the National Archives (AVIA 7/602 and 603) reveal in great detail the care taken to make sure that Worth Matravers was ready on time. The TRE Superintendent, Arthur Percival Rowe, known as Jimmy, worked immensely hard, sending off letters, memos and instructions to his superiors and to his own staff, and to one man in particular, Mr J.E. (Joe) Airey, a senior manager, who was the luckless recipient of many of these.

An airfield was essential for the new organization. RAF Christchurch was considered and Bernard Lovell paid a visit both to Worth itself and to Christchurch to inspect their facilities. He reported that 'the accommodation and situation is considered to be excellent in every respect', meaning Christchurch not Worth Matravers, which had to be built more or less from scratch. In the event, however, Christchurch was rejected in favour of the better equipped Boscombe Down, its main deficiency being its single grass runway, which was also too short for the heavier aircraft, particularly Wellingtons, the staple types used by the TRE at Boscombe Down. Nevertheless, it was used later in the war by American P47 Thunderbolt fighter-bombers to prepare for D-Day, by which time the runways had been greatly improved. In 1940 it had just one building, twenty feet square, to accommodate the air and ground crews needed to fly and service around twenty aircraft.

Land at Worth Matravers was requisitioned and two local farmers suffered the loss of much of their acreage. Mr Airey was asked to check on the electricity and Rowe told him that 'one of the bottlenecks will be the provision of electric supply and I should be glad if you would chase this. Please also write a letter to the Southern National Omnibus Company for my signature, telling them more or less what is going to happen and asking for season ticket rates.' The outcome of the latter enquiry was that the bus company's timetable was inconvenient for the workers at Worth Matravers as the route ran to Worth village, which was an eight minute walk from the site, and the fares at 1/- (one shilling) ordinary return and 7d. (seven pennies) workers' return were reckoned to be too high. At today's values these would be £1.96 and £1.27 respectively. Further prodding by A.P. Rowe and J.E. Airey resolved the problem: the bus route and times were changed and the fares reduced.

Mr Rowe then became concerned with cycling and on 19 January 1940, he sent a memo about it, again probably to Joe Airey: 'The site of the new station is approx. four miles from Swanage, starting from sea-level and rising to 400 ft. above sea level on the site. This will indicate that the outward journey from Swanage is a steady climb and to gain information a two-way journey by bicycle was carried out, the outward journey taking twenty-five minutes and the return trip being done in ten minutes'. As Eric Ackermann did not have a bicycle he would be travelling to work mainly by car, but probably also on the newly rescheduled bus service.

Throughout the summer of 1940 building work was frantic, with the erection of huts and towers as well as earth barriers for protection against air raids. Worth would need six CHL (Chain Home Low) twenty foot towers, five huts, two laboratories, drawing offices, a communications building and a first aid room, and presumably, though not mentioned, somewhere for rest, refreshment and mild recreation. The TRE was to expand so rapidly, that by the time of its move to Malvern in May 1942, it had grown from an initial staff of 200, to 2,000, and reached 3,500 by the end of the war. Many of the staff, including Eric, lived in Swanage.

It was not only civilian staff who had to be accommodated, though to help with this the Air Ministry had begun house-hunting for them in April, but also a small group of airmen of No. 32 Maintenance Unit, who were due to arrive from RAF St. Athan. To round it off, it was noted that 'The Southern Railway provided valuable assistance in unloading the equipment from Dundee at Swanage Railway Station and this was gratefully acknowledged by the Superintendent, A.P. Rowe'. Dundee was finally evacuated on 4 May and two days later Worth Matravers started operating.

The date of the move was timely, because just four days later the phoney war was swiftly transformed into something far from phoney and became a horrifying reality with the German invasion of the Low Countries and France. Within six weeks those countries were defeated and occupied, leaving Britain's nearest neighbours in German hands. As far as the air defences were concerned, the enemy now controlled all the airfields in France, Belgium and Holland, just a short flying time away.

Eric arrived with his TRE colleagues and he moved into lodgings at 128 High Street, Swanage, a small house in a Victorian terrace, with a splendid view from the rear of the house over the bay. The row of houses even had a name, Gordon Villas. The photograph of the house, taken in May 2010, shows some modernization, but the basic structure is as Eric would have found it seventy years earlier.

Marriage soon followed and on 3 August 1940 he married Dorothy Radcliffe of 28 Bushey Road, Harlington, at Harlington Baptist Chapel, Middlesex. They had met while Eric was still at Southall College where she worked as a secretary. Dorothy's father was William Edward Radcliffe, described on the marriage certificate as an Employment Manager working for the Fairey Aviation Company, for which Eric's maternal grandfather had also worked. The bridegroom's occupation is shown as a Radio Research Engineer. He and his wife were both 20-years-old. He was now firmly settled at Worth Matravers and until his marriage had been living in rooms which were suitable for a bachelor and a civilian, though not for a newly married man. Not only did his marital status change, but also his role within the TRE, which was to develop in ways he could not have foreseen when he first joined the organization.

128 High Street, Swanage, where Eric lived until his marriage in August 1940.

Eric and Dorothy on their wedding day, 3 August 1940.

He now needed a house for Dorothy and himself where they could begin their married life and he found one in a 1930s development east of the centre of Swanage. This was to be their home for the next two years. Despite the threat and indeed the actuality of bombing raids, Swanage was a very pleasant place to live, a quiet seaside resort, though not as quiet as it had been, before the arrival of several hundred scientists and their support staff, a unit of the RAF and the appearance of large quantities of strange buildings and masts on the cliff top near the town.

The couple were now living further from Worth Matravers than Eric's lodgings in High Street had been. Not having a bicycle, and anyway, probably not fancying such a long cycle ride to work, particularly the uphill section, Eric acquired a car soon after his wedding. This was a Morris 10/4 series 2 coupé model, first manufactured in the 1930s and a popular runabout of the period. The windscreen was hinged at the top, so that it could be opened to allow a bracing breeze to cool the driver and passenger, an asset in those pre-air conditioning days. It was a suitably dashing vehicle for a young RAF officer and his bride and it was his pride and joy, though not for long, as they soon sold it for £5, replacing it with something more sumptuous and imposing. This was a 4-door Vauxhall 14 Saloon. Eric certainly liked cars and his sons remember that he had several impressive vehicles in Germany in the 1950s.

3 Bonfields Avenue in 1941, Eric and Dorothy's first home, where they lived from 1940 to 1942.

A favourite place for the TRE staff to go for lunch, or after work was the Square and Compass pub in Worth Matravers. The pub was known to its regulars as the Sqump, and to the scientists as the Sine and Cosine, after the mathematical terms used in their research. Eric and Dorothy were regular customers and Dorothy remembered it with great affection, recalling that the drinks and meals were served through a small hatch and not over the bar counter. They still are. The pub has since been modernized but this has not spoilt its appearance as a traditional English country pub. It was as

Eric and Dorothy's Morris car outside their Swanage house.

This is their next car, a Vauxhall 14, though not this particular vehicle, whose number plate appears to be German.

The Square and Compass in 1940.

And in 2010.

important a refuge for the hard-pressed scientists of the TRE as the pubs near their stations were to the aircrews of Fighter and Bomber Command and it made its own small contribution to the war effort by feeding and refreshing some of the country's finest scientific brains.

Having departed from Bawdsey because of fears of aerial attack, and then returning to the south of England eight months later, after the largely wasted interval in Dundee, the TRE was off again two years later, and in May 1942 made its final wartime move to Malvern in Worcestershire, requisitioning Malvern College for the duration of the war. The reason was the same as that which caused the departure from Suffolk. This time, however, it did at least retain its name, though only for two years, becoming in 1944 the Telecommunications and Radar Research Establishment. Further name changes continued after the war, and all of these must have kept the rubber stamp industry doing brisk business and what started as the Bawdsey Research Station back in 1936, became in 2000, after many more name and organizational changes, an establishment split into two entities, QuinetiQ, a private company, and the government owned Defence Science and Technology Laboratory.

RAF Boscombe Down was the base for No. 109 Squadron with its Vickers Wellington bombers, which were to figure prominently in Eric Ackermann's two years there. The relationship between the TRE and the squadron was crucial and Michael Cumming in '*Beam Bombers*' writes that, 'Together, TRE and No. 109 formed a remarkable duo, with Oboe their common ground, the one unable to succeed without the other and both contributing their expertise, and, sadly, their lives too, civvies as well as in uniform'.

Eric at work in the dispersal hut at RAF Boscombe Down.

This photo of Dorothy was taken in 1943 for her MI5 identity card. By this time she and Eric had left Dorset and were living in London, although by then Eric was mainly in North Africa, from where he frequently returned to report to Dr R.V. Jones.

This is a blurred picture of Eric in uniform with Dorothy, taken in the garden of 3 Bonfields Avenue.

Oboe needs a brief explanation. It was the code name for a British aerial blind bombing targeting system, based on radio transponder technology. It came into operational use in December 1941 and was similar to the German X-Gerät system. It required two stations at locations in England which were some distance apart to send a signal to the bomber which carried a radio transponder. The transponder then transmitted the signals back to their original stations and the time it took for the signals to complete the round trip gave the distance to the bomber, so giving it a better chance of finding the target.

Eric Ackermann's close association with the squadron may have given him a taste for service life and it also got him into the RAF by the back door after his apparent rejection in 1939. Such an adventurous young man may have felt too, that, having endured a large number of hazardous flights, he did not wish to remain a ground-based boffin. Maybe he also liked the uniform. Who wouldn't have been proud to wear the same uniform as the Few of the Battle of Britain in 1940? Eric's wife Dorothy says he wore his uniform for much of the time, even when working at Worth Matravers. At Boscombe Down he had to, this being an operational airfield and Eric an operational

Grade	Name	Married or Single	Number of Children	Station
J.S.Os (Contd)	Mr J. E. Curran	M	–	
	Mr E. D. Fry	S		
	Mr J. Ingham	S		
	Mr F. C. Thompson	S		(Marconi) Peterabam
	Mr T. A. Blackett	S		"
	Mr D. O'C. Roe	S		"
	Mr E. W. Bristow	M	–	"
	Mr J. Brooks	S		"
	Mr N. G. Callen	S		"
	Mr M. M. Barber	S		"
	Mr G. A. Rennie	M		"
	Mr W. M. Williamson	M	1	"
	Mr G. Chapman	M	–	"
	Mr J. A. W. Stroth	S		"
	Mr H. F. Symmons	M		"
	Mr P. Taylor	M	–	
	Mr F. Kay	S		
	Mr D. W. Millington	M		Dundee
	Mr J. N. Marshall	S		Dundee
	Mr W. Pickwick	S		
	Mr D. J. Wootton	S		
	Mr D. D. Williams	S		Dundee
	Mr R. Aspinall	S		
	Mr E. G. Ackermon	M	–	Dundee
	Mr J. B. Birks	M		
	Mr D. Watson	S		
	Mr G. C. Sutton	S		
	Mr E. Rollinson	S		
	Mr J. L. Putnam	S		
	Miss M. O. Francis	S		B.R.S.
	Mr J. H. Smith	S		B.R.S.
	Mr A. T. Llewellyn	S		Dundee
Assts I	Mr F. E. King	M	1	R.A.E.
Assts II	Mr H. Grayson	S		Dundee
	Mr T. A. Gifford	M	1	Dundee
	Mr R. A. Russell	S		B.R.S.
	Miss E. B. Sudbury	S		B.R.S.
	Mr O. G. Williams	S		Dundee

This undated list from the W.B. Lewis Archive in the Liddell Hart Centre for Military Studies at King's College, London. Eric is shown as a Junior Scientific Officer based in Dundee and is married. This is confusing as he had moved to Worth Matravers three months before his marriage. His name is fifteenth from the bottom of the page. It shows that were some scientists who were still at the Bawdsey Research Station and on this page at least there is no one at Worth Matravers.

Another undated list from W.B. Lewis's papers, showing Eric's name sixth from the bottom of the list, followed by his date of birth and of his appointment, his salary and the section where he worked.

officer, but at Worth Matravers this was something of an affectation. Despite this there are very few photographs of him in uniform.

The TRE, now settled in Dorset, had to seek ways of obtaining as much information as it could about the newly captured German airfields, which were now only a short flying time away. In particular, they were concerned with the types of aircraft flying from France and the navigational beams they used. To do this, the RAF now had to fly almost daily missions from Boscombe Down to France, the Low Countries and even Germany, with the RAF aircrew taking with them some of the TRE's civilian scientists. Although the flying time from Boscombe Down to northern France was short, for the many investigative and bombing flights which 109 Squadron was to undertake, they were as dangerous as any other flights over enemy territory, no matter how near or far they were.

Just as the RAF used the time bought by the Munich agreement to increase its strength and improve its radar countermeasures, so did the Luftwaffe. During the winter of 1938/39 an experimental flying unit, No. 100 Air Signals Battalion (Luftnachrichten-Abteilung 100) was established to train pilots in the use of two radar systems, Knickebein (Crooked Leg) and X-Gerät (X-Apparatus) which were to cause the RAF considerable trouble in the early months of the war. Knickebein was able to bend the beams to lock onto a bombing target, and an aircraft flying at 20,000 feet could receive the signals 270 miles away, with the range increasing the higher the aircraft flew. The beams were only a third of a degree wide, resulting in an accuracy of one mile in 180.

X-Gerät operated on a higher frequency and used a series of beams, each named after a river (Weser, Rhine, Oder and Elbe) to find the target, the target was located when three of the beams intersected. This was a more accurate system than Knickebein and it was used to great effect in raids on Birmingham, Wolverhampton and Coventry in 1940. The two systems were eventually defeated by the work of scientists such as R.V. Jones and Robert Cockburn and many others. To get to the point when the scientists could overcome the enemy's beams, Eric Ackermann's job was to fly sorties over the radar stations in France to investigate at first hand how they could be blunted.

We shall see below how often he made these flights, as did others, and how dangerous they could be. This was not just passive reconnaissance from a safe distance but low-level flights over the German bases themselves.

The TRE staff were initially required to work seven days a week until some lightening of the burden was allowed and Saturday was made a day off to allow those who were off duty on Sunday to participate in what were called the 'Sunday Soviets', which A.P. Rowe established. These were held every Sunday at the Grosvenor Hotel in Swanage and later at Malvern College after the TRE had moved there, and Rowe invited senior military personnel to meet with the rest of the research engineers and scientists working with the team. The meetings were informal and even the most junior staff were encouraged to contribute their ideas. A photograph of one of the meetings at Malvern College was discovered in the papers of Dr W.B. Lewis, housed in the Liddell Hart archive. Dr Lewis became the Superintendent of the TRE after Rowe's retirement.

Eric Ackermann was not present at this meeting and he was never to go to Malvern, for reasons given later. Nevertheless, he probably did occasionally attend the Sunday Soviets at the Grosvenor Hotel. Sadly, this majestic hotel, which in the 1930s had been a favourite of Enid Blyton's, who set some of the Famous Five stories in the Swanage area, is no more. It was demolished in the 1960s, a victim of architectural vandalism. Its replacement is a particularly unappealing block of flats.

Later in the book there is a photo which includes a large number of senior RAF officers and some distinguished Civil Service scientists, including Lord Cherwell, who is seated fifth from the left. A.P. Rowe, wearing glasses, is seated next but one to him, with an Air Commodore sandwiched between them. There are two Air Vice-Marshals, five Air Commodores, six Group Captains and twenty-two civilians of varying degrees of importance and civil service rank.

Before leaving the Grosvenor, it is worth mentioning that W.H. Penley, writing in his article *'The Early Days of Radar'*, places the photograph not at Malvern College, but in the Grosvenor Hotel and the date as 26 October 1941. He also says that Lord Cherwell attended the meeting to tell A.P. Rowe that is was essential for the RAF to 'have a self-contained device in bombers which would allow them to navigate and strike targets deep in Germany.' The point is not where and when, but what the photograph signifies – an informal gathering of civilian and military experts, engaged in brainstorming. This particular photo is probably an exception and the meeting may have been a more formal high-level conference than most of the others held in both Swanage and Malvern.

It is hard to imagine, for instance, that such an important man as Lord Cherwell, the government's Principal Scientific Adviser, would bother to come down to Malvern or Swanage, all the way from London, to attend an 'ordinary' run of the mill 'Sunday Soviet'. Nevertheless, this is the only photograph we have and so it must suffice. Similarly, those thirteen senior RAF officers were hardly there for something routine, or an informal chat, or even an unscripted brainstorming session.

Possibly following Lord Cherwell's instructions, more work on this 'self-contained device' followed and tests were successfully carried out in a Blenheim. So much so that one of the scientists involved, P.I. Dee, a Principal Scientific Officer in Group 12 (10cm systems), rushed into Rowe's office to tell him and Rowe exclaimed 'This will win the war'.

This was a large claim, made in the excitement of the moment, but insofar as the bombing campaign which really took off in 1942 was concerned, it was of incalculable importance. And if you believe that the bombing of Germany between 1942 and 1945 shortened the war, then Dee was certainly right, despite the enormous cost to Bomber Command in terms of lives lost. He was yet another of those young scientists who achieved great distinction later in his life. In 1943 he was appointed to the Chair of Natural Philosophy at Glasgow University and in due course he was awarded the CBE and became a Fellow of the Royal Society. This was very like R.V. Jones, who received the same award and later held the same chair at Aberdeen University.

The TRE housed as much brain power in its own specialisms as Bletchley Park did in the field of decryption and many of those who worked in these places (including Bawdsey, Dundee and Malvern) went on to have spectacularly successful careers in the world of scientific and technological research. Eric Ackermann stands comparison with any of them and in his own varied and unexpected way his achievements were at least equal to theirs.

Ernest Putley, a senior colleague at the TRE, described Rowe as 'a complex character with a strong sense of mission, so difficult to work with'. He was both a brilliant physicist and also a meticulous administrator (his concern over bus routes, fares and cycling to and from Worth Matravers illustrate this). His health suffered and after the war he moved to Australia, becoming the first Scientific Advisor to the Australian Government and also the Vice-Chancellor of the University of Adelaide. He returned to England on his retirement and died in 1976 at the age of seventy-eight.

A 'Sunday Soviet' meeting in Malvern College, again from the Lewis Archive. Lord Cherwell is seated third from the left in the front row with A.P. Rowe next but one to him and an Air Commodore sandwiched between them.

He was another man, like R.V. Jones, who deserved a knighthood. Instead, like Jones, he was awarded the CBE. The British have never, until recently, been overgenerous with awards and Dr Jones, who did as much as anyone to bring about victory, was left out of the honours he so richly deserved. Even Sir Robert Watson-Watt, the inventor, or at least the man who made it work, only received a knighthood and never a peerage.

It is hardly surprising, given the stress he must have been working under, that Jimmy Rowe occasionally got cross and on 13 July 1940 he let fly with this volley to Dr Bowen:

A.P. Rowe, with a photograph of Hermann Goering on the wall and Monty's photograph of Rommel in his caravan in North Africa.

'I was astonished yesterday to find that a considerable number of the staff are using the canteen for tea and refreshments in the middle of the morning. No man in normal health needs refreshment in a morning so short as one from 8.45 am to 1 pm and in general the Canteen is not to be used in the morning. This instruction needs, of course, to be interpreted with common sense. If a member of the staff is feeling unfit or has been working out in the wet or cold, there is no objection whatever to his use of the canteen.

I think everyone knows that I am strongly in favour of tea in the afternoon. In most cases, however, it will save time if the tea is made by the junior member of staff concerned, or by use of the very willing members of the typing pool.'

A.P. Rowe

The reference to members of the typing pool, who would all have been women, was just about acceptable in those days, but would have landed Mr Rowe in a good deal of trouble if he had written it today. Attention to detail, even to the extent of checking who was in the canteen when they shouldn't have been, was typical of Rowe: if genius is an infinite capacity for taking pains, then he was certainly that.

Eric Ackermann may have been expecting to see out the war as a scientist at Worth Matravers and elsewhere, but his youthful career took a decisive turn when he was given an honorary commission as a Pilot Officer in the Royal Air Force with effect from 11 September 1940. Official confirmation appeared in the *London Gazette* of 26 September, with the actual gazetted date being 26 August. Eric is in good company, at least as far as the interesting and aristocratic names of some of the other officers are concerned. The service numbers of all but two of those in this small extract are consecutive, the exceptions being Eric and the aristocratic Pilot Officer, Lord Auckland. It looks like a production line, which in a sense it was, given the speed with which new pilots had to be trained. Eric is alone in having no number at all and he had to wait until 1950 for this important addition to his identity, by which time he was a Squadron Leader. His number was 192868.

He makes his first appearance in the Air Force List for December 1940 as a newly-minted Pilot Officer and his name remained there for the next twenty-five years. His entry is brief:

Hon. P.O. Seniority 11/9/40. (Ad)(V.R.)
[i.e. Admin. Branch (Volunteer Reserve)]

There was a condition attached to his commission and his service record states that the 'council had approved his appointment to an Hon. Commission in the A & SD Branch, RAFVR., in the rank of P/O, with permission to wear uniform only when flying in armed service aircraft, and not in the normal course of his ground duties.'

The restriction on wearing his uniform is clear enough, but Dorothy Hartnell-Beavis has recalled that he was in uniform for most of the time at Worth, as well as at the RAF station and on airborne operations. These conditions seem unfair, excluding him from the usual privileges extended to officers and underlining the fact that he was only granted a commission and the accompanying uniform, to protect him if he was ever captured by the enemy. It is as if the Air Ministry was warning him not to think he was a real officer and his rank and uniform would carry no weight at all with the rigid RAF hierarchy.

Eric was commissioned because his work was to involve flying over enemy territory as a scientist/observer and it was realized that if he fell into enemy

The *London Gazette* for 26 September 1940 recording Eric's commission as an Honorary Officer.

hands as a civilian and wearing civilian clothes, he would have been treated as a spy and been tortured and either executed or sent to a concentration camp. There was an incident in November 1941 when an aircraft of 109 Squadron, with another civilian scientist/honorary officer on board, was shot down and the crew, with one exception, were captured and sent off to PoW camps. This, if nothing else, shows how important Eric's commission was, though there were other practical benefits as well.

From 1950 to 1965 his name appears in both the grandly named British Imperial Calendar and Civil Service List and the Air Force List, even though he had left the RAF in 1960. He never appeared in the RAF's Retired Officers List. Honorary officers were not granted that privilege, and so, having left the air force, they disappeared from sight. There is just one document, the minutes of a meeting held at RAF Watton in 1961, which gives his name as Mr E.G. Ackermann. His progression up the Civil Service List corresponded to his regular promotion in the RAF lists. Until 1950 he was too junior in the Civil Service hierarchy to be included.

The details of the two ladders in his career are:

1951	Not listed
1952–54	Ministry of Supply. Senior Scientific Officer. Seconded to another unnamed department, probably the Air Ministry.
1955–56	Ministry of Supply. Principal Scientific Officer – seconded as above.
1960–65	Air Ministry. Principal Scientific Officer – seconded as above.

His RAF promotions, as recorded in the Air Force List and the *London Gazette*, are:

11 September 1940.	Commissioned as Honorary Pilot Officer.
11 January 1943	Promoted to Flight Lieutenant. [the Air Force List missed out his promotion to Flying Officer, although Keith Ackermann recalled that he certainly did not skip this rank.]

14 June 1949   Promoted to Squadron Leader.

27 January 1954   Promoted to Wing Commander (Secretarial Branch).

2 February 1960.   On this date the London Gazette records the end of his career in the RAF as:

'Commission relinquished (class CC). Wing Commander (on cessation of duty): E.G. Ackermann, GM (192868) 28 September 1959.'

Keith Ackermann explained that Eric's 'increasing RAF rank came alongside his promotions in the Civil Service, there being equivalent ranks in both the armed forces and the relevant branches of the Civil Service'. The other civilian scientists in the list had an impressive range of academic and professional qualifications, but Eric had to make do with the George Medal, an honour, nevertheless, which his colleagues could not match. He had also acquired practical experience in the field which they did not have.

From his arrival at the TRE he appears regularly in a variety of official records, and many of these sources are quoted below. He also features in several books published after he had left the RAF, including R.V. Jones' *'Most Secret War'* and its companion volume *'Reflections in Intelligence'*, published in 1978 and 1989 respectively. *'Most Secret War'* is dedicated to Eric and seven others singled out by Jones for their achievements and qualities which he particularly admired. The dedication describes him as a radio observer and Dr Jones regarded him not only as a courageous officer, but also as an innovative scientist and someone who never shirked any task presented to him. The fact that several of these tasks were to take place after the war reinforced his view, although the dedications do refer specifically to the dedicatees' wartime actions. Others in the list worked for the Special Operations Executive, and for the French and Polish Resistance. It is a somewhat random list of people who performed with great bravery, but the only one whom Eric would have known was Harold Jordan, with whom he is bracketed much later in his career in a public speech by Dr Jones.

Here is the full dedication, given in capital letters, as in the book:

TO ALL THOSE IN NAZI-OCCUPIED EUROPE WHO IN LONE OBSCURITY AND OF THEIR OWN WILL RISK TORTURE AND DEATH, LIKE 'AMNIARIX' (JEANNE ROUSSEAU, VICOMTESSE DE CLARENS), LEIF TRONSTAD, THOMAS SNEUM, HASAGAR CHRISTIANSEN, A.A. MICHELS, JEAN CLOSQUET, HENRI ROTH, YVES ROCARD, JERZY CHNIELEWSKI, AND THE AUTHOR OF THE OSLO REPORT: TO RECONNAISSANCE PILOTS LIKE TONY HILL: TO RADIO OBSERVERS LIKE ERIC ACKERMANN AND HAROLD JORDAN: AND TO THE MEN OF THE BRUNEVAL RAID. FOR 'COURAGE IS THE QUALITY THAT GUARANTEES ALL OTHERS'.

The earliest reference to Eric in *'Most Secret War'* is to an incident some months before he officially joined the TRE, when he and a fellow engineer were part of a team tracking the German battleship the *Admiral Graf Spee* as it steamed westwards through the English Channel:

'This watch [on wavelengths across the Straits of Dover in September 1939] was undertaken by some young workers from the Telecommunications Research Establishment, including D.J. Garrard and E.G. Ackermann, and it was almost immediately fruitful, for they detected radar-type transmission on a wavelength of 80 centimetres, which appeared to be ranging on our convoys and directing the fire of the German guns.'

The ship reached the Atlantic Ocean and set off southwards, where for several months she harried shipping in the south Atlantic and regularly sank British merchant ships. Eventually she was tracked and attacked off Montevideo in December 1939 by three Royal Navy ships, *Achilles*, *Ajax* and *Exeter*, and was so badly damaged that her captain ordered her to be scuttled. This was a boost to British morale and a rare success in the early months of the war.

Eric Ackermann and Derek Garrard could hardly have made a better start to their careers than under the sharp eye of R.V. Jones, who was to make sure that he employed them again and again during the war years and beyond. The two were to remain firm friends for the rest of their lives and they became part of a group of scientists who were to work together and keep in touch for more than thirty years. In the May 1942 Director's Chart for the TRE, Garrard is shown as a Senior Officer working in the

The *Admiral Graf Spee* at the 1937 Spithead Review.

Outside Duty (OD) Group. Affiliation to this group probably meant that he was not at Worth Matravers all that much, but was working on special assignments, rather as Eric himself would be later in the war. In 1945 R.V. Jones recommended Garrard for the MBE, though it seems that the award was not granted. This is another example of the British reluctance to recognize important achievements.

Jones reveals in his book that shortly before the bombing of London began on 7 September 1940, the cryptographers at Bletchley Park had 'broken a new line of Enigma traffic', which included

Dr Reginald Victor Jones, Eric's superior officer during and after the Second World War and also a lifelong friend of Eric and his family.

accounts of a direction finding beam and a very specific reference to one with the electrifying name 'X- GERÄT' (X-Apparatus), which used a series of beams to locate a target, and was being fitted to an aircraft whose callsign is identified as belonging to 'Kampfgruppe 100', a unit which had attempted to attack Birmingham on 13/14 August 1940. The TRE first intercepted radar transmissions on 28 September 1940, while searching in the Dover area.

The transmissions came from a set being used to direct the fire of German long-range batteries located between Calais and Boulogne onto convoys in the English Channel. Dorothy remembers that Eric was detached to Dover to carry out these interceptions and she and their dog Myfanwy, whom they called Fum, sat in a seafront shelter watching the shells coming over from France. Dorothy, again inevitably accompanied by Fum, also went with Eric on his detachments to RAF stations in Suffolk, Stradishall and Mildenhall. Dorothy said that he was able to get her into the stations without being stopped and checked.

The TRE was organized into twenty-six groups, based mainly at Worth Matravers, but also in the neighbouring villages of Leeson and Durnford. Eric's lowly position in the hierarchy is revealed in a comprehensive list of its staff in 1942, held on the Purbeck Radar website. His name is once again spelt with one 'n', and he is shown as being a Junior Scientific Officer in Group 6 which was responsible for countermeasures. The list does not mention his honorary RAF commission and indeed in every staff list which has been traced his RAF rank is omitted. He was of course a civilian at Worth Matravers and only metamorphosed into an RAF officer at Boscombe Down.

In charge of group 6 (and also group 5, the other counter-measures group) was one R.W. Cockburn, who headed the team of scientists and engineers developing radio countermeasures for the Royal Air Force. Robert Cockburn later received the

Congressional Medal of Merit, the highest United States honour for war service that any civilian, whether American or foreign, can receive, and was knighted in 1960. He was ten years older than Eric and a man with a forceful character who must have had an influence on the burgeoning young scientist. Dorothy remembers him in unflattering terms.

In the same list, but appearing in a mysterious group called 'Elsewhere', are two distinguished RAF officers, Group Captain John 'Cats' Eyes' Cunningham and Wing Commander (later Group Captain) Guy Gibson. Also in 'Elsewhere' were Sir John Cockcroft, Sir Henry Tizard and Sir Robert Watson-Watt. Their category is not surprising as elsewhere is where they mostly were. They are described as 'people included for their significant role (but stationed elsewhere).'

The TRE was able to recruit the finest scientists in the country in much the same way as Bletchley Park did with mathematicians, crossword puzzler solvers and others with the right kind of brain. There were other famous names on the list: Sir Alan Hodgkin, FRS, and Sir Bernard Lovell (both Group 12, 10cm systems), and Sir Martin Ryle, FRS, later the Astronomer Royal and a Nobel Prize winner for physics (Group 25, Post Design Services). One can therefore see something of the circles in which Eric was moving, however far down the pecking order he was.

As well as the alphabetical and group lists, there is also the Director's Chart dated 12 March 1942. This shows the complex organization of the TRE. All these lists are held by the Purbeck Radar Museum Trust and are reproduced with the Trust's kind permission.

Among other subsequently distinguished scientists are Philip Dee, mentioned above, who designed the Automatic Gun-laying Turret; Robert Dippy, a pioneer of radio navigation who developed GEE; Frank Jones, who worked on the Oboe blind bombing system; Sir Bernard Lovell, (also referred to above) whose greatest achievement was the building of the radio telescope at Jodrell Bank; E.G. Bowen, who in 1935 had developed the first radar that could detect an aircraft, and, since this list must end somewere, Sir Robert Cockburn, who developed the radar jamming system known as Window and called chaff. His obituary described this work as 'a main contributor to the reduction of civilian [air raid] casualties'. These are just a few of the extraordinary and dedicated people with whom Eric worked at Worth Matravers.

5 Countermeasures

Surname	Initials	Title	Group	Grade	From	Full Name, Awards & Notes
Alder	N.L.		5	AIII		?Norman? Alder
Allen-Williams	D.J.		5	AIII		
Bagnall	I.A.		5	AIII		
Cockburn	R.		5	SSO		Sir Robert (Bob) Cockburn
Hall	P.D.		5	AIII		Peter Hall
Hardwick	J.		5		EMI	
Heaton	W.		5		MAR	
Mayer	D.W.F.		5	AIII		
Norman	W.J.		5	AIII		
Russell	V.		5	AIII		
Thorne	T.G.		5	SO		George Thorne

6 Countermeasures

Surname	Initials	Title	Group	Grade	From	Full Name, Awards & Notes
Ackerman	E.G.		6	JSO		
Barthorpe	C.H.		6	AII		
Belham	N.D.N.		6	AII		
Cockburn	R.		6	SSO		Sir Robert (Bob) Cockburn
Court	G.W.C.		6	AIII		
Curran	J.E.	Miss	6	JSO		
Farvis	W.E.J.		6	SO		Prof John Farvis
Fishwick	W.		6	JSO		
Forster	H.J.		6		MAR	
Garland	L.P.M.		6	I/A		
Hampshire	J.G.		6	AIII		
Hawkins	G.A.		6	I/A		
Moncrieffe	I.A.		6	AI		
Platt	D.C.		6	AIII		
Silversides	R.G.		6	AIII		

Part of the TRE staff list for 1942. Eric worked in Group 6 and its alphabetical arrangement places him at the top.

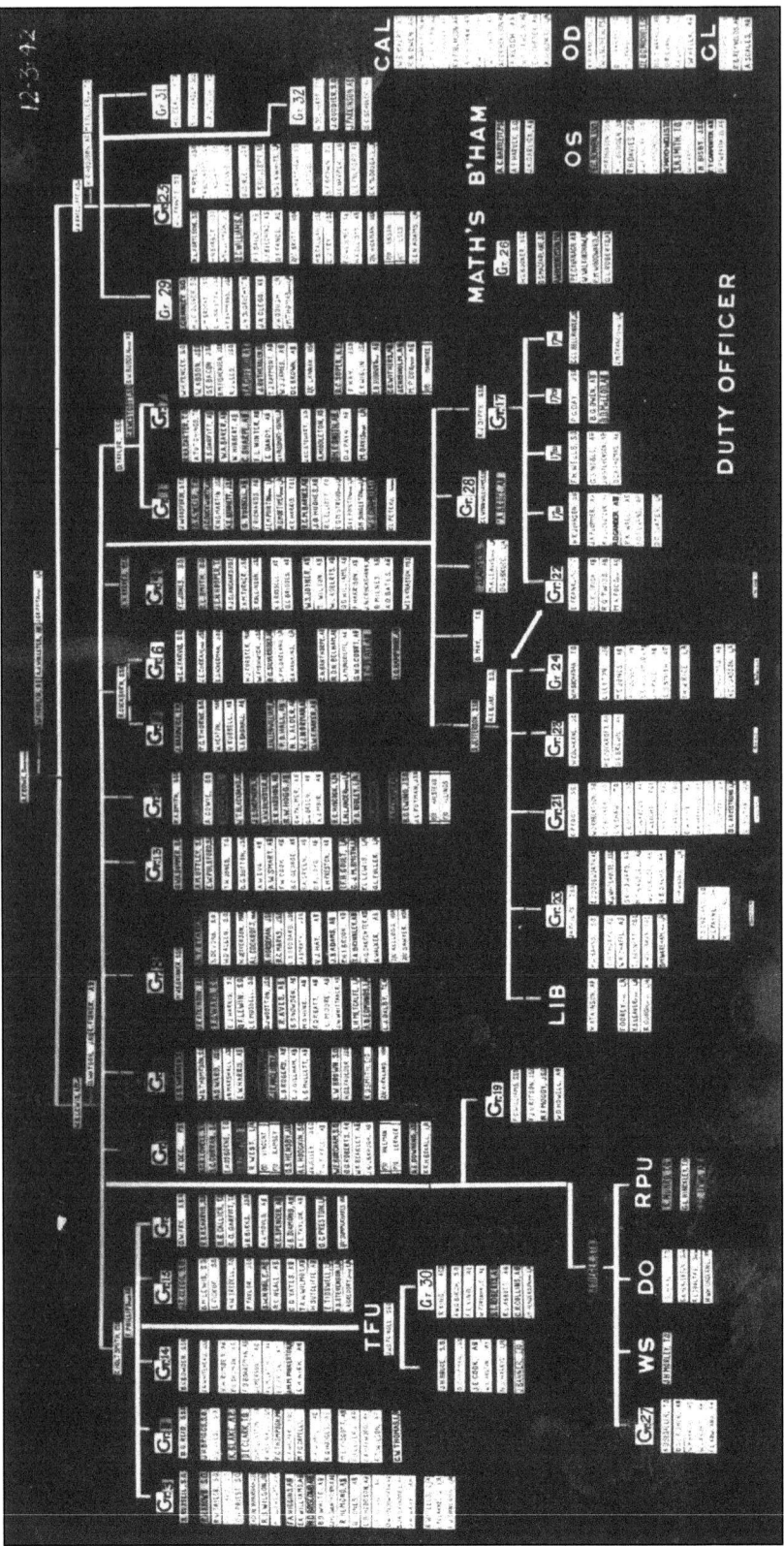

The Director's Chart for March 1942. Eric is listed in Group 6. Reproduced by kind permission of the Purbeck Radar Museum Trust.

Back now to R.V. Jones, who writes that the 'RAF unit which had made the original sortie to discover the Knickebein [Crooked Leg] beams in 1940... had taken to flying down the beams in order to bomb the transmitters, and thus to making radio and radar observations over France. Specialist observers from the Telecommunications Research Establishment had volunteered for the flights, and had received RAF commissions in case they were lost on operations'. Eric was one of these observers. The X-Gerät beam referred to above was superior to Knickebein as it had a longer range and it eventually took over at least as far as the more distant raids were concerned.

Eric reappears in Jones' book where he is described thus:

'An even earlier observer on radar listening flights was Eric Ackermann, who in two years made more than ninety flights, including more than forty on which bombs were dropped against the beam stations. Most of his later flights were over the Main Belt, listening for Würzburg transmissions. Not only did he hear these transmissions very frequently over the Main Belt, but he also concluded that some of the flights were radar-controlled'.

Würzburg was the code name given by the British to the German ground-based gun-laying radar system for the Luftwaffe and the German Army. It entered service in 1940 and one of the Würzburg stations was based just across the Channel at Douvres-la-Délivrande, in Calvados.

In 1941 Eric Ackermann made his debut in RAF Form 540, the Operations Record Book (ORB), which every unit had to keep, although his first flight from Boscombe Down was on 22 September 1940, just eleven days after his commission was gazetted. He flew twice on the following day, and both of these flights were with the Blind Approach Training and Development Unit (BATDU). This information was discovered in the logbook of the pilot, Flying Officer Henry Cundall, of whom more later. The BATDU was being used in 1940 to investigate the Lorenz and Knickebein system, but was disbanded on 30 September, to be replaced immediately by the Wireless Intelligence Development Unit (WIDU), a part of the RAF whose name did not exactly conceal its function. Both units were commanded by Wing Commander (later Air Vice-Marshal) R.S. Blucke, a highly decorated officer who went on to command No. 1 Group, which had the largest complement of Lancaster bombers of any Group. By the time Air Vice-Marshal Blucke retired in 1952 he had been awarded the CB, CBE, DSO and AFC.

Until very recently Eric had been a newly qualified electronics scientist and a civilian. Now, seven months after joining the TRE, he was airborne and his first two recorded flights took place while the final stages of the Battle of Britain were being fought not very far away from his own flight path. By this time the Luftwaffe had switched its attacks from airfields to bombing London and on a clear night Eric and Dorothy, at home in Bonfields Avenue, must have been able to see the bomber streams converging on their target and the fighters rising up to meet them.

Following a common pattern in wartime, the WIDU was another unit destined to disappear almost before the ink on its new official writing paper had dried. It lasted ten weeks and was replaced, or rather absorbed, by No. 109 Squadron. This had been a not very conspicuous squadron in the First World War, and it came to life again on 10 December 1940 when it was re-formed with the stirring motto *Primi Hastati* (The First of the Legion). Its earlier undistinguished existence, when it was never required on the Western Front, had lasted less than a year, from November 1917 to 19 August 1918, a curious date to disappear, as it was at the point in the war that the Allies had halted the Germans' rapid advance and began to push them back the way they had come.

In the Second World War the squadron had a more glorious existence, beginning with its work at Boscombe Down, carrying out secret operations against the Luftwaffe's radio navigational beams. It then operated the RAF's 'Oboe', the radar-based ground-controlled, blind-bombing system used in high-precision attacks on German industrial centres, and, after moves to RAF Stradishall and then to Wyton in 1942, became one of the original units in the Pathfinder Force, flying Mosquito aircraft. They took part in the thousand bomber raid on Cologne on 30/31 May 1942. Things had certainly looked up for this previously unconsidered squadron and by the end of the war it had flown more than 5,500 sorties. Its crews greatly distinguished themselves and were awarded one VC, twenty-eight DSOs and 175 DFCs. After the war it was re-equipped with Canberras which it flew during the Suez operation of 1956. The squadron was disbanded on 31 January 1957.

Eric now moved from the two multi-initialled units to a real flying squadron and he first appeared in 109's ORB on 2 June 1941, where he was shown as a Pilot Officer (c). Between the date of that first flight in which his name is mentioned and the last on 25 February 1942, he appears in the ORB crew list on only seventeen occasions, compared with R.V. Jones' statement in *'Most Secret War'* that he made at least ninety flights, on forty of which bombs were dropped.

The long interval between September 1940 and June 1941 is hard to understand, unless it is because any intervening flights were just not recorded in the ORB, or that he did not fly at all during that period, which is highly unlikely. Five other flights have been traced which are not shown in the ORB. There were the two with the BATDU and at least three others which for some reason are not in the 109 Squadron ORB. Three of these are listed in Group Captain Henry John Cundall's Flying Log, when Cundall, then a Pilot Officer, was the pilot and captain. A few flights appear with their full crew list but most of them name only the captain, so Eric's other flights were probably in this group. As he left Worth Matravers sometime in 1942, his flying career so far would have been very intensive, with most of the ninety plus flights Jones refers to being compressed into less than eighteen months.

There are brief entries on the purpose and length of each flight, for example: operations on the 30s and the 40s, a trip for the TRE on GAL, trips for the Y Service, and several Ruffian flights. Ruffian was the British name for the German X-Gerät beam system operating from the Cherbourg area. Each beam was identified by the name of a leading Nazi such as 'Himmler', 'Heydrich', 'Goering'.

Although the ORB does not usually state where the aircraft went, though there are exceptions, it does give take-off and landing times and the length of most of the flights shows that they were over occupied France and occasionally even further afield, reaching Holland on at least one occasion. Most of the flights were at night.

David Cumming's book *'Beam Bombers: the secret war of No. 109 Squadron'*, published in 1998 explains Eric's commission:

> 'Having a TRE man go missing in such circumstances, someone privy to so many secrets, prompted a rethink about the wisdom of sending over enemy occupied territory any more of these specialists (who swapped 'Mr' for an RAF commissioned officer rank and their civvies for service dress)'.

The practice quickly ceased and these quasi-officers seem to have been grounded. Eric was the exception. He is mentioned in Cumming's book in a reference to a letter from the Squadron Commander, Squadron Leader Hebden, recording his appreciation of the work of TRE in devising Oboe, a ground-controlled bombing system, and concluding it with 'Pilot Officer Ackermann of TRE at all times has given invaluable help.'

The 109 Squadron flights were carrying out a variety of tasks, from testing Oboe, to jamming enemy signals, to intelligence gathering. Each of the flights had a crew member with radio expertise and this is why Eric's training and skills were invaluable. The scientists who undertook these hazardous flights seem to have been well regarded and not disdained as mere civilians.

In her book *'The Enemy is Listening'*. Aileen Clayton refers to 109 Squadron and mentions Eric Ackermann by name:

> 'Each of the Wellingtons of No 109 Squadron engaged in these investigations carried special radio personnel. Among these were men such as the young scientist Eric Ackermann, who had already made several flights to monitor transmissions from radar stations, and who had been given an honorary commission in the RAF in case he had the misfortune to be shot down.' She then writes: 'flying with experienced investigational pilots such as Flight Lieutenant C.O.V. Willis, the young scientist, Flying Officer E.J. [sic] Ackermann, and other special operators, including civilian personnel from TRE, made long and dangerous sorties listening to beam transmissions.'

By now Eric was flying in larger aircraft than the Anson, though it was in that aircraft that he began his flying career in September 1940. 'Faithful Annie' was the RAF's all-purpose workhorse. It was in service from 1935 to 1968 and 11,020 of all types were built, making it only second to the Wellington for the number of twin-engined aircraft to be built.

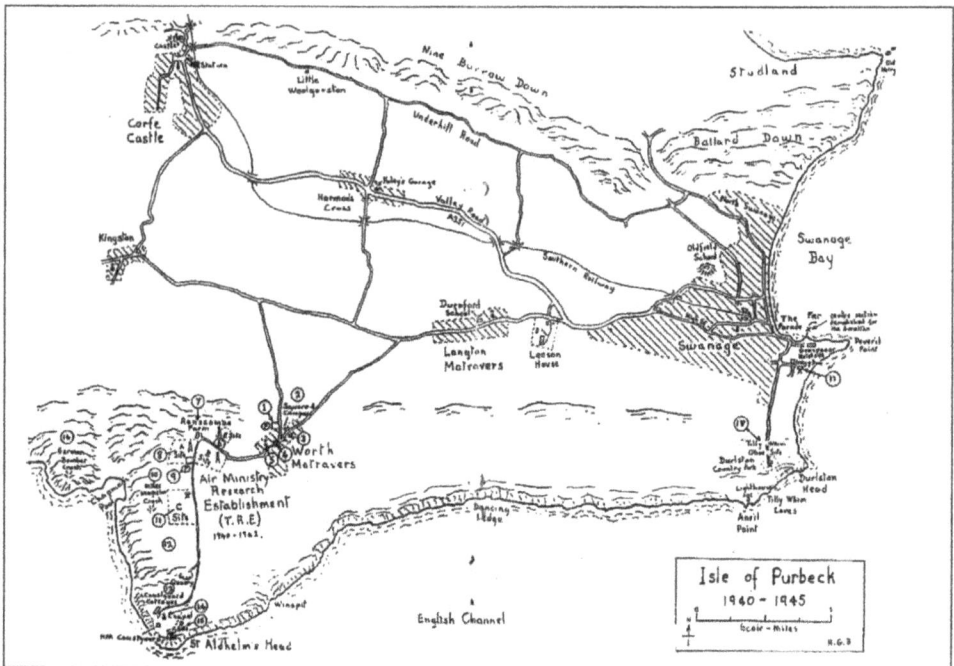

A sketch map of the Isle of Purbeck showing Worth Matravers on the left and Swanage on the right. Reproduced by permission of the Purbeck Radar Museum Trust.

The Vickers-Armstrong Wellington, used by Boscombe Down for investigative flights, was the RAF's main bomber at that point in the war. It was more suitable for the kind of operations which the TRE and 109 Squadron were requiring and Eric flew most of his flights in Wellingtons of different types. It remained in service until 1945, though it was superseded in the European theatre by the Lancaster in 1942. It went through several modifications during its operational service and 11,474 of all types were built. Eric was to fly from Boscombe Down in Marks T, X and Z, which could easily be fitted with the detection and interception equipment he needed. It could accommodate a crew of six or seven, including scientist/observers like Eric and their specialist equipment. The scientists made no contribution to the actual flying of the aircraft, but were just as busy as those who did.

In the early stages of the war the Wellingtons were heavily employed on bombing raids on Germany, until they were superseded for European operations by the Lancaster. They took part in the first bombing raid over Germany on 4 September 1939 and more than half (559 out of 1046) of the aircraft on the 1000 bomber raid in May 1942 were Wellingtons.

When not flying from Boscombe Down, Eric worked here in the cluster of buildings on the left of the map above, near the beautiful Jurassic Coast of Dorset, which must

The TRE at Worth Matravers. Both photographs were provided by the Purbeck Radar Museum Trust. The only buildings to survive today are a row of cottages at the bottom right of the lower photograph, amongst a group of farm buildings.

have done something to ease the strain of working under the extreme pressure which affected everyone working at the TRE.

Nothing remains of the TRE's buildings and aerials at the site, except the row of small cottages on the right of the photograph at the top of this page, on the edge of a field. In the far distance in both photographs the tiny shape of the eighth century St. Aldhelm's Chapel can just be seen.

Some of Eric's 109 Squadron flights, which are shown with his name in the Operations Record Book, are listed below, together with the three others which are not in the ORB, but are recorded in Group Captain Cundall's flying log. They are all included, as collectively they contain useful information about these operations and a wider picture of 109's activities, and for that matter, Eric Ackermann's own heavy workload.

Here now are Eric's recorded flights from 1940 to 1942.

22 September 1940. Anson
Crew: Pilot Officer Cundall, Squadron Leader Bufton, Pilot Officer Ackerman, Sergeant Philips, Leading Aircraftman Walker
Night flight – 3 hours 45 minutes.
Special duty: Channel East.

23 September 1940.
Same crew as above.
Night flight – duration: 3 hours.
Special duty: Channel East.

[There is then a long gap before the next entry mentioning Eric and this can only be because the compiler of the Form 540 decided to omit the crew details. These forms frequently depended on the diligence of the writer and how much time he had and are therefore frequently inconsistent.]

5 May 1941. This flight is not recorded in the ORB so no more details of it are available, but Eric wrote a report about it after the flight: TRE Report 5/26/ EGA. Details of Installation of Search Equipment in 109 Squadron Wellingtons, 5th May 1941. The report has not survived.

7 May 1941. As for the above flight with a further report.
TRE Report 5/16/EGA.
First report on 53cm Würzburg Transmissions by TRE observer in 109 Squadron aircraft on 7 May 1941. Report written on 14 May 1941. [This report is reproduced at the end of this chapter.]

2 June 1941. Wellington T.2552.
Crew: Pilot Officer Reece (Captain), Pilot Officer Ackermann, Sergeants Gent, Bucknall, Moffatt, Snape, Edwards.
Took off 2240, Landed 0215.
Operations on the 30s.
[Pilot Officer Reece later became Group Captain (Rev.) A. Reece, DSO, OBE, DFC, AFC.]

8 June 1941. Wellington T.2552.
Same crew.
Took off 2300, Landed 0230.
Operations on the 40s.

11 June 1941. Wellington T.2552.
Same crew.
Took off 2310, Landed 0215.
Trip for TRE on G.A.L

15 June 1941. Anson W. 1891.
Took off 2330. Landed 0030.
Trip on the Ruffians.

1 July 1941. Wellington T.2552.
Crew: Flying Officer Cundall, Pilot Officer Ackermann, Flight Sergeant Holy, Flight Sergeant Sewell, Sergeant Morgan.
Daylight flight – duration 1 hour 10 minutes.
Special duty: Local.

2 July 1941. Wellington T.2552.
Crew: Flying Officer Cundall, Wing Commander Hancock, Pilot Officer Ackermann, Flight Sergeant Sewell, Flight Sergeant Holy, Flight Sergeant Sandifer, Sergeant Harrison.
Took off 2230, Landed 0345.
Special duty: Den Helder, Amsterdam. 'Y' service.
(There was a Knickebein station at Bergen-op-Zoom and this was probably the reason for the operation.)

4 July 1941
Crew:Flight Lieutenant Willis, Pilot Officer Ackermann.
Took off 2335, Landed 0340
Y service trip.

7 July 1941.
Crew included Flying Officer Cundall and Pilot Officer Ackermann
Took off 2230, Landed 0345.
Carried out a trip for the 'Y' service.

6 August 1941.
Wellington T.2552.

Crew: Flying Officer Crane, Pilot Officer Ackermann, Flight Sergeant Sandifer, Flight Sergeant Holy, Sergeants Morrison, Cornforth, Matthieson.
Took off 2220, Landed 0020.
Carried out a 'Y' service trip.

16 August 1941. Wellington T.2552.
Crew: Flying Officer Grant, Pilot Officer Ackermann, Pilot Officer Maygothling, Flight Sergeant Adam, Sergeants Sewell, Blacker, Thornhill, Snape, Matthiesen
Took off 2040, Landed 2140.
'Y' service.

17 August 1941. Wellington T.2552.
Crew: Flight Lieutenant Willis, Pilot Officer Ackermann, Flight Sergeant Huntley, Sergeants Dicks, Hall, Bowen, McDonald, Matthieson
Took off 2045, Landed 0100.
'Y' service trip.

13 October 1941. Wellington T.2552
Crew: Squadron Leader Banks, Pilot Officer Ackermann, Sergeants Dunmall, Bowen, Storey, Edwards
'Y' service trip.

29 October 1941. Wellington T.2552.
Crew: Flying Officer Northen, Flying Officer Ackermann, Flight Sergeant Holy, Flight Sergeant Sandifer, Sergeants Morrison, Sewell.
Took off 1900, Landed 2100.
'Y' service trip. [Eric's rank is given as Flying Officer, though he reverts to Pilot Officer on his next flight.]

5 November 1941. This is the flight referred to later in this chapter. Eric Ackermann should have been on it but he was withdrawn from it on the previous evening.

21 November 1941. Wellington T.2552 crashed at RAF Oakington. The crew of six were all killed. Eric had flown in this aircraft on most of his flights so far, the most recent being only three weeks before. One of those on board was a civilian scientist doing the same kind of work as Eric Ackermann.

22 November 1941. Wellington Z.1048.
Took off 1115, Landed 1240.
Carried out a special duty flight.

29 December 1941. Wellington Z.1048.
Took off 1430, Landed 1600.
Special duty flight.

6 January 1942. Wellington Z.1048.
Took off 2110, Landed 0030.
Special duty flight.

9 January 1942. Wellington Z.1048.
Took off 1240, Landed 1540.
Special duty flight.

25 January 1942. Wellington Z.1113.
Took off 1900, Landed 2135.
Special duty flight.

28 January 1942. Wellington Z.1113.
Took off 1800, Landed 2200.
Special duty flight.

31 January 1942. Wellington X.9913.
Took off 1915, Landed 2120.
Special duty flight.
25 February 1942. Wellington Z.1041.
Took off 2050, Landed 2330.
Ruffian flight.

This may have been Eric's last flight with 109 Squadron – it is certainly the last in the squadron ORB, despite R.V. Jones' statement that he completed at least ninety.

Reporting on the flight of 7 May 1941, Eric writes that he was 'using a Wellington aircraft fitted with the G.E.C. superhet receiver and a conical aerial.' He describes the aircraft's route from Boscombe Down over Christchurch to the French coast and then inland into Brittany, and finally back via Jersey and Guernsey and he includes a map showing the positions of the enemy 53cm RDF stations.

The flights were dangerous and at least one aircraft was shot down. This occurred during the night of 4/5 November 1941, when Wellington T.2565 was damaged by a stray shell fragment which hit an engine while over Pontivy in Brittany. The scientist on board as the TRE's representative was Flying Officer Howard Gooding Cundall, another honorary officer, not to be confused with Henry Cundall, who was Eric's pilot on several flights. Howard was a few months older than Eric and their careers were running along similar lines until this event. He had joined the TRE on 14 May 1940 (on a salary of 45 shillings per week, considerably less than Eric's at £4 per week) and worked in Section 3(ii) Responder Beacons.

The Wellington was beyond saving and the crew bailed out. They landed safely and made their way to the coast, a journey which took them nearly two weeks. Once there they found a rowing boat to which they added a makeshift sail. They put out to sea but were seen by the Germans and captured, though one of them, Sgt Mackenzie, who was the co-pilot, escaped and managed to reach Spain from where he made his way back to England and was very soon in action with 109 Squadron once again. The crew was now one short, something the Germans did not notice and neither did they realize that there was now only one pilot, nor that the crew had gained a gunner. This was Howard Cundall who had successfully concealed his real identity as a civilian scientist and passed himself off as one of the aircraft's complement of gunners.

Two of the crew, Flight Lieutenant Lester Bull, DFC, and Flight Lieutenant William Grisman, took part in the great escape of 24/25 March 1944. They were both captured and were among the fifty officers shot by the Gestapo on Hitler's direct orders in one of the worst atrocities against PoWs in the western theatre of the war. The perpetrators were arrested after the war and twelve of them were hanged as war criminals by the British occupation authorities. The event has been well documented but it never fails to arouse horror.

There are several twists to this story. One is that on the evening before the flight Dorothy and Eric Ackermann gave Lester Bull and Bill Grisman a lift from Boscombe Down to Salisbury, where they both lived, not knowing that they would never see them again. Dorothy remembers that Bill Grisman's wife was pregnant and father and child were never to meet. The Germans were meticulous record keepers and were callous enough to note the cremation records of these two gallant officers. (These records are now retained in the National Archives in London.) They appear to have been signed even before the men were killed. In March 2012 a memorial to Flight Lieutenant Bull and three others who were captured on the Czech border was unveiled. Grisman was not one of this group as he was captured separately from Bull and killed in a different place.

Another twist is that Eric himself was due to fly the following evening on the doomed flight, as the observer scientist, but he was ordered back to Worth Matravers to be in

43932 F/L Lester G Bull DFC, British, born 7-Nov-1916, 109 Sqdn (shot down 5/6-Nov-1941, Wellington IC, T2565) recaptured near Reichenberg, murdered 29-Mar-1944 by unknown Gestapo, cremated at Brux.

45148 F/L William J Grisman, British, born 30-Aug-14, 109 Sqdn, (believed shot down 5/6-Nov-1941, Wellington IC, T2565) recaptured near Gorlitz, last seen alive 6-Apr-1944; murdered by Lux, cremated at Breslau.

Photographs of the two officers who were captured when their aircraft was shot down over France in November 1941 and were later shot by the Gestapo when they escaped from Stalagluft III. Eric and Dorothy had given them a lift in their car the evening before their aircraft took off from RAF Boscombe Down.

attendance during a visit by Air Chief Marshal Sir Philip Joubert de la Ferté. Sir Philip was at that time Commander-in-Chief, Coastal Command, but until the summer of 1941 had been the Assistant Chief of Air Staff, responsible for the practical application of radar in the RAF and as Eric Ackermann was by now a considerable expert on radar, his presence at Worth was required. Eric's withdrawal from the flight not only preserved him for future exploits, but, of more immediate significance, illustrated the value of his honorary commission, should this ever happen to him. Had he, and not Howard Cundall, been on board the Wellington, he would have been captured and possibly ended up in Stalag Luft III.

In their book; *'MI9: the British secret service that fostered escape and evasion 1939–1945 and its American counterpart'*, M.R.D. Foot and J.M. Langley write that after Cundall's capture:

> 'His main difficulty was in passing himself off as a genuine flight lieutenant (as which he was dressed) among his fellow prisoners. He clearly knew a lot about wireless, eventually becoming the secret wireless maintenance officer in Stalag Luft III in Sagan, and building a transmitter, or rather collecting the parts for it; but the camp history states categorically that the transmitter was never assembled for use.'

The official history of the camp, retained in the National Archives as document AIR 40/2178, rather contradicts Foot's statement and states that on arriving at Sagan from Oflag XXI/B at Schubin in April 1943, Flight Lieutenants Lou Barry and Howard Cundall had with them parts of a receiver which they smuggled through in various pieces of luggage, a biscuit tin and a medicine ball. They had assembled the parts by the end of April and had hidden them in a wall in Barry's room in barrack 69. In December 1943 they rebuilt the receiver and fitted it into the top of a desk in the same room. Another set was made from spare parts by June 1943 and was kept in the false bottom of a box where Barry kept his clothes. He was appointed Head of the Camp's Radio Department from April 1943 to January 1945 and Cundall was placed in charge of operating the radio and they regularly listened to BBC news bulletins from the set in the wall of Barry's room. Their activities and the two radios were never discovered. They even kept the radios in working order and undetected on the brutal forced march westwards, when the camp was evacuated by the Germans in January 1945, a quite remarkable achievement.

Foot's comment that the transmitter did not work is either ignoring the stated fact in the National Archives document that two receivers did work, or that he never found that particular section in the file, which is unlikely. Probably both accounts are partly right and both transmitter and receivers were operated successfully. It is a 'what if' comment, but it is more than likely that had Eric Ackermann been on that flight and ended up in Stalag Luft III with Barry, he would have done much the same with the radios as Cundall did. Given his fascination with anything electrical and particularly with radio transmission, he could hardly have kept his hands off the equipment.

How he would have relished such a challenge, though he would have hated the grim confinement of a prison camp.

Lou Barry would come to know and work with Eric Ackermann after the war when he was stationed at the signals units at Uetersen and Hambühren and detached to Obernkirchen. He was a Hungarian linguist and was later to play an important role in the RAF's intelligence gathering efforts. He is remembered fondly, at least by the airmen who knew him, for having both a very beautiful wife and an almost equally beautiful Mercedes car. He was always willing to stop and give airmen lifts when he passed them struggling back to camp after an evening out. While we are with Stalag Luft III it is worth noting that it housed another officer who would come to work with Eric after the war. This was Flight Lieutenant P.S. (Paddy) Engelbach, of whom more later.

The third and more remote twist is that a cousin of Eric's wife's future husband, Michael Hartnell-Beavis, was also a prisoner at Stalag Luft III. This was Squadron Leader Francis John Hartnell-Beavis, DFC, of No.10 Squadron, who was shot down on the night of 25/26 July 1943. His DFC was gazetted three months later. He was an architect and when the Luftwaffe allowed the creation of a memorial to the murdered officers, he designed it and it was erected in the local cemetery.

Howard Cundall is not to be confused with the other officer with the same surname and first initial who also served with 109 Squadron at the same time and who was Eric's pilot on several of his flights. Henry John Cundall, then a Flying Officer, was a career officer and a pilot. He was commissioned in 1938, and from late 1940 until 1942 flew regularly with 109 Squadron. Group Captain Cundall, as he later became, continued to fly with a number of squadrons throughout the war, and remained in the RAF until 1961 when he retired. He was a much decorated officer, with the CBE, DSO, DFC and AFC. He died in December 2001, aged eighty.

Howard Cundall was dressed as an officer on his final flight and he must have had the appropriate identity documents when he was arrested in France, but the *London Gazette* had not at that time actually reported his commission and indeed did not do so for several years. It took until 28 December 1945 for him to be officially gazetted as an officer, when at long last the following entry appeared with the effective date of his commission given as the very day on which he abruptly landed on French soil. His belated *London Gazette* entry is given as:

ROYAL AIR FORCE VOLUNTEER RESERVE
GENERAL DUTIES BRANCH
Appointment to commission.
As Plt. Off. On prob.(emergency):-
Howard Gooding CUNDALL (117264). 5 November 1941

The delay may have been due to his capture and imprisonment, but the backdating helped his arrears of pay if nothing else. It is a small matter now, but to Cundall in November 1941 it could have made a whole lot of difference to his immediate future prospects in German hands. And another oddity: Cundall was immediately given a service number: Eric still had to wait several years for his.

After the war Howard Cundall resumed work in the Civil Service, his career closely shadowing Eric's, and although he rapidly returned to civilian status, he is listed in the Air Force List in 1948 as an Experimental Officer working for the ADI(Science) at the Air Ministry. He worked his way through the Civil Service ranks along very similar lines to Eric to reach the rank of Principal Scientific Officer at the Department of Trade and Industry in 1973, specializing in automation and processes. He appears in the same 1948 staff list as Eric Ackermann in the 1940s and mention is made of this in a later chapter

Just to round off this chapter, there is an intriguing document in National Archives file AVIA 7/603, written at around the time that Eric was leaving Worth Matravers, Boscombe Down and his and Dorothy's home in Swanage. In it the tireless A.P. Rowe had drafted for discussion the following memo, dated 12 March 1942. It shows that even the apparently dour and unsmiling Mr Rowe could summon a laconic touch in his memo-writing from time to time:

'Memo in the event of a surprise raid and the effects on the civilian staff.
They could: destroy vital papers, sabotage secret apparatus with which they normally work.
Invasion:
We all run
We all obey the general instructions to civilians and 'stay put'.

Certain indispensable individuals run and reassemble elsewhere.

Apart from the indispensables, we stay on the station and fight to the best of our ability.
We all stay and fight'

The indispensables were probably relieved to know that they did not have to stay around and be bombed. The dispensables, on the other hand, had both to accept their category and remain behind to be a target for the raiders. There was, of course, a genuine threat and Rowe, as usual, was taking precautions.

As it happened, Worth Matravers did have to be evacuated in a hurry, when, as Dr W.H. Penley writes, the Prime Minister and the Cabinet believed that a German Parachute Division, which had been assembled on the Cherbourg Peninsula, was about to descend on the TRE:

'and capture us and our equipment. At the end of April the team leaders were called together and told that we had to leave before the next full moon! Malvern College had been chosen for our new home, and a few of us went straight up there to plan and arrange the modifications – benches, power supplies, telephones etc.

– to convert the buildings into laboratories. Pickfords arrived in force; we packed up, and after one false start, left for Malvern early in May'

George Millar, writing about the celebrated raid on the Bruneval radar station in France, in February 1942, describes the rush to move and quotes A.P. Rowe on the effect this had on Worth Matravers and the future of the TRE:

'There were, we were told, seventeen trainloads of German parachute troops on the other side of the English Channel preparing to attack TRE. The Prime Minister said we must leave the south coast before the next full moon. A whole regiment of infantry arrived to protect us. They blocked the road approaches, they encircled us with barbed wire, they put demolition charges in our secret equipment, and they made our lives a misery. My own time was spent in discussions as to whether we should die to the last scientist, or run. These events made us co-operate in the task of finding a place where we could get on with the war in peace.'

This swift departure was based on more than just a mild dose of panic brought about partly because of a raid on a radar site in France. On 27/28 February 1942 the Bruneval Raid took place, officially called Operation Biting. This was a combined operations attack by parachute on the radar station at Bruneval near Le Havre, which was satisfactorily destroyed. All three services were involved. The Royal Navy took the soldiers off the beach and back to safety, the RAF, flying 51 Squadron Whitleys from RAF Thruxton in Hampshire, transported the Army element, C Company of the 2nd Battalion Parachute Regiment paratroopers, to the drop zone to carry out the attack. The Paras were commanded by Major John Frost, a distinguished soldier who later took part in the Arnhem landings in September 1944.

The raid was a success, with only light casualties (two killed, six wounded and six captured) and the varied units which took part had cause to be well satisfied with their night's work. It would have been too much to expect the Germans to take this reverse without doing something about it, such as attacking Boscombe Down, or the TRE, or both, but surprisingly there was no immediate retaliation, though there was an aerial attack later in the war. The Germans apparently did not believe that the British could be so foolish as to place a sensitive unit in such an obvious and vulnerable place. The authorities were not to know this and the move went ahead.

A slight downside was that the Bruneval raiders were irritated, as they felt that the German defenders had been alerted by the RAF flights in the nights immediately preceding the raid. Given the success of the raid, there is nothing to show that the flights made any difference to the readiness of the defences. After the war a German paratroop leader stated that the Bruneval operation was outstandingly the best, both in conception and execution, of all the British commando operations.

Malcolm Stewart, who served under Eric's command in Germany many years later, recalls that Eric was held in awe by the airmen in 646 Signals Unit on account of his involvement in this or a similar raid, though there is no evidence that he did in fact take part.

Malvern in Worcestershire, and more specifically Malvern College, was selected for the TRE's new home and the college was requisitioned for the duration. Its beautiful 250 acre grounds in the shadow of the Malvern Hills were rapidly disfigured by the usual collection of wooden huts which always mushroomed wherever there was a wartime military installation.

Eric was meant to go with TRE to Malvern and he and Dorothy were offered a flat in Malvern. Dorothy remembered that it was 'horrible' and Eric was unwilling to go there. They did not want to leave their house in Swanage, though with the departure of the TRE at Worth Matravers, there was no point in remaining in Swanage, even if he had been allowed to.

Dorothy believes that it was then that R.V. Jones began to figure more prominently in their lives and that he became directly or indirectly Eric's employer. They decided to leave Malvern and moved to better accommodation in 35 Ennismore Gardens, Kensington, which was to remain their home for the rest of the war, although much more Dorothy's than Eric's, as he was away on missions overseas for much of the time.

Meanwhile, 109 Squadron moved to RAF Stradishall in March 1942, taking its Wellington aircraft with it. The Wellingtons and two Ansons continued to fly on similar radio and wireless detection operations in enemy air space and while up there they also tested new radar aids. Not only that, but the crews remained much the same, except apparently, for Eric. The new Mosquito fighter-bombers came into service around this time and were added to 109's strength. The squadron's operations in the early summer of 1942, as already noted, were such that Eric's expertise was not required. If these dates do apply to Eric, then the chronology of his life in 1942 falls neatly into place,

The Bruneval Radar station. This photograph was taken by Flt. Lt. Tony Hill on 5 December 1941.

because he was shortly to go to North Africa for part two of his RAF career.

At Malvern, the TRE seems to have had rather different responsibilities, at least as far as flying operations were concerned. The nearest RAF station was at Defford near Worcester and it housed the Telecommunications Flying Unit (TFU). This had moved from RAF Hurn in Hampshire to Defford in May 1942, presumably to coincide with the arrival of the TRE, so that it could be its flying base. It appears from the unit's records that the kind of co-operational flying there was more the testing of radar in the air than its more aggressive role at Boscombe Down had been. There it had mainly been

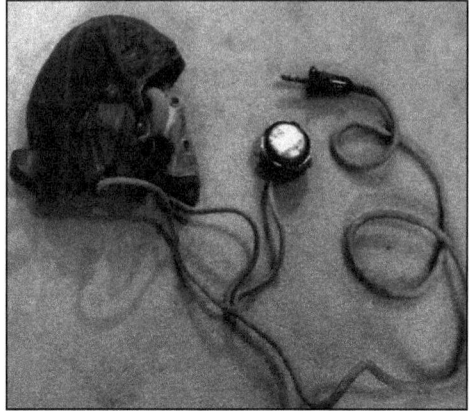

Eric's flying helmet, photographed in his brother Keith's house in 2009. It is now in the possession of his sons.

to seek out radar and then either attack its ground stations or record what they were capable of doing. Another difference was the number of civilian scientists who went on flying operations, and there is a note of a complaint in the unit's ORB about the

The radar memorial on the cliff top at Worth Matravers.

A commemorative hassock in the parish church of St. Nicholas of Myra in Worth Matravers.

number of these wishing to go airborne. Clearly the flights cannot have been all that dangerous for the authorities to set their scientists' lives at risk in such quantities. The TFU's flights were much more over home territory than venturing to France. Despite this, however, some of the Defford flights were dangerous, as a memorial in the nearby village records:

'DEDICATED TO THE MEMORY OF THOSE ROYAL AIR FORCE AND CIVILIAN PERSONNEL WHO LOST THEIR LIVES IN THE FURTHERANCE OF RADAR RESEARCH WHILST SERVING WITH THE TELECOMMUNICATIONS FLYING UNIT, LATER, THE RADAR RESEARCH FLYING UNIT, AT DEFFORD AIRFIELD, 1941–1947'

With that, Eric's operations shifted from England to the one theatre of war where British and Commonwealth land forces were engaged in fierce fighting. The desert campaign, which had swung to and fro over the previous two years, was at the point when the Allies' fortunes were about to change for the better following the appointment of Lieutenant-General Bernard Montgomery to command the Eighth Army and the subsequent victory in October at the Battle of El Alamein. Eric probably arrived shortly after El Alamein, though another version claims that he did not get there until the following February.

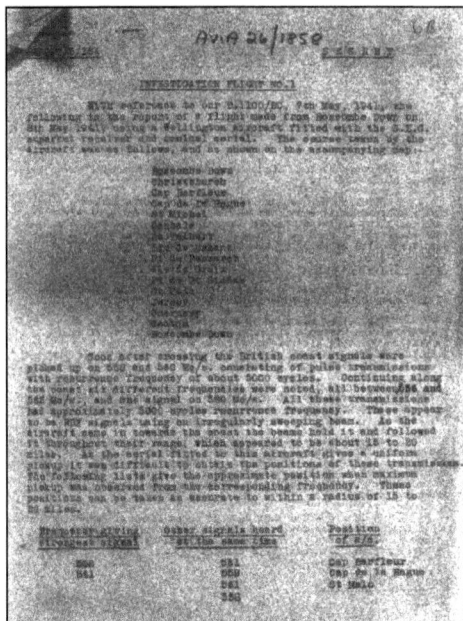

Eric's report on a flight he took with 109 Squadron from RAF Boscombe on 7/8 May 1941.

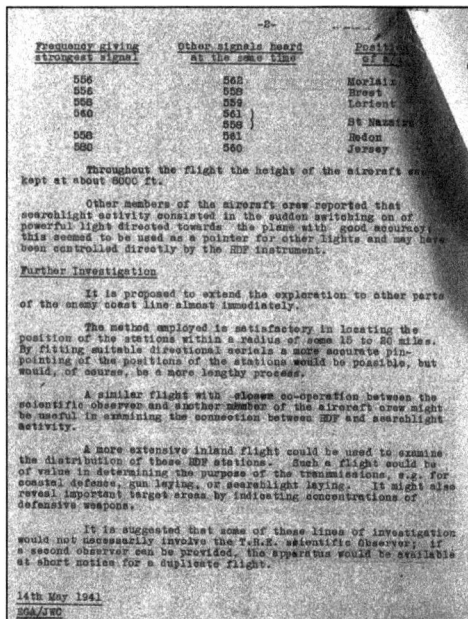

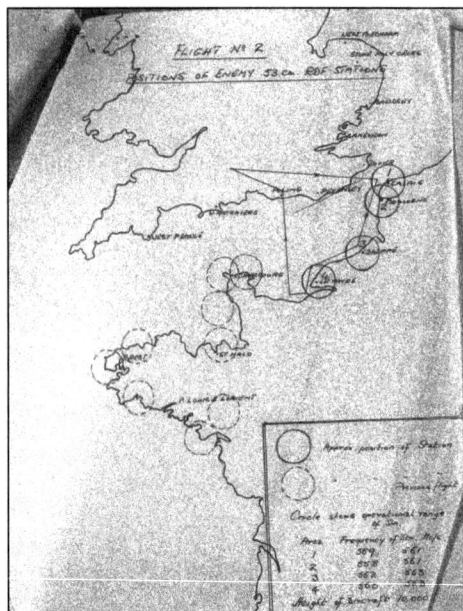

Chapter Three

North Africa and Italy:
Torch, Husky and Avalanche

The battle for North Africa and for control of the Mediterranean was already more than two years old when Eric Ackermann arrived. It had begun on 14 June 1940, when British forces crossed from Egypt into the Italian colony of Libya after Italy's declaration of war on France and the United Kingdom four days earlier.

The course of the campaign swung one way and then the other for the next three years. At first, the British Army, commanded by Major General Richard O'Connor, swept aside the Italian forces, capturing 130,000 prisoners and nearly 400 tanks. Then, on 6 February 1941, Lieutenant General Erwin Rommel arrived in Libya to take command of what became known as the Afrika Corps. The Italians had to be rescued and the Afrika Corps provided the bolstering needed to avoid a drastic defeat. For more than two years the two sides fought to gain the advantage, with each advancing enormous distances and then being forced to retreat. A key factor in this long struggle was the problem of supply lines. The further the armies advanced, the longer and more vulnerable these lines became, until they could not be defended and the pendulum swung the other way. The crucial breakthrough for the Allies was victory in the second Battle of El Alamein in October and November 1942, which forced the German and Italian troops westwards, out of Egypt and Libya and into Tunisia.

On 8 November, just as El Alamein was being won, American and British forces launched an attack from the other direction, from the west going east. Operation Torch was an amphibious landing at Casablanca in French Morocco and Oran and Algiers in Algeria. The occupying Vichy French forces offered only slight resistance, so allowing the Allied troops to push forward to contain any German breakout westwards. This had the effect of squeezing the enemy between the forces coming from the west and Eighth Army advancing from the east. It was immediately successful and by the end of the day its initial objectives had been achieved.

There were, however, another eight months of fighting, including the prolonged and bloody Battle of Kasserine Pass (19 February to 23 March), until Montgomery's Eighth Army and the US II Corps were able to begin their final advance westwards. Enemy forces eventually surrendered on 13 May 1943. By the end of the campaign the Allied forces had expanded to include Indian, South African, Canadian, Polish, Australian and New Zealand troops, with their accompanying air power.

The RAF, under the overall title of the Middle East Air Force, was scattered across the widely dispersed commands of Egypt, Iraq, Malta and Aden. With the outbreak of open war in North Africa in June 1940, it was far too small to get involved with much open conflict with the Italian air force and so concentrated more on ground support and reconnaissance. As John Rawlings writes in his *'History of the Royal Air Force'*, the RAF had to 'equate its attempt to dominate the front line with avoidance of unnecessary losses'.

A successful attempt to seem aggressive, without having much in the way of aircraft to be aggressive with, was shown when a single Hurricane was able to convince the Italian reconnaissance aircraft that the RAF was actually much stronger than it really was. This was done by switching the Hurricane rapidly from airfield to airfield and by increasing the reliance on accurate intelligence. This was very similar to the RAF's effort in Malta, where just three Gloster Gladiator aircraft , named Faith, Hope and Charity, were able to hold off the Italian and German Air Forces until reinforcements arrived.

The launching of Operation Torch showed that the RAF's 'Y' facilities had scarcely improved since 1940, when, to quote John Rawlings again, 'the war became real in North Africa'. There were just four units thinly spread across a vast area. These were No. 276 Wing, based in Cairo, No. 162 Squadron, which, with its numerous detachments, had to cover signals intelligence from the air throughout the Middle East and therefore the whole of the theatre, and two Wireless Units, No. 351 in Gibraltar and No. 371 in Freetown, Sierra Leone, in West Africa.

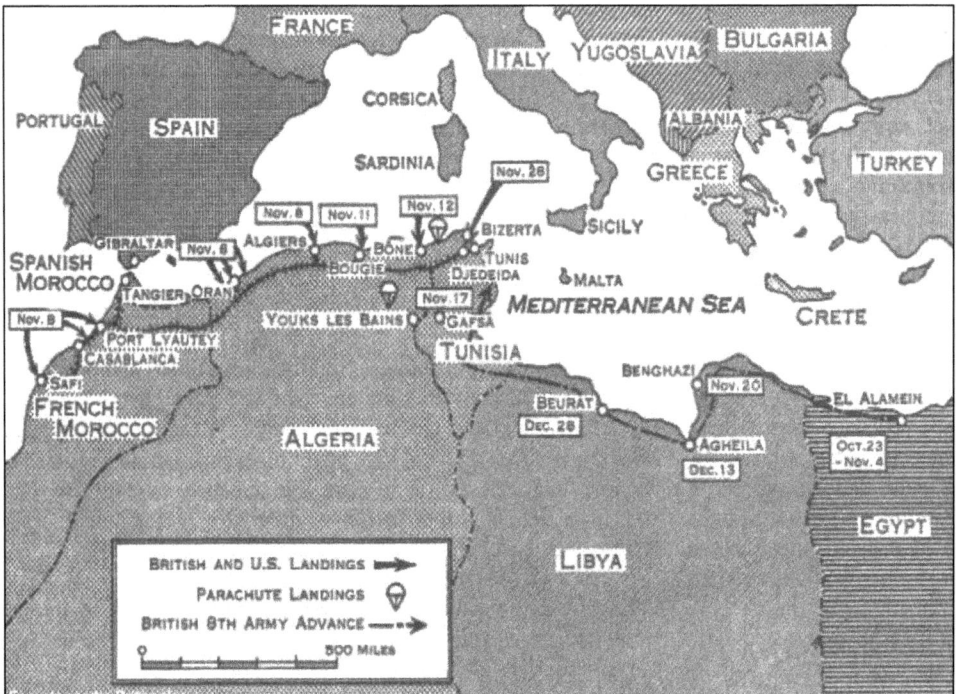

This map shows Operation Torch and the areas of the North African campaign in which Eric was particularly active.

The deficiencies to which this led are described by F.H. Hinsley, in *'British intelligence in the Second World War'*, in which he writes about the Torch landings:

'neither W/T nor R/T produced noteworthy results during the actual operations. The *Bulolo* [HMS *Bulolo*, a communications ship] failed to receive Cheadle's signals and it turned out that her W/T and R/T groups were too inexperienced, and perhaps too seasick, to be able to cope unaided.'

Hinsley goes on to say that this did not matter much at the time, as the landing was a success, but it most certainly did a little later:

'With the Allied advance to Tunisia, it was discovered that the Y units were inexperienced and poorly trained and that the staff appointed to AFHQ and First Army HQ, to direct their work, was also inadequate. The US Y units turned out to have little training: such were their deficiencies that in January 1943 they had to be stiffened by British Y staff or temporarily integrated into British units. But the British units themselves were not much more experienced or any better organized during the first crucial months after the landings'.

One of the stiffeners described by Hinsley was Eric Ackermann, and, four days after the successful conclusion of Operation Torch, No. 380 Wireless Unit (WU) arrived at Port Algiers and at last we have some precise information about his whereabouts after he left Worth Matravers and RAF Boscombe Down. This came not from any official record, but from an airman who served with him. Ted Lines was aboard the troopship SS *Cameronia* with 380 WU and although he is not sure if Eric was actually on board the ship, he does know that he was in Algiers on or around the day they arrived. He was probably already there and it is more likely that he flew out rather than waste his and the Air Ministry's time by undergoing the tortuous, slow, dangerous and very rough voyage. It was not only the airmen on board HMS *Bulolo* who were seasick, but also those who had to cope with appalling weather on board the *Cameronian*.

On arrival the weary airmen were marched from the docks up to the top of the hill to the city itself, where they found a beautiful villa, or more properly, a chateau, the Chateau Béraud, which was reputed to have been built by Napoleon for his mistress. Their CO announced that they would commandeer it, only to find that the Army had got there first, presumably having taken up residence three or four days earlier, after their successful invasion. The new arrivals were nevertheless graciously allowed to sleep in the orchard and were given a plentiful supply of red wine to help them over their disappointment. The owner of the chateau, Monsieur Boissy, had three daughters and a son. One of the daughters, according to Ted Lines, a very beautiful young lady, formed a brief and unreciprocated attachment to Eric and another was serving with the Free French Army in Algeria as an interpreter, while the third daughter was working for the US Army in Casablanca.

Bert Evans, another 380 WU veteran, remembers Eric, or Ackers as he calls him, as an adventurous, lively and somewhat unpredictable officer, not behaving at all like one would expect an officer to behave. This confirms Ted Lines' view and that of others who came to know him much later. Bert does not recall Eric being around at the time of 380 WU's arrival in Algeria and believes that he only came across him in February 1943, which coincides with the time shown in the official record. In fact, Eric probably arrived in Algiers in November 1942, flew back to the UK to report on the state of the Y service in North Africa and then flew out again.

He had been promoted to Flight Lieutenant a few days before leaving for North Africa in February, the *London Gazette*, referring to him as a Flight Lieutenant (Hon.). The relevant Operations Record Book notes his return to North Africa:

24 February 1943.	Flight Lieutenant ACKERMAN arrived from U.K.
1 April 1943.	Flight Lieutenant ACKERMAN left for U.K.
21 May 1943.	Flight Lieutenant ACKERMAN returned from tour of forward area

It may have been just a coincidence that Eric Ackermann arrived in North Africa at precisely the time when, according to Hinsley, the 'Y' service was not performing up to standard during and after Torch. A combination of poor conditions and what were described as 'lousily organized' communications, limited its effectiveness even then, until 380 WU was sorted out. Again according to Hinsley:

'the normal R/T and W/T parties in the *Bulolo* did what they could with RAF traffic and provided occasional warnings of GAF [German Air Force] attacks before the establishment of the radar early warning [system], but the service they provided was limited'.

In other words, for Torch, the RAF was depending entirely on a seaborne signals intelligence service with inexperienced and seasick operators, who anyway, were unable to receive signals from the Y service intercept station in Cheadle in Staffordshire. All this can hardly have escaped R.V. Jones' notice and one has to conclude that Eric Ackermann once again assumed the role of Jones' roving fixer. Certainly, when in North Africa, he was Jones' personal representative for all aspects of scientific intelligence and was initially attached to 380 Wireless Unit for five weeks. He came to North Africa with all the authority of the Air Ministry, answerable to no one but Jones himself, and after a few weeks to acquaint himself with the W/T and R/T problems he set out to see what was happening in his immediate area. The 'forward area' from which he returned on 21 May was probably La Marsa, on the north–east coast of Tunisia, which he would have used as a springboard for visits to other units and in particular No. 381, which was now based there.

No. 381 Wireless Unit, being concerned with R/T rather than W/T, had a considerable number of linguists. Indeed, according to Sidney Goldberg, who served with the unit, there were thirty-eight senior NCOs, who between them, had a knowledge of no fewer than ten languages. Sidney himself, who was born in Germany, had his own obvious role to play in this. He writes in the proceedings of the RAF Historical Society for 1993 that he and some of his fellow linguists – six in all – were called the Refugees, as many of them were German-born, although having Polish passports. He remembers that there were many others serving in the Field Units, subordinate to the Wireless Unit. Sidney goes on to write that 381's main client was 242 Group and among the 'recipients of our work were Group Captain D.F.W. Atcherley, Flight Lieutenant E.J. [sic] Ackermann, a scientist working for R.V. Jones and Dr Roxbee Cox from the TRE, Malvern.'

It took a while to sort out the muddle arising from Torch, but there was a further improvement when, on 26 February, two days after Eric returned to Algeria from the UK, the unit was reinforced by six wireless operators arriving from Gibraltar and again in April, more were transferred from 276 Wing Headquarters, based in Cairo. With the war in North Africa now at a crucial phase, the strength of a small Sigint (Signals intelligence) unit had become a serious matter and increasing such an outfit, even by six, would have made a significant difference.

There were postings the other way too. On 2 April, three officers attached to 380 WU from No. 192 Squadron followed Eric back to England. Their task had been to identify German radar signals, thereby replicating Eric's work with 109 Squadron during the previous two years. The squadron operated over the Bay of Biscay and the Mediterranean in 1943, again establishing a link with Eric Ackermann, which was to be re-forged long after the war. 192 Squadron was disbanded in August 1945 but reformed in July 1951 and was based at RAF Watton, the station to which Eric was posted when he finally left Germany in 1959.

Another connection was that on 11 May, one Pilot Officer Beavis arrived by air from 276 Wing, (also in the previous month there were several more postings from the Wing to the Wireless Unit, including the aforementioned wireless operators for which Eric may have been responsible). Beavis, whose full name was Michael Hartnell-Beavis, although he never used the first part of the double-barrel, was with Eric later that summer and was still around ten months later in Italy. On a personal level too the link became closer later on, at least indirectly, when Hartnell-Beavis became Eric's first wife's second husband.

Two rudimentary sketch maps from National Archives files showing RAF signals dispositions just before Operations Husky and Avalanche (the invasions, respectively, of Sicily and mainland Italy) are shown later in this chapter. They show, if not much else, the huge area which the Allied forces had to cover and the sparseness of the land units where the RAF (and the Army) intercept teams had to keep watch on the enemy and predict his next move, something which they had failed to do earlier in the campaign.

No. 381 Wireless Unit's task was to monitor the shorter range R/T traffic and to provide tactical information for the locally controlled fighter formations of the North-

Western African Air Forces. The unit had landed at Bone in Algeria on 7 December 1942, and made its way to Ain Brahim, just on the Tunisian side of the border, arriving on Christmas Day. After four months at Ain Brahim the unit moved eastwards to La Marsa, becoming operational there on 15 May. Its task is made clear by the list of its equipment in the ORB: a VHF portable direction finder and three prime movers, two VHF receiving tenders, and a converted intelligence van able to work with a W/T MF and HF interception tender. It had eighty-six personnel on its strength, with Flight Lieutenant S.L. Hill in command, three intelligence officers, three code and cypher officers, one computer officer, a signals warrant officer, and seventy-seven other ranks.

Aileen Clayton, in *'The Enemy is Listening'*, describes Eric Ackermann's work in tracking German radar signals:

> 'Details of the positions of the enemy radar stations were carefully recorded, as were their types and their efficiency. From this data the Operational Research Section compiled charts and maps indicating the best approach to follow, with the ranges of the various radar stations. To help with this task we were fortunate in having in North Africa, as a scientific advisor on enemy non–Morse transmissions, one of the most capable colleagues of Dr R.V. Jones. He was the enthusiastic and courageous young Eric Ackermann, who had already made many flights over the Western Front investigating enemy radar signals.'

Dr Jones states in his commendation for Eric's George Medal that he made more than ninety flights and as his operational flying career would have largely ended when he left North Africa and Italy, the majority were between 1940 and 1943. He was also going to and from England to report to Jones and to be briefed on his next mission, working with the wireless units which were under the administrative and operational control of 276 and 329 Wings. The two Wings, which were themselves responsible to the Air Ministry's department DDI 4, had 113 stations listening in to Luftwaffe W/T channels and thirty more intercepting their RT signals.

By now (i.e. late 1943) there were Y stations all across the Mediterranean theatre, from Algiers in the west, to Aleppo in Syria, taking in Tunisia, Malta, Sicily, Calabria, Benghazi, Cairo and Alexandria on the way. Eric was involved in a large part of this huge area, which kept expanding as the Allies conquered more and more territory. No. 380 Wireless Unit was disbanded on 30 June and was absorbed into 329 Wing, as was its close relation, 381 WU, which lost its separate identity and as the record says, 'is now known as No. 21 Field Unit'. The sequence of Wireless Unit numbers was maintained, however, with the formation of No. 382, commanded by one Flight Lieutenant Sidney H. Ottley, which operated in the Low Countries and Germany in 1944 and 1945, and to which Eric Ackermann was attached in those years.

Changes were in hand and on 8 July 1943, Wing Commander David Davies, the Officer Commanding 276 Wing, wrote a paper classified as Most Secret and with the title 'Moves and renaming of numbers four and five field units.' It is more than that, however, and it does refer in one section to Eric Ackermann, though only by implication and without naming him. This seems to be the only time when Eric upset a senior officer, and even much later when he came up against someone much higher up than Davies, he got away with it.

'On arrival at 276 Wing to take over command, the commanding officer [Davies} had no knowledge at all of the organization of the 'Y' service. He was instructed by the members of the wing at that time and also by AI4 Middle East. This instruction gave the impression that the 'Y' service was naturally controlled from the Air Ministry, DDI4, and that the DDI4 representative in the Middle East [This must refer to Flight Lieutenant Ackermann] was the officer designated as AI4. This officer was responsible to the Air Ministry for the implementing of their general policy with regard to 'Y' matters and combining this policy with that of the CSIO [Command Signals Intelligence Officer] with regard to local operational requirements'.

Davies goes on to deal with the future of 380 and 381 Wireless Units and actual and possible operations in the Middle Eastern theatre, including the invasion of Sicily and Sardinia, or, alternatively, Crete, Greece or the Aegean and the participation of Turkey in the war. Summing up, he recommends the establishment of 329 Wing, which duly took place on 30 June. There is no need to go into the rest of the report, but Davies had earlier expressed himself strongly on the subject of civilians in uniform. Eric's regular commuting to and from London must have been the reason for him to have a rant about such people. At a meeting held at Mediterranean Air Command Headquarters in Algiers on 13 May 1943 (the same day as the German and Italian surrender), his views on civilian officers are recorded in the minutes:

'Wing Commander Davies had experienced severe difficulties in his control of these personnel, as they are of the nature of civilians in uniform who did not regard themselves as owing allegiance to the senior RAF officer on the spot, but rather to GCCS (the Government Code and Cypher School, i.e. Bletchley Park), through the Bureau. It is requested that a clear directive be issued from Air Ministry on this question. It should give him [i.e. Davies] complete control of these individuals on the lines of other RAF mixed civilian/uniformed establishments, and it is further suggested that all vacancies should, in future, appear as RAF ranks with provision for civilian substitution.'

Having to put up with a mere Flight Lieutenant who was the personal representative of Wing Commander Davies' ultimate boss was obviously galling. Davies had arrived to take over the Wing with no prior experience of signals intelligence and interception work, and this apparently freelance officer, only 23-years-old, was coming and going without the CO being able to regulate his movements. There is also a touch of jealousy and of Davies' feeling out of his depth in dealing with his unwelcome and somewhat ephemeral visitor.

Michael Beavis crops up now and again and he seems to have had frequent contact with Eric throughout the latter's time in the Mediterranean theatre and well into 1944. Another recurring name is that of Section Officer (equivalent RAF rank: Flying Officer) M.K. 'Rusty' Goff, a WAAF officer whose duties meshed with Eric's on his frequent visits to North Africa and on a joint visit they made to Gibraltar. She had been sent from the RAF's Y service station at West Kingsdown in Kent to Cairo and then on to Tunisia. She must have been a formidable person to work with, and Bert Evans certainly agrees with this assessment, though he also describes her as friendly. Aileen Clayton gives a brief clue in, *'The Enemy is Listening'*:

> 'One of the first WAAFs to arrive in North Africa had been Section Officer M.K. 'Rusty' Goff, who had been posted over to join the Field Units operating in the Cap Bon area [this is a peninsula in north-eastern Tunisia]. But to her chagrin, when the unit moved over to Sicily for 'Husky' [the Allied invasion of Sicily], she was not allowed to go with them. However, when the Italian naval vessels surrendered after the armistice [in September 1943] the energetic and irrepressible 'Rusty' flew over, first to Taranto, and then to Gibraltar, with our scientific officer, Eric Ackermann, to act as his interpreter when he examined the radar equipment on board the Italian warships.'

Rusty, described by Eric's first wife Dorothy as 'a horsey woman', and by Aileen Clayton as 'energetic and irrepressible', was a German and Italian linguist who served with No. 381 Wireless Unit and No. 21 Field Unit, as the latter's 'Y' service Intelligence Officer, where she was the only female officer on its strength. To judge from her photograph in Aileen Clayton's book, however, horsey seems a harsh description.

Before reluctantly leaving the 'irrepressible' Section Officer Goff, it is worth mentioning an event which happened when she returned to England. She was put to training American airborne monitors and from time to time had cause to criticize the paucity of their logs during operational flights. The Americans were not taking that and challenged her to do better. She accepted the challenge and went on a raid over

Officers of Nos. 21 and 25 Field Units at La Marsa, Tunisia, just before Operation Husky in July 1943, Rusty Goff is in the centre of the front row.

Wilhelmshaven. Her logs that day were so good that the 'Y' service headquarters at West Kingsdown praised them, having no idea that they were not the remarkably improved work of the Americans.

Back now to Eric Ackermann, who had the misfortune to suffer a broken arm in a road accident in June 1943. There are three versions of this. One, supplied by Ted Lines, who served with him at that time, is that he was driving a three-ton Bedford lorry to Tunisia with a small party and somehow overturned it, though how he managed to do this is not clear. The second, is from Eric's brother Keith, who confirms that Eric was driving, but says that on the way up a narrow road they met an American vehicle coming the other way which lost control and hit Eric's lorry. It seems too that Michael Beavis was a passenger. The third, which is from Bert Evans, who witnessed the event, is that Eric was driving down into Algiers from the Chateau with one of the daughters of the owner, a very attractive young lady, when one way and another, he became distracted and the car crashed, breaking the celebrated arm. Not only that, but three months later he broke the same arm again in an incident described below. He returned to the U.K. for some recuperation leave and Keith Ackermann remembered him arriving at the family's flat in Ennismore Gardens, 'with his arm broken above the elbow – a compound fracture – and his arm was plastered so as to stick out in front of him.'

Some weeks after the accident Eric gave a lift into Algiers to two airmen who were serving with 380 Wireless Unit. Ted Lines was one of them and he recalls that it was a hazardous journey, as they were in a three-tonner and their driver was driving one-handed. They were going to downtown Algiers, to the Hotel St. Georges, which was the Headquarters of the Supreme Commander Allied (Expeditionary) Force of the North African Theatre of Operations (NATOUSA), General Dwight D. Eisenhower. They were sent there for instruction on the switchboard and Ted describes what happened:

'It was a large board [with] some eight to ten positions and something new to us. We spent two or three hours operating it with the 'GI guys and girls'. It was most interesting and good experience for us.' Ted then continues; 'No arrangement had been made to pick us up to return us to our units. We left the hotel, crossed the road and started walking, not enjoying the four or five mile hike back. I suggested we stop and hail each Jeep that came along, shouting out 'Flight Lieutenant Ackermann'. The Jeep has a high revving engine distinct from any other. It was dark at the time. After the third or fourth attempt we struck oil. Eric pulled up and we hopped on board. It was pure coincidence and luck'.

Some time later, Eric drove Ted down to Algiers on his day off. They were in a small pick-up truck, with Ted sitting on Eric's left. Due to his broken arm, Eric was required to alter his driving technique. As Ted said, 'It was rather a hairy journey, to say the least.' This was partly due to the fact that when changing gear, Eric steered without being able to use his one functional hand, as it was involved with the gear stick. The injured arm, in a sling and heavily bandaged, was also hard to miss. It is hardly surprising that Ted fondly recalls Eric as 'one of the boys', though something of a loner, and, in his words, a scarlet pimpernel, which chimes with the recollections of others who served with him later in Germany.

There was another incident recounted by Bert Evans and involving five officers from 380 WU and none other than the commanding officer of the Y service in North Africa, Squadron Leader Cottam, who went one day with five other officers to the seaside resort of Sidi Ferruch. They enjoyed their swim but when they got back to the shore they found that their car, containing all their clothes, had disappeared. They then had to get back to the Chateau wearing very little, if anything at all. Could Eric have been with them? It would have been in character if he was. There were very few officers on the strength of 380 WU, although Eric's ambivalent status rather kept him apart from the others. Cottam was promoted to Wing Commander shortly after this escapade and commanded 329 Wing.

In readiness for Operation Husky – the invasion of Sicily – which began on 10 July, Sidney Goldberg's 21 Field Unit moved to the nearby airbase of Korba on 5 June and it is possible, though again it cannot be confirmed, that Eric was there as well. Peter Ackermann believes that his father did take part in Husky at an early stage, although the relevant ORB does not mention him. He does reappear in August, when the 329 Wing's ORB records his movements, or some of them, during August and September, leaving out, as usual, several intervening dates:

24 August 1943.   Flight Lieutenant Ackermann and Pilot Officer Beavis and three other ranks proceeded by road to La Marsa [Tunisia] for intelligence duties.

28 August 1943.   Flight Lieutenant Ackermann and Pilot Officer Beavis returned from La Marsa by road.

24 September 1943.   Flight Lieutenant Ackermann returned from UK as representative of AM ADI (Sc.).

The third of these entries clarifies Eric's position, vis-à-vis Wing Commander Davies. He was responsible, not to the commanding officer of the wing, but to the mysterious individual at the Air Ministry whose job title is hidden in this formidable set of initials. This, it hardly needs saying, was R.V. Jones, who, to spell it out in full, was Air Ministry Assistant Director of Intelligence (Science) (AM ADI [Sc]). For good measure they also managed this time to spell Eric's name correctly.

Husky took just seven weeks and was virtually over by the time Eric was noted as being back in Algeria. He was certainly still in Tunisia organizing the 'Y' service in its monitoring of Luftwaffe signals, and this was work he could better carry out from North Africa, rather than in Sicily itself. This does not rule out the possibility that he might have flown to and from the new battle front, while still maintaining some sort of headquarters at Ain Brahim, La Marsa or Draria.

The four weeks between the second and third entries were taken up with planning the amphibious invasion of the Italian mainland, which was given the name Operation Avalanche. It was launched on 9 September and Eric was there on the first day, playing a courageous part in the operation when he landed on the beach at Salerno and dashed ashore from an American landing craft of which he was, according to his wife Dorothy, the commanding officer. He seized what he was looking for and then returned to the landing craft, having in the process re-broken the same arm which had suffered a compound fracture in that road accident three months earlier.

Dorothy remembers too that the American soldiers on board the landing craft were jumping off into the sea and each in turn was using Eric's arm as a lever to swing himself overboard. For an RAF officer to be in command of an American landing craft seems improbable, but there is no evidence to contradict this, although it may be hidden in American records which have not been consulted. Maybe Eric just jumped at the chance of more excitement and volunteered for the operation and/or the chance of grabbing some interesting equipment may have been too much to resist. Perhaps they just needed an officer, any officer, to take charge and he was available.

The arm must have recovered sufficiently for such a valuable item of Air Ministry (and Civil Service) property as Eric Ackermann to have been placed in the dangerous position of having to come ashore under heavy fire on the first day of one of the most important landings of the entire war, but Eric's qualities of courage and specialist knowledge meant that he and he alone could do what his masters required of him. R.V. Jones specifically refers to this action in his personal handwritten commendation for the award of the George Medal in these words:

'[Despite his broken arm] he nevertheless went forward to examine captured radar stations until, according to his own signal, he was unable to proceed further owing to stiff German resistance.'

No. 329 Wing was disbanded on 23 December 1943 after one of the briefest lives of any operational unit, just five months. Its achievements did not go unnoticed, as Lieutenant General Andrew 'Tooey' Spaatz, the Commander of the Allied North-West African Air Force, paid this tribute to the Wing:

'The organizational and operational efficiency of 329 Wing RAF has contributed materially to the successes of the North-West African Air Force in all phases of the North African, Tunisian, Pantellerian and Sicilian campaigns. You and your personnel have displayed an unusually high degree of efficiency. This has been confirmed repeatedly by the high order of your work, as well as by my personal visits to elements of your command.

  The high order of your work has contributed most definitely to the air operational successes in the various campaigns and has reflected great credit on 329 Wing of the Royal Air Force.'

This is a generous tribute and well deserved, as it was only with help from 329 Wing that the Americans' Sigint work was brought up to scratch. 329 Wing was a signals unit, and while a flying unit might have been more obviously prominent in catching the commander's attention, for a secretive, behind-the-scenes part of the war effort to be praised in such glowing terms, is something that must have made its personnel proud of what they had achieved. General Spaatz had come across some of the units involved in the 'Y' service personally a year earlier in Algiers, as Ted Lines has related earlier and maybe he remembered the impressive drill movements displayed by Ted and his Naval counterpart then.

As it was at this time, in the autumn of 1943, that the first moves were made to secure a gallantry award for Eric, he may have enjoyed some reflected glory from General Spaatz's comments. It can certainly have done him no harm to be associated with a unit which was so highly regarded by the most senior air force officer in that theatre of the war.

That is not the end of Eric's involvement with 276 Wing. He reappears in Italy in the Wing ORB on 15 March 1944, when it reports that he, 'proceeded by road to San Savero on Temporary Duty and returned the same day.' No. 276 Wing had taken over from 329 Wing in December when it was still in North Africa and in January was settling into its new headquarters in Conversano, 30 km south-east of Bari and 7 km from the Adriatic coast. Although he had his George Medal by this time, there is no mention of it in the 276 Wing records, nor does Eric reappear in the wing's records and his immediate movements remain something of a mystery.

Possibly his trip to San Savero was to visit a field unit there. These were Sigint units, subordinate to the wing, and were scattered about the immediate area. It could have been No. 14, as his old colleague, the recently promoted Flying Officer Michael Beavis, 'proceeded' there by air on 4 April. Indeed, when Eric made his final appearance in an Operations Record Book for the Mediterranean theatre, he was returning to No. 14 Field Unit, from the UK to Draria, on 6 April. So between mid-March and early April he had been in Italy, gone home and returned to Algeria. Beavis was posted back to the same Field Unit on 31 May and remained there until 21 July, when he left by air for Naples en route for the UK.

As Beavis crops up from time to time in the story, it is worth mentioning that when a Wing Intelligence Officer, Flight Lieutenant W.R. Edwards, visited the same Field Unit a few days earlier, he reported that Flying Officer Beavis, 'works very long hours, as intelligence staff is barely adequate for requirements. Beavis is making a separate report on the subject of the wireless operators'. Was Edwards' visit prompted by Eric's report on his own inspection?

The role of the Field Units and their personnel was set out concisely in National Archives file (AIR 23/1265 – Field Units – General). They were required to perform at a very high-level of efficiency and the relevant files make no bones about the demands placed on them, with no allowance made for their difficult conditions of work in the desert:

'They had to pass immediate operational intelligence to the operations [headquarters] with all possible speed.

Pass daily to HQ, summaries of operations logs for research purposes and longer term intelligence in general.

'Interpreters. These men should be encouraged to work as a team and should be hand-picked, not only particularly for their colloquial knowledge of the language, but for initiative in the intelligence and operational part played by the Y service. At the end of a watch it has proved of great value for the duty officer to interrogate the operators on the traffic taken during the period. It is considered essential that the intelligence and duty officers doing this should have themselves an intimate knowledge of the language.

'Daily reports to be made up at the end of the last watch and transmitted to HQ by W/T on one time pads. Closest contact must be maintained at all times with controllers and a spirit of mutual confidence should be fostered.'

With all this to worry about, it is hardly surprising that Michael Beavis was having to work so hard. We do not know if Eric ever went to RAF Conservano, but if he did he would have found a station equipped to allow its personnel to pass their leisure hours in an impressive variety of activities by way of physical, spiritual and intellectual sustenance. There were cricket and football pitches, they could play darts, whist and bridge, enjoy tombola, films and amateur dramatics in the Gremlin Arms, or join the male voice choir. There was also a library and a church. To help with the catering, the minutes of the commanding officer's conference of 17 January 1944 records that, 'Six fat pigs arrived after quite a pleasant journey'. For whom, the pigs or their swineherds? The other ranks enjoyed watching their football team beat the officers 1–0, while one day, two teams of sergeants, the Impossibles and the Improbables, fought out a gritty goalless draw. The RAF, and no doubt the army too, played cricket in the most unlikely places, but Eric seems to have had no interest in either cricket or football. For what it is worth, on the day Eric visited San Savero, he was accompanied on the return journey by an itinerant chiropodist, so the RAFs' feet were cared for as well as their social, intellectual and spiritual needs.

Nothing to do with the story of Eric Ackermann, but nice to read nevertheless, is a report dated 27 August 1942, that the 276 Wing Sports Officer visited Squadron Leader W.R. Hammond at Headquarters RAF Middle East (in Cairo) to obtain sports kit. The squadron leader should need no introduction to anyone with even a passing interest in cricket, as before the war and until 1946 he was England's premier batsman. Wally Hammond served in the RAF throughout the war and reached the rank of wing commander, though he was kept well away from any danger. He even managed to play some cricket, particularly at the Gezira Sports Ground in Cairo. The Second World War was, for some people, a very pleasant few years.

As a footnote it is worth recording that the wing had a magazine called '*Der Feind hoert mit*' – *the Enemy is listening in* – which is, but for one word, the title of Aileen

Clayton's book. The September 1943 issue has an unflattering cartoon of Hitler on the cover and also some useful hints for those using R/T in the air.

A further point is that 276 Wing became 276 Signals Unit at Brazzacco in the north-eastern province of Udine in 1946 and moved to RAF Habbaniya in 1947. Eric is noted as visiting Habbaniya for one week from the 1 to 8 December 1948, on detachment from the British Air Forces of Occupation (Germany).

The difficulty with researching the years from mid-1942 to mid-1944, is that Eric was moving around North Africa and Italy on specific missions, as directed by Dr Jones back at the Air Ministry. It must have been difficult for senior officers such as Wing Commander Davies, operating in more conventional units, to pin him down. He seldom stayed in one place long enough for anyone to make an entry in the relevant Personnel Occurrence Report or the Operations Record Book (RAF Form 540). He was frequently airborne, flying back to London to report and then, after a short break and sometimes enjoying some leave with Dorothy, he was back out again to the Mediterranean. During one of these leaves, as Dorothy recalls, they were walking in St. James' Park, not far from their home in Ennismore Gardens in Kensington, when an American officer, out enjoying a morning canter, was thrown from his horse in front of them. Eric went to his rescue, somehow saw to the horse, and then took him (the American officer, not the horse, whose fate is not known) back to their flat for rest and recuperation. The American became a regular visitor to the flat whenever Eric was home on leave.

Eric's next documented adventure is one of the most controversial episodes in his life and one which took him back to England, then on to yet another part of the world which was new to him.

Before reaching that point, however, it is appropriate to go through the labyrinthine process which led to the award to Eric of one of his country's highest awards for gallantry.

Chapter Four

The George Medal

E ven at this stage of the conflict, Eric Ackermann was having a good war and he had so greatly distinguished himself that he was awarded the George Medal (GM), which was gazetted on 14 January 1944. Correspondence about the recommendation for the award is retained at the National Archives in document AIR 2/5021 (Ground Gallantry Awards, October 1943 – January 1944) and records the discussions about which award he should actually receive. These reached the highest level in the Air Ministry and also bothered the War Office and College of Arms as well.

The problem lay in deciding on an appropriate award for a man who was technically a civilian and was therefore disqualified from receiving an award which could only be given to 'real' commissioned officers. The DSO, which he probably deserved, was ruled out because its terms of reference did not include the kind of the operations in which he was engaged. The OBE was considered, but discarded as being inadequate recognition, and so in the end the George Medal was settled on.

The GM was introduced on 24 September 1940, by King George VI, as a second level decoration. It was, and still is, primarily a civilian award, though it is also granted for actions by servicemen and women for which purely military honours are not normally granted. The official description says that it is awarded for 'acts of great bravery in, or meriting recognition by, the United Kingdom'. Sometimes it is granted for a single act, but in Eric's case it was for continuing bravery over a lengthy period, covering the three years since he began flying in 1940.

The full text of the correspondence and the citation is given below, as they provide some information about his activities, though the wording of the citation in the *London Gazette* is brief (just thirty-nine words), and is deliberately vague. Security, particularly in Eric's area of work, had to be maintained and so details of any operations in which he distinguished himself had to be left out. This is the citation in full:

'Honorary Flight Lieutenant Eric George Ackermann, Royal Air Force Volunteer Reserve.

'For three years Flight Lieutenant Ackermann has been employed in special duties, both in this country and the Mediterranean area. He has completed these tasks often under most difficult conditions and the results have been worthy of great praise.'

Even at this important point in his career, higher authority was uncertain about the spelling of his name. The original draft of the citation had some corrections and a second 'n' is added to his name in the revised version. The *London Gazette* is almost the only source to get it consistently right.

The full commendation, drafted in his own handwriting, by R.V. Jones, and included in the Churchill College archive, is:

'Flight Lieutenant Ackermann has been concerned for three years with intelligence regarding enemy radio navigation and radar stations. In September 1940 he was a member of a small party which for a time recognized German radar transmissions. During 1941 and 1942 he flew as a special observer on many investigation flights over enemy territory, including more than forty sorties on which bombs were dropped. Many of these involved flying into the heart of the German night fighter defences to ascertain the methods of control, and include detailed observations of night fighter attacks. Early in 1943, Flight Lieutenant Ackermann went to the Mediterranean area to organize investigations and flights to locate enemy radar stations prior to the invasion of Sicily and Italy.

'In June, he sustained a badly fractured humerus through a road accident in the course of his duty, but this accident only interrupted his work for a fortnight. Later, while he was still recovering, he landed at Salerno on the first day of operations, where his arm was again broken during an enemy attack. He nevertheless went forward to examine captured radar stations until, according to his own signal, he was unable to proceed further owing to stiff German resistance. Flight Lieutenant Ackermann has volunteered for every dangerous operation connected with obtaining information about German radar stations, and has shown continuous courage, coolness and resource. His observations have been of a high order of accuracy, even under difficult and dangerous conditions and of great value to the subsequent programme of radio countermeasures.

'Note. Flight Lieutenant Ackermann is a civilian in the employ of the Ministry of Aircraft Production, holding an honorary commission in the Royal Air Force Volunteer Reserve. The Admiralty and War Office have been consulted regarding his eligibility for a DSO and the Admiralty consider that there is a fair case for the award of a service decoration, having regard to the fact that such decorations have been awarded to officers of the Corps of Naval Constructors, who are civilians, but hold naval rank while serving at sea. The War Office consider, however, that the DSO statute was not intended to cover a civilian holding an honorary commission and that a civil award would be more appropriate for a person who normally performs his duty as a civilian and not as an officer.'

This reveals all that we are likely to know and it is a tribute to Dr Jones' generosity, that it was he who set things in motion, rather than a senior air force officer. It is debatable whether Eric normally performed his duty 'as a civilian and not as an officer.' Rather the reverse, one would have thought. It certainly worked, for on 5 October 1943, the

Assistant Chief of the Air Staff (I) wrote the following to the Director General of Personal Services, unknowingly stirring up a hornet's nest and perhaps creating a precedent in the complex world of gallantry awards:

'I attach for your consideration a recommendation that the gallant conduct of the above named officer merits recognition.

'In the normal way such a recommendation would have been included in my list of recommendations recently submitted to CAS [Chief of the Air Staff], but in view of the fact that Flight Lieutenant Ackermann's commission is an honorary one and that he is technically a civilian employee of the Ministry of Aircraft Production, I am doubtful as to the nature of the award for which he may be eligible.

'I suggest that his outstanding service merits an award on the level of DSO or GM and, if you agree, I should be grateful if you would forward the recommendation to the proper quarter.'

A handwritten note is attached:

'PS to PUS

'As this officer holds an honorary commission we presume you will arrange for the attached recommendation to be considered (probably a GM or OBE would be appropriate). 14.10.43.'

Four days later, on the 18 October, the Assistant Permanent Secretary wrote to the Permanent Under-Secretary as follows:

'On PUS's instructions I have consulted Sir Robert Knox. He was inclined to the view that as Flight Lieutenant Ackermann was being recommended for gallantry in operations against the enemy, he might properly be awarded the DSO [Distinguished Service Order]. The Warrant for the DSO refers to the holding of a commission and the rule that holders of honorary commissions – in general they do not take part in operations – should get civil and not military awards is a semi-official arrangement adopted by Departments as a matter of convenience.

'Sir Robert recommended, however, that, before going ahead with the DSO recommendation, we should take the Admiralty and the War Office into our confidence and tell them what we proposed to do.

'PUS would be glad, therefore, if, subject to DGPS's concurrence, you would initiate action on these lines.'

Sir Robert Uchtred Eyre Knox was the Secretary of the Political Honours Committee. A question remains as to what was so political about Eric's award. Possibly it was because Eric was that rarity, an honorary officer who had been on operations, lots of them. Sir Robert's names in full are immensely impressive, but despite his apparent grandeur he did not in the end persuade his colleagues that Eric should receive the DSO, despite the fact that he had, in the words of the DSO Warrant quoted above, taken part in operations.

A civil servant with the less exotic name of Simmons then wrote to F.S. Yuill of the Air Ministry on 29 October 1943, using the conventional Civil Service mode of salutation of the time, the unadorned surname and also, perhaps unsurprisingly, misspelling Eric's surname:

'Dear Yuill.

'You wrote to me on the 19th about a recommendation for a gallantry award to Honorary Flight Lieutenant E.G. Ackerman.

'MAP [Ministry of Aircraft Production] strongly endorse the recommendation, which we think should be for the GM; in our view the OBE would not be appropriate.

'I may add that Ackerman's work is thought very highly of, and the recommendation for an award is wholly in keeping with what his official superiors would have expected.'

On 2 November, the Air Ministry, possibly in the person of F.S. Yuill, wrote to R.M.Y. Gladowe, Esq, CVO, which took the process several steps nearer to its conclusion:

'Dear Gladowe,

'We have received a recommendation for the award of the DSO or GM to a civilian employee of the Ministry of Aircraft Production who holds an honorary commission in the RAFVR. The services rendered, which are of a secret character in connection with radio, including flying as an observer on more than forty missions on which bombs were dropped, also landing at Salerno on the first day of operations, when he went forward to examine and capture Radiolocation stations.

'Knox is inclined to think the DSO might be awarded, but has suggested that the Admiralty and War Office might be consulted. I should be grateful if you will say whether you have any precedent for the grant of this decoration to an honorary officer, or whether you have any views on the subject.'

The issue was finally settled and on 7 January 1944, when Sir Robert Knox sent a memo:

'I write to inform you, for record purposes, that the King has approved the following awards for gallantry:

'GM: Honorary Flight Lieutenant Eric George Ackermann, ADI (Science)'

The *London Gazette* then recorded the award in its issue for Friday, 14 January 1944 and the relevant entry is reproduced here. It consists of a mere forty-one words, giving away very little about the work in which he had been and still was engaged. The *Times* announced the award on the following day, and Eric was included in a list of five officers and one airman receiving the George Medal.

A short time later, Eric and his wife Dorothy went to Buckingham Palace for the investiture by King George VI, an event she remembered with great pride. The whole procedure, from the first airing of the commendation, to the concluding event of the investiture, took some four months. It was a lengthy

THIRD SUPPLEMENT
TO
The London Gazette
Of TUESDAY; the 11th of JANUARY, 1944

Published by Authority

Registered as a newspaper

FRIDAY, 14 JANUARY, 1944

Awarded the George Medal.

Honorary Flight Lieutenant Eric George Ackermann, Royal Air Force Volunteer Reserve.

For three years Flight Lieutenant Ackermann has been employed on special duties both in this country and the Mediterranean area. He has completed his tasks often under most difficult and dangerous conditions and the results have been worthy of great praise.

The *London Gazette* of 14 January 1944 recording the award of the George Medal to Flight Lieutenant Ackermann.

process, partly because of Eric 's unusual status, but it all worked out in the end and Flight Lieutenant Ackermann was at last the deserving holder of a very high award for gallantry. Just to round this off, at the end of the war Eric also received seven campaign medals: the Defence Medal, the 1939–1945 Star, the War Medal 1939–1945, the Air Crew Europe Star, the France and Germany Star, the Africa Star and the Italy Star. Not a bad effort for an honorary officer still without a service number.

Chapter Five

Eric Ackermann and the Flying Bombs

This chapter is about an operation involving Eric Ackermann after he left Italy in the early summer of 1944. On his return to England he reported to the Air Ministry and to R.V. Jones, who had another ace up his sleeve to keep him busy and sent him off somewhere very different.

The story is about a mission which lasted more than two months and although Eric's part in it turned out to be slight, it is worth telling, because it shows how far up his own particular ladder – as something of a roving scientist in uniform – he had progressed.

In late 1942, a new threat, the flying bomb appeared and from that followed an operation in which Eric's part was abruptly and inexplicably curtailed. The British were aware, through RAF reconnaissance flights, that the Germans were building pens from which to launch a new kind of bomb with a greater destructive power than anything ever seen before.

The first successful test firing of the V1 (Vergeltungswaffe –vengeance weapon) was in October 1942 and two months later the first test launch took place. Constantly referred to by German propaganda as the 'wonder weapon', it became, by 1944, a last-ditch attempt to reverse the course of the war by forcing Britain to surrender and therefore to deal once and for all with the threat of an invasion of north-western Europe. One of the launch sites was at Peenemünde on the Baltic coast. In August 1943, the RAF attacked it for the first time with 598 aircraft. This and many subsequent raids caused considerable damage, which seriously delayed the full firing programme; which did not take place until the following June.

The first salvo of V1s fell on London on 12 June 1944. Then, on 18 June, which was a Sunday, a V1 fell on the Guards Chapel during the morning service, killing 121 of the congregation and the Coldstream Guards Band, including its Director of Music. Not only was this an appalling tragedy, but the bomb fell alarmingly close to the Houses of Parliament, 10 Downing Street and Buckingham Palace. The next day the Prime Minister set up the Crossbow Committee to report on these new weapons and come up with the measures needed to counter their threat. Churchill appointed Duncan Sandys as Chairman and it included the Chiefs of Staff, the Commanders-in-Chief of the various Commands, other senior serving officers and several scientists, of whom R.V. Jones was one. Jones, incidentally, described the problem thus: 'the pilotless [missile] is a problem in defensive intelligence', a neat summary.

Trials at Peenemünde continued after these attacks on London and inevitably some went considerably astray. One of these landed in neutral Sweden on 23 June 1944 and after it exploded – luckily it fell in open country – the remnants were collected by the Swedish police and the British Embassy was permitted to examine them.

Within a few days Crossbow was considering what to do about the so-called Swedish bomb, whose explosive power can be appreciated from information given by the Embassy to the Air Ministry, which reported this on 24 June, quoting the Swedish press:

'1. Thirty-five kilometres N.W. of Kalmak. Violent explosion made crater several metres wide and 1.5 metres deep. Explosion heard over fourteen kilometres away. Two metres long shell of projectile found 300 metres away from crater. Several explosions were heard whilst projectile was flying and pieces of iron have been found scattered over an area four square kilometres.

'2. I am endeavouring to obtain more details and will send further report as soon as possible.

'3. Do you intend sending expert to Sweden?'

The RAF's attacks on the Peenemünde site since August 1943 had caused so much damage that Hitler was persuaded to move the trials to a new location far away and safe from air attack. For this purpose Himmler placed an SS training camp at the disposal of the rocket organization. This was located at Blizna, sixty-five miles east of Cracow in south-east Poland, with the unthreatening name of Heidelager (camp on the heath). The Blizna site was supplied with rocket components from factories in Stettin, Frankfurt, Breslau, Eberswalde and Königsberg and at least one in Poland itself.

R.V. Jones began prodding the Air Ministry and the Crossbow Committee to investigate Blizna and to find out from remnants left by the trial launches as much as they could about the V-1s, which were now constantly attacking London and south-east England. This was by now a feasible operation, as Russian troops were advancing rapidly through Poland and would reach Blizna within a few weeks. It was a very active site: between the first test there on 5 November 1943 and the last on 30 June 1944, no fewer than 204 tests were carried out, of which eighty-four took place in June. At the peak of its activity as many as ten missiles a day were fired and most of these appear to have been successful.

After a two-week delay, the Air Ministry finally replied to the Embassy signal on 7 July asking Flight Lieutenant A.H. Burder, who was on the Air Attaché's staff at the Embassy in Stockholm, for his preliminary views on this new weapon which he was inspecting. Burder replied on the following day with the information on the technical details of the projectile. On the same day, another of the Air Attaché's staff, Flight Lieutenant G. Wilkinson, together with Burder, sent two signals with more technical information and on 10 July a further signal was despatched, with Wilkinson recommending that:

'we should endeavour to obtain loan remainder W/T equipment for examination in United Kingdom. I shall endeavour to arrange this, but I shall need your authority to give Swedish written undertaking that equipment will be returned within half time, say two months and that a full report of British examination of equipment will be given to Swedish authorities.'

Sweden, as a neutral country, was cautious about being seen to co-operate with one of the warring parties, although it was not at all averse to supplying Germany with iron ore, timber and other essential war materials, partly because it was good for trade, but also to dissuade Germany from annexing the country.

Parallel with the information from Sweden, the Deputy Chief of the Air Staff, Air Marshal Sir Norman Bottomley, sent a message from the

The rocket site at Blizna.

Headquarters of the MAAF at Caserta in Italy to Air Marshal Sir John Slessor, Commander-in-Chief, Middle East Air Force, on 7 July:

'Fragments of German long-range weapon which may be the rocket have been found by a Polish source at a point some eighty miles east of Warsaw. It is of utmost importance for us to obtain these as they include radio which may assist in planning countermeasures. Would like you to consider laying on Dakota to pick up, similar to operation Wildhorn, to bring back this equipment. Enquiries being made as to exact location to enable you to select clandestine landing ground. Further information on this will be sent to you direct from Poland through the SOE [Special Operations Executive] link at Bari.'

Slessor replied the next day. 'Action being put in hand at once'.

Bottomley then responded on the 10 July, suggesting that the flight would be difficult and an aircraft capable of defending itself would be needed. He suggested a Beaufighter, Mosquito, or Mitchell, rather than a Dakota. He concludes:

'Chances of success of the project would be immeasurably changed if aircraft could use Russia. Would it be possible, for example, to use one of the American bomber bases in Russia. SOE here consider that they could make their arrangements fit accordingly. In this event Dakota could be used without escort'.

This was a separate operation and had nothing to do with the Blizna site, but it shows how desperate the British were to get hold of bomb parts so that they could develop countermeasures. Just to tidy up this part of the V-bomb story, on 11 July, Air Marshal Bottomley signalled an officer named Elliott at the Air Ministry, saying that SOE had asked the Poles for detailed particulars, landing ground and weight of stores to be carried. It is included because it shows the determination of the British to gather as much information as they could on the V-weapons and, in this particular case, the extraordinary courage of the Polish SOE agents.

Elliott duly obliged and on 14 July Mediterranean and Allied Air Forces Headquarters at Caserta in Italy signalled the Air Ministry to say that:

'SOE London have now heard from Poland that proposed operation will be ready for mounting from 20 July onwards.

'Landing ground will be same as that used for Wildhorn II. Load to be picked up consists of 50 (R) kilograms of equipment and one man.'

A Polish resistance agent, Jerzy Chmielesewski, made an epic 200 mile journey by bicycle, carrying the parts in a sack on his shoulder, to reach a landing ground near Tarnow which was more or less adequate for an RAF Dakota flying from Brindisi to land, collect him and the parts and eventually get them and him to RAF Hendon to hand over the priceless booty. It was an immensely courageous ride through the German lines which were retreating westwards in the face of the advancing Russians.

To provide almost the perfect (or more properly, given the circumstances, imperfect) climax, the aircraft's wheels got stuck in the mud and it could not take off. A crowd of local people dug the mud away with spades and bare hands and some farmers produced planks torn down from the fences surrounding the houses and made a crude runway, and then the Dakota was able to drag itself off the ground. While all this was going on a German patrol, attracted by the noise, had to be disposed of by some of the Poles who were guarding the hectic work going on in the muddy field.

While signals were flying to and fro between Italy and the Air Ministry about the other find of V-bomb parts and at the risk of interrupting the flood of signals between Stockholm and London about the Swedish bomb, a document in the Jones archive merits examination and is an example of the prodding referred to above. It is the first glimpse we have of Jones' interest in this matter and he writes forcefully in an undated, unsigned and handwritten memo to the Chief of the Air Staff, Sir Charles Portal:

'You will have seen the various signals about the projectile [which] recently fell in Sweden. They show beyond doubt that it is a long-range rocket with radio control. Similar projectiles have fallen in Poland and the Secret Military Organization there has rescued various components.

'Through the good offices of our Air Attaché in Stockholm, the Swedes have allowed two of my officers to examine the fragments recovered. This examination has been very valuable, but I am convinced that our hope of uncovering the details of the very complicated radio mechanism is to have the components brought to this country. They can then be examined in the laboratory and perhaps combined with other radio parts which we are trying to bring back from Poland and compared with other German radio control systems to which they show similarities.

'I believe that the acquisition of all available components is a matter of vital interest to the defence of this country, and that we should not hesitate to pay any reasonable price which would satisfy the Swedes. Our best hope of arranging this is as [illegible] Staffs, rather by Foreign Office channels, and we can probably obtain American support if necessary.

'Probably if we offer the Swedes the results of our examinations, together with any radio jamming equipment which we may subsequently design, the additional price in, say, Spitfires, may not be unduly high.

'Perhaps you would consider action along these lines.

'The Germans have for some months been trying out the long-range rocket from the SS camp near Drbice [i.e. Debice, the handwriting is unclear at this point].

'The Russians are now within [illegible] miles of this camp and should they take it soon, they may acquire important details of the long-range rocket, such as [the] nature of the launching point and of the radio [illegible, could be wavelength]. Both these are at the moment very serious intelligence problems.'

On 11 July, the Chiefs of Staff Committee wrote to the Prime Minister urging him to approach Marshal Stalin personally, and to ask him to arrange for the preservation of the installations and equipment at, 'the experimental station of Debice and, after its capture by the Soviet armies, to grant us full facilities to examine these installations and equipment.' In his letter, Churchill informed Stalin for the first time of the German rocket weaponry being tested in Poland and he asked that Soviet troops, which were then some fifty kilometres from Debice, should be ordered to preserve any rocket and other hardware found at the site, once the Soviets had captured the area. Churchill further asked Stalin to allow a team of British experts to visit the site to examine the hardware. Stalin agreed to all of this, but at the same time ordered his own army intelligence to prepare to evaluate these items. He also made sure that Russian intelligence officers would reach the scene before the British.

The Air Ministry too was stepping up a gear and on 11 July sent a signal to its Stockholm Embassy saying they attached 'highest importance to obtaining radio equipment' and that the guarantees required by the Swedes were agreed. The Chiefs of Staff Committee met on the same day and its members, Field Marshal Sir Alan Brooke, Marshal of the Royal Air Force Sir Charles Portal and Admiral Sir Andrew Cunningham, agreed a report under the aegis of the Crossbow Committee. The key paragraphs in the Chiefs' report were these:

'There is firm evidence to show that the Germans have been conducting trials of the flying rocket from an experimental station at Debice for a considerable time. This station is in the path of the advancing Russian Armies and, should their advance continue at anything like its present rate, the area will be overrun in the next few weeks.

'The Germans will almost certainly destroy or remove as much of the equipment at Debice as they can, it is probable that a considerable amount of information will become available when the area is in Russian hands.

'We therefore also suggest that strong representations should be made to the Russian Government with a view to the preservation of such apparatus and installations at Debice as they are able, and to ensure that after the area has been overrun, they give us every facility for its examination.

'This too is a matter for political negotiation, but we attach so much importance to it that we think it wants a personal approach from the Prime Minister to Marshal Stalin.

'We, therefore, recommend that:-

i. 'The Foreign Office should ask the Swedish Government whether they would be prepared to release the fragments of what is believed to be a flying rocket for transmission to this country, as a matter of urgency.

ii. 'The Prime Minister should send a personal message to Marshal Stalin, requesting him to arrange for the preservation of the installations and equipment remaining at Debice after its capture and to grant us full facilities for their examination.'

Churchill duly sent his signal to Stalin at 1255 hours on 15 July, using much the same wording that the Chiefs of Staff had suggested:

'There is firm evidence that the Germans have been conducting trials of the flying rocket from an experimental station at Debice in Poland for a considerable time. According to our information, this missile has an explosive charge of about 12,000lbs and the effectiveness of our countermeasures largely depends on how much we can find out about this weapon before it is launched against this country. Debice is in the path of your victorious advancing armies and it may well be that you will overrun this place in the next few weeks.

'Although the Germans will almost certainly destroy or remove as much of the equipment at Debice as they can, it is probable that a considerable amount of information will become available when the area is in Russian hands. In particular, we hope to learn how the rocket is discharged, as this will enable us to locate the launching sites.

'I should be grateful therefore, Marshal Stalin, if you could give appropriate instructions for the preservation of such apparatus and installations at Debice as your armies are able, to ensure after the area has been overrun, and that thereafter you would afford us facilities for the examination of this experimental station by our experts.'

Meanwhile, back in Sweden, the radio equipment which the British Embassy had managed to secure was on its way and was despatched to Britain on 15 July by Mosquito in eight diplomatic bags. The value of the Swedish missile, as far as the British were concerned, was that they would be able to assess the effect of a flying bomb no matter where it came from and to use the Blizna bits and pieces to work out details of the construction and operation of the bomb itself. It was already apparent that the bombs could hit targets within ten miles of the target area.

On 18 July, a report prepared by ADI (Science) – R.V. Jones – for the Chiefs of Staff and the Crossbow Committee, stated that photographic reconnaissance had been made of Blizna (or Debice), the experimental firing station in Poland, and the photographs were being interpreted. An SOE operation to Poland to pick up certain electrical equipment and plans, had been successfully completed. This was the operation referred to in the MAAF signal of 14 July.

The Prime Minister took the chair at a meeting of the Crossbow Committee on 18 July. Those present show its importance: R.V. Jones, the Chiefs of Staff, Duncan Sandys (Minister of Supply), Herbert Morrison (Home Secretary), Lord Cherwell (Churchill's wartime science adviser), Robert Watson-Watt, Major General Sir Colin Gubbins (executive head SOE), and other important people. The Prime Minister stated that, 'Marshal Stalin has agreed to render us all assistance to obtain information from Debice when the Russian Forces capture that area.'

A signal from the British Embassy in Moscow on 27 July stated that there should be no delay over visas and urged that the party be sent to Moscow Airport by aircraft specially detailed and not by routine air services. The Ambassador, Sir Archibald Clark Kerr, then stated firmly:

'And also for reasons of prestige I would like to make strongest plea that aircraft of British, repeat British manufacture, with RAF, Repeat RAF crew be selected. In view of rapid advance by Soviet forces into Poland, consider party should leave UK just as soon as all arrangements are complete. They should proceed here rather than to any intermediate or shuttle base owing Soviet system of centralized control of everything Moscow also location our missing contact which has direct WT point to point with you.

'Unless you have in mind a Polish interpreter who is hundred per cent British national, with British name, strongly advise against including one in party.

'Soviets most repeat most suspicious of UK émigré Poles, furthermore, suggest Polish interpreter not important. Will supply interpreter from my staff.

'Major General Slavin has been detailed by Marshal Stalin to make arrangements this end.

Later that day came the news from Moscow that:

'Slavin is sick and his deputy knew little of what was going on and has as yet received no directive from higher authority. Impressed on him we must avoid delay on issue of visas for passengers and crew, and clearance for aircraft to enter Soviet territory, I can only reiterate my earnest hope that it is RAF and a product of the British aircraft industry. No British built aircraft with service crew has ever flown to Russia and RAF kudos consequently depressingly low in comparison with USAAF.'

Everything was now in place for the mission to get on its way, although it may have occurred to the committee setting up the team that alerting Stalin to the value of the Debice station might cause him to go in for double-crossing. At that stage in the war, however, he was still considered a more or less trustworthy ally. Subsequent events were to disprove this optimistic view. The mission was to be headed by Colonel T.R.B. Sanders, who appears in the Army List as retired, but in fact was working for the Ministry of Supply as an engineer and an expert on the V-bombs. He had earlier submitted his own report to the War Cabinet on the threat of the bombs. The composition of the party was mixed, and apart from Colonel Sanders, they were: Lieutenant Colonel A.D. Merriman, Flight Lieutenant C.H. Burder, G. Wilkinson and E.G. Ackermann, as well as two civilians and four US officers. Later on three more RAF officers were added as interpreters.

The two senior officers, Sanders and Merriman, were considerable figures. Terence Sanders (1901–1985) was educated at Eton and Trinity College, Cambridge, stroked the victorious Cambridge crew in the 1923 Boat Race and later co-wrote a history of the Boat Race, published in 1959. He was a member of the British coxless fours team which won the Gold Medal in the 1924 Olympic Games in Paris. His civilian profession was as a University lecturer in engineering and for good measure he was also a Fellow of Corpus Christi College, Cambridge. He was awarded the CB in 1950.

Arthur Douglas Merriman (1892–1972) was a Royal Engineers officer and a bomb disposal expert working for the Directorate of Scientific Research at the Ministry of Supply. He was awarded the George Cross in 1940 after removing explosives from a bomb dropped on Regent Street on 11 September 1940 (the same day that Eric Ackermann received his commission). Burder and Wilkinson, who were Air Intelligence officers in the Embassy in Stockholm, had been involved in the story since the experimental bomb had landed in Sweden and so it was logical to include them. Dr Jones managed to get Eric Ackermann added, as he writes in *Most Secret War*:

'.... Air Intelligence Officers were included in a balancing rather than a primary capacity. One was Wilkinson, who had examined the Swedish rocket, and was obviously a good choice; and I nominated, as my personal representative, Eric

Ackermann, who would be best qualified of the whole party to look at any aspects of radio control which I suspected might be used to fly a rocket along a beam.

'In briefing Ackermann, I warned him that I thought the party had already been rendered ineffectual by its composition [Duncan Sandys had taken over the nomination of most of the party from Jones, who was understandably peeved] but that he should continue with it as long as there seemed any hope. It would be well at this point to dispose of the fortunes of the party as they progressed eastwards. Their first signal, on 31 July, from Headquarters of British Forces in the Middle East included the ominous sentence, "Party amalgamating well and very hopeful of good results". This naiveté did not augur well for matching the wiles of the Russians'.

Dr Jones had previously, by implication, paved the way for Eric Ackermann to be included when he minuted the Chief of the Air Staff, saying that:

'It is most desirable that some Air Intelligence Officers, with a full knowledge of our background, should immediately inspect the camp in the event of its capture. You may consider, as I do, that this matter is of sufficient importance to justify a personal approach to Stalin by the Prime Minister.'

Could it have been an intervention by Winston Churchill that persuaded the Crossbow Committee to include Eric in the mission? Nick Ackermann says his father had told him many years later that he had met Churchill in 1944, possibly when Eric was in London receiving his George Medal, or maybe the Prime Minister, who took a close interest in such matters, knew of Eric's achievements thus far in the war. Anyway, Eric was in the team because he knew about aircraft flying along a radio directed beam, which was how the flying bombs were sent on their way. He was therefore as familiar with this aspect of the missiles as anyone else and probably more than most of them.

The final launch at Blizna took place on Monday, 24 July and five days later, on Saturday, 29 July 1944, Sanders' party took off from RAF Bovington in Hertfordshire, in a Liberator with a double crew for the tortuous journey to Blizna, travelling via Newquay, Cases Air Base, Cairo and Tehran where they arrived on Monday, 31 July. At this point they experienced difficulties in obtaining visas to travel to Poland and these had to be obtained from the Russian Consul, which inevitably took a long time. This was despite the British Ambassador in Moscow's assurance that visas would not be a problem.

The brief outline of the mission is taken from the official diary written by Colonel Sanders. On 4 August, Eric's name appears in the official diary where Sanders writes that Flight Lieutenant Burder had, 'visited me and asked my permission to send [the] following message:

'Personal from D of I(R) with Col. Sanders consent. Situation static.

'Possibility of American plane leaving shortly for London.

'Request permission to return and continue work in England pending clarification of position if there have been no further developments by the time the plane starts. Please signal instructions.'

Dr Jones' version of the events and Eric Ackermann's reaction to them, as recorded in *Most Secret War*, clarifies the latter's strong views and his frustration at the delay after four days on the ground in the heat of Tehran:

'On 3 August a signal from Tehran announced that the Russians were holding them up, because the party had left London without obtaining visas, and part of the signal ran, "Position regarding visas unchanged … still confident that Mission will obtain extremely valuable technical information if allowed to visit sites." Four days later the party was still in Tehran with most of them down with dysentery, with two actually in hospital. By this time Ackermann managed to get an independent signal to me saying that the Mission was quite hopeless because of its incompetence, and requesting my permission to return. Since there was plenty of work for him to do on the Western Front, I readily agreed.'

Sanders then writes, 'Burder was followed by Flight Lieutenant Ackermann who had drafted a longer but somewhat similar message to Dr Jones in which he asked Dr Jones for his views and instructions, indicating that it might be well for him, Ackermann, to return home to report'.

Sanders refused to send either of these reports to London as he felt they would confuse the situation at home and it was unlikely that a reply would be received before the plane left. Why Eric himself should ask to be allowed to go back home is extraordinary and out of character for someone who had already proved himself to be far from lacking in courage or a sense of adventure. It is equally extraordinary that Jones should have agreed so readily to Ackermann's return, given his glowing reasons for wanting him in the group in the first place. He may, however, have been half expecting the news as he had already expressed his doubts over the mission due to interference by Duncan Sandys over its make-up. Possibly too, Eric hoped, having got back to England and presented his report, that he would be sent back out again. This did not happen and his participation in the operation was effectively ended.

The next day Sanders decided that he would send Ackermann back home with despatches and to give a full report of what had happened to date; 'I decided against sending Burder home as I felt that he would be of more use to the mission if it went forward and of less use in London than Ackermann'.

On 7 August at 0600 hours, 'Saw Ackermann off. Gave him despatches and verbal instructions concerning events of preceding twenty-four hours'. Meanwhile, as R.V. Jones had written, both Burder and Wilkinson had gone down with dysentery, so the

RAF component of the mission was either in hospital or on the way home. Another report, written by Sanders' son, suggests that Eric was recalled for political reasons, although there is no hint as to what these might have been. Nevertheless, Keith Ackermann shared the younger Sanders' view.

Sir Harry Hinsley, in British Intelligence in the Second World War, discusses a dispute between Duncan Sandys, the Minister of Works and Chairman of the Crossbow Committee and R.V. Jones. Sandys wanted to be shown the intelligence raw material as and when it was received. Jones felt that this could not be granted and although he was supported by Lord Cherwell, he lost the battle. Nevertheless, he was allowed to remain on the Crossbow Committee.

Two less likely reasons for Eric's recall, which are no more than surmise, are that somehow he did not fit in or was difficult to handle. Was this an echo of Wing Commander Davies' unease with Eric and other civilian scientists in uniform during the North African campaign? The other possibility is that Sanders may have felt that Eric's Germanic name would upset the Russians, bearing in mind the British Ambassador in Russia's warning against including anyone with a Polish name. The Germans were not exactly welcome in Russia at this time either. Another possibility is that Eric was not comfortable with the mission and was missing the action in France in which he had already been involved.

While all this was going on and Eric's immediate future was being determined, a parallel Soviet mission of aviation specialists left Moscow on 5 August and joined the Soviet Army which was aiming to reach Blizna, where it arrived on the following day, which happened to be the day before Eric Ackermann's abrupt departure for home. It now seemed that the way was clear for the intrepid group to proceed into Poland, once the visas and other permissions had come through from the Russians. These eventually appeared on 11 August, by which time the mission was seriously short of personnel due to sickness and Eric's departure.

The Soviet experts now had had four clear weeks on the site before the British mission finally arrived on 2 September, five weeks after leaving the UK. They found that the Soviet officers had not made much progress in discovering what the rocket parts actually meant. Their finds meant nothing to them and it was left to Sanders' team to help them out. Indeed, without the British officers and their maps, their search would have been fruitless. Boris Chertok, a leading Russian scientist and one of the team who would be inspecting the rocket parts later on in Moscow, wrote that had it not been for Churchill's letter to Stalin, the Soviet Army would have passed the site without realizing what was there.

The mission found rocket remnants and had them crated up and sent on to Moscow. On 18 September Sanders sent a signal to R.V. Jones:

'Russian Headquarters were undoubtedly a little sceptical about the existence of such large rockets until they saw us recovering and recognizing parts. This has made deep impression on the Russian officers with us.

'We may cause a minor sensation in Russian technical circles when we return to Moscow with the parts. Probably this is all to the good as regards future relations between the three countries.'

Unfortunately, in view of what was to happen to the parts while they were being packed up to go to Britain, this optimistic view was rapidly shattered. The three countries which Sanders mentions are the Soviet Union, Great Britain and Poland, and post-war events in Europe would later show that the Russians behaviour over the rocket parts was a small part of a pattern which was revealed more fully once the war was over.

According to a Russian source, when the Director and Deputy Director of the NII-1 Research Institute saw the treasure; 'they could hardly believe their eyes. The size and capabilities of the combustion chamber was far beyond anything Soviet engineers could dream at the time.'

Even this late in the day when it seemed that nothing more could go wrong, it did. Sanders had to report to Jones on 27 September that, 'the

A forthright warning notice in Polish and German at the Blizna site.

Russians have temporarily lost main part of our R[rocket] specimens in transit between Blizna and Moscow but they have promised to do all in their power to see that they follow us without undue delay.' He had not been informed of this until his team reached Moscow and writing on Tuesday, 21 September and due to leave on the following Tuesday, with or without the parts, he says: 'Parts or no parts, we must leave and the parts would have to follow.' His exasperation and loss of trust in the Russians is obvious in this entry in the official diary.

A farewell party was held on Monday, 25 September at which one Colonel Makarov, 'apologized very much (!) [the exclamation mark is Sanders'] for the loss of our rocket parts, said that they had been located and steps were being taken to get them to Moscow.' They did reach Moscow and were crated up and despatched to go to London. At last, then, after so many vicissitudes, it seemed that the exercise was going to end happily. Almost inevitably, however, this was not to be. The party was further delayed in Moscow due mainly to the customary problems with visas which forced them to remain for a further five days. The final dénouement was taking place even while the party was waiting to leave.

Boris Chertok recalls in his autobiography *Rockets and People*, that he inspected the components gathered by the British at Blizna in Moscow on the evening before they were dispatched to Britain. He also claims that he and four other experts inspected the cargo before it was handed over to the British Embassy and found to be in order.

British officers inspecting rocket parts at Blizna.

Nevertheless, the Russians, when packing up the mission's finds to send them to the UK, removed them and replaced them with car parts, or, in R.V. Jones' version, aircraft parts, although he did later write that; 'when opened they were found to contain not parts of rockets, but old scrap parts of motor cars. The Russians had their own agenda regarding German rocket research.' It was simply that the Russians intended to appropriate the finds for themselves and place them in the NII-1 Research Institute in Moscow under heavy security on the evening before they were dispatched to Britain. Under whose instructions and when the rocket components were then switched for car parts remains a mystery. It was, however, a taste of things to come and an example of what co-operation with its allies really meant to the Soviet Union.

The exhausted and frustrated party finally arrived back at Bovington on 1 October. Their fury at discovering the substitution of rusty bits of cars for their valuable booty of rocket parts can be imagined. It is ironic to note that just before they left Colonel Sanders had noted in his diary that:

'We all parted on the best of terms (This is what really irritated Dr R.V. Jones).'

It was an epic expedition which ended in inglorious failure through no fault of the participants, but due entirely to the duplicity and constant delaying tactics of the Russians, though that would not have been much consolation for the weary travellers on their return. Sadly, it was in the end a waste of time and resources, except that the Allied officers were at least able to take photographs of the rocket parts on the ground at Blizna and make notes of what they saw.

R.V. Jones gave a bleak summing up of the whole business, writing in *Most Secret War*, that:

'as Wilkinson told me on his return, the Russians accompanied our Mission throughout the visit to Blizna, and Poles who might not have talked to the Russians gladly came forward to talk to the British, only to have their names taken by the

Russians to be listed for their pro-British sympathies. So the Mission probably did positive harm and achieved no good whatsoever.'

What a contrast this is to the words of Colonel Sanders' euphoric signal to Jones on 18 September.

As a footnote, no sooner had they got back home, than Colonel Sanders and Lieutenant Colonel Merriman were involved in a similar though less problematic expedition in November 1944 to uncover the secrets of the flying bombs at La Coupole in France. None of the others who took part in the Blizna mission were involved in this, probably to their relief, although there was no chance this time of any of the double-crossing which had ruined the earlier venture. As for Eric Ackermann, he was soon off on another venture, this time in north-west Europe and at the instigation, almost inevitably, of R.V. Jones, who appears in these pages almost as often as Eric himself.

In case R.V., as Dorothy Hartnell-Beavis still calls him, comes across as something of a control freak, wilfully directing Eric hither and thither, he was nothing of the sort. Dorothy remembers him as a kind, warm and friendly and most gentlemanly man, whom she and other members of the family got to know well. We shall see later how this continued until the end of Eric's life and that R.V. kept in frequent touch with him during the many years he was to spend in America.

Before leaving the V-bombs, it is just possible that the following year Eric may have been involved in another incident, this time in north Germany after the end of the war. In the autumn of 1945 the RAF was investigating a V-2 at Altenwalde, near Cuxhaven, on the north German coast. Given his work in Holland and his attenuated role in the Blizna episode he must surely have been called on for what was called Operation Backfire. He was to some extent in professional limbo around this time – his future work with yet another venture was still developing and he was available and in the vicinity. Nevertheless, with no documentary proof, this part of the story can go no further, at least as far as Eric is involved. David Haysom found out about this from an article headed, *Heute vor 60 Jahren: Operation Backfire* in an October 2005 issue of the *Cuxhavener Nachrichten*, describing events there sixty years earlier:

[On 15 October 1945 at 1506 hours] the last German V-2 Rocket was erected onto its firing platform in the southern Wernerwald after intensive preparations by German scientists and specialists. Tracked by English radar stations the length of the German-Danish coastline, the V-2 travelled 233 kilometres towards its target in the North Sea before falling into the sea.

Maybe Eric felt he had enough of flying bombs by now and declined an invitation to attend, if indeed he ever received one.

Chapter Six

North-West Europe, 1944 to 1946

There is some evidence pointing to Eric being back in Europe during the early summer of 1944 and his son Nick believes that he was in France on, or shortly after D-Day. It would have made sense if he was, as he had already been involved in two of the three previous seaborne invasions, Husky and Avalanche. Dr Jones commented that he did not mind if Eric did come home prematurely from the Blizna Mission, writing that, 'Since there was plenty of work for him to do on the Western Front, I readily agreed [to his return]'. This implies that he was already involved in France. If he was, it was not for very long. The Blizna mission set off for Tehran on 29 July with Eric on board believing that he would be away for some weeks. It is inconceivable that such a valuable asset as Eric Ackermann was not in the thick of it from D-Day onwards, but Jones' faith in his protégé was such that it was worthwhile detaching him from the invasion of France and send him off elsewhere.

For whatever reason, things did not work out in Tehran and Eric was back home on 5 August to continue with the work he had been doing in North Africa and probably a few weeks earlier in France. In North Africa he had been working in close co-operation with two Wireless Units, numbers 380 and 381, and although these two units were not involved in Operation Overlord (they had in fact been disbanded) another of that group, No. 383 was and it landed in France on 8 August. With 383 came Sidney Goldberg, fresh from North Africa and Italy, where he had known, or known of, Eric. There were two more Wireless Units, numbers 365 and 382, which Eric would certainly to be working with, together with the parent organization of all of them, No. 84 Group. No. 365 appeared in a document dated 14 January 1944 which has the title *Formation of Signals Intelligence Organization for AEAF* (Allied Expeditionary Air Force). This organization surely cannot have ignored the presence of Eric Ackermann, a man widely experienced in signals intelligence. The document is in the early plans for D-Day, and a short extract from it says that:

'The organization will consist of an R/T unit with each of 83 and 84 Groups, No. 365 Wireless Unit for service with TAF [Tactical Air Force] outside the UK.'

This does not take our story much further, but it shows that 365 WU, at that time in North Africa, was already in line for service in Europe, as was Eric Ackermann. Nick Ackermann supports his claim that his father was in France on or around D-Day, but also says that he was with the US forces and had, 'set up radio/radar intercept networks as commander of the entire UK effort.' This is an ambitious claim, but Eric had already taken on responsibilities far beyond those ordinarily given to young flight lieutenants. He had proved himself in North Africa when he sorted out the muddle over signals intelligence and the need for reliable and prompt intelligence was just as important for Overlord as it was for Operation Torch and indeed more so. Indeed what was happening in the early stages of Overlord was similar to the same stage in Torch in November 1942, although bigger to the nth degree.

There is support for Nick's statement in an infuriatingly vague line in 84 Group's Operations Record Book, where it gives some details about the D-Day plans. It reveals that 83 and 84 Group's Y sections were to land on D-Day itself. These were in Eric's field and as he was available on D-Day, and not off on another Jones-inspired adventure, he was most likely on board a landing craft, just as he had been in 1943 at Salerno. We just cannot prove it and the dates given in the following paragraph unfortunately demolish this assumption. The plans of the two Groups could easily have been changed anyway and it probably does not matter much. Eric did get to France sooner or later, although he might have liked the kudos of landing on D-Day itself. A footnote is that the landing of RAF troops was part of a subsidiary effort, called Operation Neptune.

We do know that on D-Day a small Y detachment of linguists and wireless operators was functioning on a Fighter Direction Ship, rather as HMS *Bolulo* had done during Torch. There were also land based units when a Y detachment came ashore on D+1 and 365, 382 and 383 Wireless Units arrived on D+7, although Sidney Goldberg asserts that 383 did not appear until early August. The task of these units was to provide 84 and 85 Groups with signals intelligence. No. 365 WU, of which unfortunately no Operations Record Books have survived, covered W/T and liaised with the other Y field units in the Western European theatre. No. 383 looked after R/T and was staffed with linguists, while 382 was the second W/T interceptor. The history of 382, written, or at least signed off, by Flight Lieutenant Sidney Ottley, provides a valuable account of the events of that time.

Ottley writes that, 'there was intense activity from dawn to dusk every day with as many as twenty VHF frequencies active simultaneously.' At the end of June the unit began to move slowly eastwards, although it was held up for more than two weeks around Caen until the city was captured on 15 July after fierce fighting and massive damage to the city centre. Once that obstacle had been cleared, however, faster progress was made and by early September No. 382 was in Belgium, where the presence of the Germans' new Me 262 jet fighter was reported. In October, the unit moved to Veghel in Holland and took over the priest's house as it was, to quote the ORB, 'at the nearest siting to enemy lines which had yet been risked by an Air Ministry Y unit, which by nature of its particular business operates usually a more reasonable distance from any possible chance of surprise or mischance in the matter of its secret mission.' Veghel was near the air base of Volkel in the east of Holland, between Eindhoven and Nijmegen.

It is worth interrupting the narrative by quoting a comment made by Group Captain P.H. Holmes, the Chief Signals Officer of 83 Group, in his account of the Group's activities in 1944. The source is National Archives file AIR 37/33:

'Many signals units … had been working on a two-watch basis, eight to twelve hours on, eight to twelve hours off. They had made long treks in which little sleep was possible, and on arrival had to erect masts and aerials and to service their equipment before going on watch. This combination of physical effort and mental concentration over a long period was bound to tell. Hitherto, they had been buoyed up by the excitement of the chase, and the novelty of strange places, and the enthusiasm with which they had been welcomed all along the road and, in the circumstances, had acquitted themselves remarkably well. But now they were together again, and things were settling down to normal, the inevitable reaction set in … there was less determination and snap, and operators and traffic masters were inclined to be irritable and to "give up".'

This is not intended as criticism, but the writer is highlighting the severe adrenalin-producing stress which these units were experiencing. This kept them going and when things calmed down, the high level of efficiency which they had shown for many months fell away. Eric and his team would have gone through this, even though Group Captain Holmes is not writing especially about them. The specific period about which he is writing is the late autumn of 1944, when the RAF ground troops had reached Holland, which is just where Eric himself was.

By the time of D-Day, Eric was experienced in both radar and signals intelligence through his work in North Africa and Italy and his burgeoning interest in the V weapons was a further addition to his portfolio of expertise. So it is inconceivable that R.V. Jones would not have attached him to a Y service unit. We do know about his next documented move under Jones' direction, which is detailed in the 382 WU's Operations Record Book, when on 7 November, he is reported to be arriving at Veghel on detachment to the unit, with the specific remit to command the Signals Investigation Unit. The entry in the record describes him as Flight Lieutenant Ackermann (ADI[Sc]). Eric remained with 382 for more than five months, finally departing on 21 March 1945, 'investigations in this sphere being completed'.

Not far from Veghel was the air base at Volkel, which was built for the Luftwaffe after the Germans had occupied Holland in 1940 and was initially a diversion airfield for fighter aircraft. It became fully operational in its own right in 1943 and its squadrons flew both the Junkers 88 and the Me 262 jet fighter and for just one week – from 30 August 1944 – the world's first operational jet bomber, the Arcado Ar 234. It flew on a few bombing missions though it was mainly a reconnaissance aircraft. One of the type made the very last Luftwaffe flight over England in April 1945. From Eric's professional point of view it was interesting as it had been a V-1 launch site.

The SIU was made up of two officers, twelve sergeants and nineteen other ranks – a total of thirty-three. Ten of the sergeants were linguists, officially described as Clerk Signals Linguists and the other two were Code and Cypher sergeants. Of the other ranks, eight were W/T operators, eleven were MT drivers and cooks, two were general duties airmen and there was an RAF policeman and a wireless mechanic. The name of the second officer is not given. Brian Lagden, who served in the Y service from August 1939 to the end of the war, met Eric there and recalls their meeting after an interesting period in France in 1940:

'I started in Y at 61 WU Cheadle [on] 26 August 1939, went to France with Y section AASF, BEF in November 1939 (a pointless exercise if ever there was one!). Got out of France late, in June 1940, by the skin of our teeth! Some of our guys who were at a remote D/F site to the south got out via Gibraltar on a collier, which I believe they picked up at Bordeaux!

'Next I got transferred to the R/T side of Y and installed H/F D/Fs at Eastbourne and Gorleston HDUs. From Gorleston I was transferred, in 1943, as a flight sergeant to fill a warrant officer vacancy on 382 WU, then being formed and equipped at Rugby. We were part of 2nd TAF in anticipation of Normandy and were, basically, the Y satellite of 83 GCC, the Group Control Centre, which also had radar satellites, of course. Our interception work was mainly fighter R/T traffic.

'A very interesting encounter on that unit [the SIU] was with a Flight Lieutenant Eric G. Ackerman [sic], who was a boffin (from DSREI I assume). He was trying to determine the exact nature of the control signals used to direct the V-2s. He had a couple of large trucks of very sophisticated equipment and was attached to us in Holland just for domestic purposes. His recently trained wireless operator was taking all day and having a hard time contacting the Foreign Office station they were using to report their results and he appealed to our CO for help in both equipment and operating ability. I was able to set up our spare 300 watt w/t transmitter and a decent antenna and remote control it from EGA's office van. His R-1055 receiver was relegated to the role of keying monitor (!) and we brought in an AR-88 to take care of the receiving end. I appointed myself radio operator and believe me, that was some experience. The SOE Operator at the London end was some operator.'

Brian continues for a few more sentences, though what follows is not relevant to the Ackermann story, except that 382 WU went on 'a Cook's Tour through Europe, winding up in Schleswig', which Eric himself reached also in 1945. After the war Eric returned to Holland with Dorothy to attend a reunion of members of the Dutch Resistance in Amsterdam and she remembers meeting its head, who told her that on one occasion he had to spend a night up to his neck in a canal to escape capture.

It is possible that when the Volkel air base was liberated by the Allies, Eric may have moved from the priest's house at Veghel to carry out the work to which he had been assigned – examining the remains of the V-1 launch sites and even rockets themselves, which had been fired from there. He soon had company and some welcome protection when No. 174 (Mauritius) Squadron of the RAF arrived to carry out attacks on German bases in Holland and Germany with its Typhoon ground-attack and fighter aircraft.

Meanwhile, on 1 January 1945, the Luftwaffe launched Operation Bodenplatte (Baseplate) from airfields just over the German border. This was a last-ditch attempt to destroy the aircraft of the USAAF and the RAF and make the way clear for German ground forces to resume the attack which had been stalled further south in the Battle of the Bulge in the Ardennes and retake the initiative from the Allies, as well as providing a considerable boost to German morale and Goebbels' propaganda machine.

Volkel was scheduled to be attacked, but the German aircraft of Jagdgeschwader 6 (Focke-wulf 190 and Me 109s) could not locate it, though other airfields nearby were found, including Heesch, a short distance from Volkel, where considerable damage was done to RAF aircraft on the ground, but none at all to the pilots. On the other hand, the Luftwaffe suffered severely, losing its pilots as well as its aircraft. The German attack failed, partly due to the inexperience of the many new young pilots who were now taking the place of the veterans who had been lost.

Control from the ground was erratic and the marksmanship and the navigation of the pilots were poor, so once the Allies had recovered from the initial surprise of a totally unexpected attack, they were able to get aloft and shoot them down. It was a blow from which the Luftwaffe was never able to recover and was its last attempt to mount a major attack and recover air superiority. Allied intelligence, surprisingly, failed to anticipate the operation. They were aware that something was pending, but did not identify when and where it would be launched. As it was, the Allied air forces suffered barely a pinprick, even though Allied troops did not get across the Rhine until March 1945.

Sometime in the spring of 1945, Eric Ackermann moved from Holland into Germany, though we do not know exactly when because his name does not surface again until July. During that period, he had crossed the Rhine and moved eastwards with the British forces and reached Bad Eilsen, a pleasant spa town which had been chosen as the headquarters of the British Air Forces of Occupation (Germany), the direct successor of the 2nd Tactical Air Force. The 2nd

Eric in Holland in the winter of 1944/45, probably at Veghel.

TAF became BAFO(G) on 15 July and its role changed from being a fighting unit to one of occupation. R.V. Jones seems to have had Eric installed at Headquarters, but he was also operating in the small town of Obernkirchen, a short distance away, where he was to live for the next thirteen years.

He spent his first six months billeted at the Gasthaus zur Alten Bückeburg, which was situated behind the railway station in Obernkirchen and had been requisitioned by the British forces. He then moved into a house in Obernkirchen at 27 Admiral-Scheer-Strasse. The street was named after Obernkirchen's most distinguished son, Admiral Reinhard Scheer, (1863–1928), who commanded the German High Seas Fleet in the Battle of Jutland in 1916. It was a splendid property and was one of the many requisitioned houses in the town. No. 27 had belonged to a mine owner who had lived there in some style. It had a large garden, so much so that when the house was sadly demolished in the 1960s, the site was big enough to be replaced by a school with a sizeable playground.

Such a large property meant that this young man, living on his own, needed staff and in due course a cook, a gardener and a general handyman were taken on. This was an unusual amount of domestic help for a junior officer, although Eric was never a typical flight lieutenant, nor was he to know at that early stage that he would be there for far longer than the usual two or three year tour of most service personnel.

Eric was not much in Obernkirchen in those early days. He was frequently out and about in the British Zone, fulfilling the mission given to him by R.V. Jones by collecting equipment and arranging its transportation to his new workplace. There are occasional clues in the official documents about his activities in 1945, some of which are believable, but cannot be proved.

One clue concerns the 314 Supply and Transport Column (STC), which, together with Nos. 309 and 317 STCs., was known as the Pickfords of the RAF, with an appropriate motto, 'Any Load, Anywhere, Any Time'. No. 314 moved huge quantities of equipment from the Hamburg area and elsewhere to B Squadron of No. 2002 Air Disarmament Wing (ADW) at Obernkirchen. There are two documented instances of this in 314's Operations Record Book. On 16 July 1945, six 3-ton vehicles carried CAT 1 equipment from Lübbecke to Obernkirchen. Category One material was required for intelligence and research purposes and was therefore just the kind of booty for which Eric was searching.

On 10 September, twenty 3-tonners went to No. 31 Air Equipment Park at Altona, near Hamburg, to take unspecified equipment to the same destination. The STCs certainly lived up to their motto, carrying everything from people (displaced persons, the RAF Gang Show and airmen going on leave and coming back), to petrol, coal, furniture, bedding, consignments of toilet rolls and so on ad infinitum.

Eric was not alone in Obernkirchen in 1945, as the aforementioned B Squadron of No. 2002 ADW had taken up residence. These wings, of which there were eight covering the 60,000 square miles of the British Zone, were set up to clear away the debris of war abandoned by the Luftwaffe. There were parallel units for the Army and the Royal Navy. The ADWs' finds were then sent to the appropriate base in the British Zone for further examination, or for onward despatch to the United Kingdom. An arrangement, agreed to reluctantly, provided for a considerable quantity to be re-routed to the French Zone.

The wings relied heavily on local information to track down their quarry, but they also roamed widely and randomly over their own specific areas seeing what they could find. Local people were often keen to ingratiate themselves with the occupying forces by revealing the hiding places of the more portable items, including, in one case, the former station commander of a former Luftwaffe base (Uetersen, near Hamburg) who was found hiding in a barn.

Eric's house at 27 Admiral-Scheer-Strasse in Obernkirchen.

Aero engines were discovered in a railway siding, again near Uetersen, and six more, in mint condition, had been secreted in the loft of a village bakery. Of more direct interest to Eric Ackermann would have been sixteen wagons of V2 spirit found abandoned on an Autobahn and a quantity of signals equipment hidden in a railway tunnel. Anything which was liable to explode, of which there was a great deal, was detonated on site. The alarming term 'bomb cemetery' crops up frequently in the records and these were sometimes dug out on former Luftwaffe bases.

B Squadron 2002 ADW moved from Detmold to its new headquarters on 31 May 1945, having obtained permission from the 9th US Air Force. At that time the area was still occupied by US forces, though a few days later, on 9 June, the parent wing passed from 9th Air Force control to 2nd Tactical Air Force, just as 21st Army Group took over from the 9th US Army.

The Squadron's investigated at least two firms in Obernkirchen itself. The Neuhotte Glass Factory and J.H. Bornemann & Co. The latter made locomotive and pump parts and both were inspected though neither attracted Eric's attention. There was, however, a general comment made in the Squadron's records in July 1945 that: 'Further items of technical intelligence and research value are being uncovered and shipped to UK for scientific examination and the rest to RAE Farnborough and elsewhere.' By the end of November things were running down and "Nothing of interest" recurs in the official record. Eric's source of this electronic manna from heaven had dried up.

Nevertheless, the summer and early autumn of 1945 must have seemed like a very long Christmas, with presents arriving almost every day. Eric now had a heaven – or at least Luftwaffe – sent opportunity to work with highly advanced German (and Italian) signals and other electronic equipment to use in his R.V. Jones' mission to set up an intercept system in the British Zone.

Colin Gammon was stationed at Obernkirchen with the Air Scientific Research Unit between 1949 and 1952 and he corroborates the recollections of another airman, Charlie Olito, about the contents of the Gasthaus zur Alten Bückeburg, a building which was to feature large in the story of Eric's new unit.

The hall in the Gasthaus was full of electronic equipment which Eric had either retrieved independently, or which the ADW had obligingly directed his way. Furthermore, and to assist the process in retrieving enemy war matériel, when the WUs were disbanded in August 1945, their Signals Interpreters re-mustered to become Interpreters with the ADWs. Given his earlier service with the WUs, Eric may have been able to use their particular skills. In the name of safety, however, anything which was liable to explode, of which there was a great deal, was detonated on site.

Colin Gammon's recollections of events four years later indicate that the cornucopia stored in the Gasthaus was never used and that it remained there for some years. This was not uncommon, as the baggage of war left behind when the conflict ended was simply cleared away, stored and then forgotten about, or just held on to 'in case'.

The whole situation about what was delivered to Obernkirchen, by whom and for what purpose, is confused. This is hardly surprising. So much war material, not to mention the millions of refugees struggling to find safety, was moving around Germany, that a few trucks destined for Eric at Obernkirchen hardly made an impression. Circumstantial evidence shows that Eric may have been to Hamburg to recover some aviation electronics, but whether he did or did not, another intriguing convoy made its way south-west from Schleswig-Holstein to Obernkirchen.

This comprised of a few Wehrmacht trucks driven by German soldiers, who must have been PoWs, towards the end of 1945 or early in 1946. Apparently at least some of the vehicles in the convoy were 'steam driven', which means that they were powered by wood. It arrived at the Decimetre Site near Obernkirchen. David Haysom has researched the incident and describes it thus:

'The troops, some of whom were in private vehicles, were accompanied by wives and small children. The trucks contained mobile communications equipment and on the roof of one vehicle there was a very large telescopic antenna. On arrival at the Decimetre Site, under the control and supervision of the British Forces, the German soldiers set up their equipment, which was subsequently used by the British. According to our information, at about the same time a small number of Wehrmacht soldiers from the Decimetre Site drove down the winding road to the foot of the hill and headed to the centre of Obernkirchen, when the police apprehended them at the corner of Eilsenerstr. (K6) and Rathenaustr (L442). The soldiers were handcuffed and led away. The fate of their families is not recorded.'

More credence concerning Eric's eager scooping-up of ex-Luftwaffe equipment is given by R.V. Jones, who writes in *Most Secret War* that:

'Ackermann's enthusiasm could sometimes present problems. At one stage he had accumulated so much equipment that he signalled me demanding three Dakotas to transport it back to Farnborough. I thought that it was somewhat out of order for my junior to expect me to arrange transport for him, so I sent a signal back saying, "Arrange transport yourself", omitting the "bloody well" that would have more correctly reflected my mind.

'To my surprise, three Dakotas shortly flew into Farnborough with the equipment. I had not reckoned with Ackermann's resource: as soon as he received my signals he went to the Chief Transport Officer [of BAFO], showed him the signal, saying: "Look Sir, Dr Jones authorizes me to arrange the transport", and promptly got all that he wanted.'

This was not the only time when Eric 'persuaded' BAFO to do his bidding by invoking the powerful name of R.V. Jones, as we shall see. There is, though, another twist to the story (Eric's life was full of strange twists). On board the aircraft was a recent recruit to Eric's unit, a young pilot officer who had been a classical scholar at Oxford University before the war. His task was to escort the aircraft home and look after them until Eric himself was able to see them. Eric had remarked to him that he wanted, 'this equipment kept on ice till I get there'. This precaution was important to Eric because he was worried that other officers might get their hands on his treasures. Unfortunately, the young man's classical education had not equipped him to deal with colloquialisms. He took Eric's instruction literally and went round the station asking for a consignment of ice, believing that his task was to prevent the temperature of the aircraft from rising. This must have become a standing joke at Farnborough. Eric's reaction is not recorded.

Not only was Eric busy establishing radar and signals detection equipment at Obernkirchen, but he was beginning to co-operate with the Americans at their bases at Frankfurt-am-Main (US Army), Wiesbaden (USAAF) and Bremen (US Navy), which were respectively the headquarters of the three services operating in the American Zone.

A document released in 2010 by GCHQ describes an agreement reached in 1946 which was entitled: *Outline of British–US communication intelligence agreement*. This seven-page report, in the words of *The Times* report on 25 June 2010: '....formed the basis for co-operation between London and Washington throughout the Cold War and beyond, in an arrangement unparalleled in Western intelligence'. *The Times* report goes on: 'The pact stressed that the exchange of intelligence would be unrestricted except when both sides agreed that specific information could be excluded'. The two sides did undertake to limit such exceptions to the minimum. The report sets out the reasons for the agreement: 'As the threat posed by Nazi Germany was replaced by a new one in the east, the agreement formed the basis for intelligence co-operation during the Cold War.' It was extended to Canada in 1948 and Australia and New Zealand in 1950.

Did this provide the opportunity for Eric Ackermann to establish contact with the Sigint community in America? His son Nick certainly believes so, writing that in 1947 Eric was establishing; 'direct secure communications with [these three headquarters] for the exchange of technical intelligence data.' In that year he went to America for the first time and visited the newly created Central Intelligence Agency.

R.V. Jones wrote that, 'his radio work in Germany was so well regarded by the Americans that it did more than anything else after the war to ensure the continued exchange of electronic intelligence between Britain and the United States.' Continuing the American connection a few years later, Nick writes that:

'In 1953 [Eric] was training US servicemen in new techniques and the following year he set up a joint US/UK Committee on Interception of Enemy Transmissions (total membership five) in collaboration with a leading civilian US scientist in electronic intelligence.'

This scientist was James Sears of the CIA and he became a close friend of the Ackermann family over the next twenty years. In 1973, Uncle Jim, as he was known to them, wrote of Eric's work as being:

'…of unusual value to me in my work, and in fact to the whole western world. I started working with him in 1952 within his operations and found that he mastered the details of his work to an extraordinary degree.

'Eric possesses that rare quality of the proper mix of the practical and the theoretical that gets the job done more effectively and more expeditiously than those highly qualified (solely) in the practical or (solely) in the theory'.

This is moving ahead and we shall return to Uncle Jim later, after Eric had left the air force. At this stage, however, it is a portent of Eric's future that from the beginning he was pushing ahead with his links with the Americans. Small wonder then that he would eventually emigrate and make a new career there. For now, however, Eric was about to set off on yet another and even more extraordinary mission.

Chapter Seven

The Long March to Lindau, 1946

Just as Eric was beginning to settle down to life in Obernkirchen events took another sharp turn, again unsurprisingly involving R.V. Jones, though R.V.'s role this time was more of a frustrated and sometimes baffled onlooker than an active participant.

It came about in this way. In the autumn of 1945 Eric visited Jones in his London office, accompanied by Dr W.R. (Roy) Piggott, who was an international leader in ionospheric physics research and also assistant to Sir Edward Appleton, winner of the Nobel Prize for Physics in 1947. Appleton was at that time the Director of Scientific and Industrial Research and had been a member of the War Cabinet's Scientific Advisory Committee.

Roy Piggott looked just like the popular image of the absent-minded professor, slightly dishevelled, with spectacles and wild hair. He was mildly forgetful about such minor matters as matching socks and doing up his shoe laces, but he was very far from being absent-minded at work. His obituary in *The Times* of 30 June 2008 describes him as:

'unfailingly courteous, patient, kind and generous, both professionally and personally. He was passionate about science, unselfish, inspirational, and full of ideas. He was a superb mentor, though frequently disconcerting his audience as he would absent-mindedly nibble elastic bands and other detritus recovered from his desk or jacket pocket, without interruption to the flow of science ideas. Everyone whose lives were touched by Piggott has their own story about the lovable, archetypal British eccentric, who will live on through his humanity and his legacies to ionospheric physics.'

R.V. Jones describes him similarly in *Most Secret War*:

'Had I known more about Piggott, I might not have been misled by his quiet air, for this proved to hide an unexpected resource. Shortly after the war, for example, he and his wife had problems cutting their baby's nails, because, whenever they tried to do so, the baby screamed her head off. One night they heard a bump, and rushed into the baby's room, to find that she had climbed out of her cot and fallen on the floor, knocking herself unconscious. Before Piggott went for the doctor he said, "Here's our chance" and cut the baby's nails.'

He and Eric made an improbable pair, though both were imbued with a spirit of adventure and insatiable curiosity. They told Jones, another scientific genius, though more conventional than Appleton, that the latter was anxious to restart ionospheric research and to co-operate with Germany and that he and they knew of an important research station located in Austria, the Institute for Ionospheric Research. This was headed by Dr Walter Dieminger, a distinguished scientist who, despite his gruelling experiences during and immediately after the Second World War, survived until the end of the twentieth century, dying at the age of ninety-three in 2000.

During the war the institute had been based in Loebersdorf, some thirty miles south of Vienna, in Lower Austria and close to the Hungarian border. After the war it fell within the Soviet Zone. Dieminger anticipated this and decided that he should get away to one of the western zones, and so on 30 March 1945:

'for fear of being captured by advancing Russian troops from the east, [he], together with ten trucks, departed from Loebersdorf with the remaining scientific equipment for the newly established centre at Ried-im-Innkreis [in Upper Austria], which had been opened in January. The journey was hazardous, with low flying aircraft attacks and hindrance from [Nazi] party bosses and, above all, lack of fuel.'

Dieminger's decision was prescient. If he had stayed where he was the Russians would have captured both him and the institute and almost certainly moved them to Moscow as part of their reparations programme. They already had form for this on their rampage through eastern Germany on their way to Berlin, which continued ruthlessly after the war ended.

Dr Dieminger himself travelled to Ried with his wife and three children in his own DKW car. On arriving there, Dieminger considered that he needed to disguise the military component of the institute's activity, and therefore decided to destroy all equipment that might be associated with military communications, or to transfer it to Kochel, a military base in Upper Bavaria. What remained was scientific equipment used for high frequency research belonging to the Fraunhofer institute.

Ried fell to the advancing American forces on 3 May 1945 after minor resistance. The Americans needed convincing that the institute had not been part of the Nazi's war machine and Dieminger's assistant managed to persuade them that its function was entirely scientific and had no military function. The staff were not interned as PoWs, but they were confined to the cloister which was their place of work. Thanks to an American 'Off Limits' sign, their valuable equipment was not stolen by local inhabitants.

From May to August 1945, the institute worked innocently enough doing watch repairs and radio and mechanical work for the local community and the occupying American forces. In August a team of scientists from America, France and Great Britain arrived to investigate its activities. It was at this point that the meeting between

Jones, Eric Ackermann and Roy Piggott took place. The two visitors told Dr Jones that Sir Edward Appleton wanted to find Dr Dieminger's laboratories so that he could restart work on ionospheric research, which was already regarded as the future for telecommunications.

The institute's value to the Allies stemmed from Marconi's discovery in the late nineteenth century that radio waves appeared to bend round the earth's curvature so that communication signals from England could be heard a very long way off. This extended the range of civil and military communications and if research was to fall into the wrong (i.e. Soviet) hands then the implications would be serious.

The importance to Appleton and Piggott and by extension to Ackermann, Jones and the Air Ministry, is clear enough. Any possibility that the Russians might get hold of the institute had to be eliminated and now that Dieminger had conveniently moved the institute to within their reach, the chance now had to be taken. The Allies had known of its existence in Loebersdorf and believed as late as the summer of 1945 that it was still there. Repatriated institute staff then provided the vital information about its move. A week's interrogation revealed what its equipment could do and this led to something of a scramble for its treasures. The French occupation authorities wanted to move part of the Ried site to Freiburg-im-Breisgau, in their own zone of Germany. The Americans wanted the institute to stay where it was in their zone of Austria, to build scientific equipment and continue atmospheric research, but at a reduced capacity. The British wanted to have it as well and in the end the Americans gave way.

Appleton had initially wanted to disband Dieminger's group and just move the equipment to the British Zone, but in the end he relented and Dieminger and his staff and their families moved, along with everything else. The chosen site, once all parties had agreed that the move should take place, was Lindau am Harz near Göttingen. It was estimated that about ten trucks would be required to transfer everything and everybody. The British would be responsible for the operation. This was in August 1945 and the inspection team promised to deliver a final decision within six weeks.

By now Eric Ackermann and Roy Piggott were persuading R.V. Jones to let them go after it, having heard that the institute was safely in Ried. This is more or less where they come into picture and began organizing their mission. One thing led to another and by the beginning of February Dr Dieminger and the much larger convoy than the ten vehicles originally estimated was assembled by Eric Ackermann and met in Munich at the other end of Germany from Eric's home base.

This is jumping ahead by about five weeks, as at the end of December, four months after he had been promised action by the inspection team, Dr Dieminger at last prepared to leave and found that:

'an endless column of Royal Air Force vehicles was waiting. We drove past the convoy and I counted seventy trucks, three armoured carriers, a large Ford car, a Jeep, a communications truck and six motorcycle outriders. It was here that I learned of the final plan: seventy trucks were there to transport the institute and every last nut and bolt from Ried to Lindau near Göttingen where, according to the Control Commission, equipment was to be assembled and scientific research continued on a small scale.'

On the evening of the same day the convoy arrived in Salzburg, where it formed a corral on the city square. The local inhabitants excitedly greeted it, probably thinking that the trucks were carrying food supplies. It was apparent now that the communications truck was there to maintain radio contact with headquarters in Bad Oeynhausen, that Dr William Roy Piggott had been given the task of organizing the transfer of the Fraunhofer institute and that a young Flight Lieutenant, Eric Ackermann, was to be the convoy commander.

We know from evidence provided by Nick Ackermann that his father was in Ried on 8 February because he recorded in his journal years later that Eric phoned him in 1985 to tell him that he met Marianna (whom he was to marry in 1948) in Ried at 8am local time on that day. It seems their meeting was not just by chance, but was somehow pre-arranged. This is a curious fact for Eric to remember after nearly forty years and for him to feel so moved as to telephone his son and tell him. Was it because this was the first time that the two of them had met, and was Ried where Marianna had settled, at least temporarily, after her horrific escape from Hungary which she herself described and which is reproduced elsewhere in this book? It looks too as if the meeting was pre-arranged and not just a chance encounter. Maybe Eric suggested that she should travel to Bad Eilsen to see if she could work with the RAF and if she did, one wonders if she was given a lift in the convoy. Nick does not say and perhaps Eric never told him.

During the next fourteen days the convoy was split into small groups and sent on to Ried, where it took three weeks to complete the loading. When assembled the convoy stretched the length of Ried. By the end of the month it was ready and on 28 February it departed, leaving the citizens of Ried without any bounty they had hoped for. It followed the same route as the outward journey – it already had clearance to go that way as a direct route north out of Austria would have taken it through part of the Soviet Zone of Germany which was very much out of bounds. There were now seventy three-ton trucks with drivers, 90,000 litres of fuel, four armoured vehicles with outriders, as well as three of the institute staff and their families who had decided to resettle in Göttingen. Altogether 200 people made the journey. Dr Dieminger followed the convoy in his own DKW private car, which unfortunately broke down on the last leg of the journey and had to be towed into Lindau.

The journey was no mean undertaking for such a large convoy travelling through war-torn Germany on ice-covered roads in the depths of winter. Inevitably there were accidents and the penultimate section from Frankfurt to Kassel suffered the worse conditions and at Kassel it was decided to split the convoy. The main part headed for Lindau/Göttingen and five trucks with the families made for Bückeburg, the headquarters of the convoy commander, Eric Ackermann, who, by the way, would have travelled in the Ford car.

David Haysom notes: 'This was a very strange decision. Why did the convoy split and take a longer and more hazardous route to Bückeburg, only to return later?' He wonders if this was because Eric wanted to grab at least a small part of the booty for his, or rather the RAF's, own use. This is not as outrageous an accusation as it might seem. After all, it was the RAF's transport which had been used, as well as the valuable time of a serving officer, so the detaching of a very small part of the convoy seems a small price to pay for an otherwise successful mission. Journey's end at Lindau was eventually reached on 3 March, where the ever-thoughtful RAF had established a skeleton staff to help unload and set the institute up in its new home in, for what it is worth, a beautiful part of Germany close to the Harz mountains.

We are lucky enough to have an eyewitness account of the whole adventure from one of the convoy's drivers, David Box, who recalled the experience in a letter to David Haysom in 2006:

'All we knew was that it was very sensitive and a professor was coming and he had organized it all. We did not get involved with any loading or unloading. Lorries had to be left and collected later. All we were told, through a little bit of gossip that always went round when on convoy, was that the Russians were after the equipment and it had to be taken out of Ried as quick as possible. It is about sixty years ago now. I was about 19-years-old at the time – memories fade and bits and pieces gradually come back to you. Also, I remember going into Salzburg and across one of the bridges. From there I think we broke up into smaller convoys. I know [there were] about seventy trucks in which 317 S & TC [Supply and Transport Column] was involved.'

We now go back to the start of it all, as the first part of the story is more curious and fraught than its conclusion, due to a strange series of misunderstandings and even accusations of impropriety. It began well enough. Appleton and Jones had known each other during the war and the former had been a strong supporter of Jones and his team in the Air Ministry. Dr Jones must have felt that he had to agree with the two emissaries and that Eric was just the man for the job. He was after all a relatively free man in air force terms, not attached to any operational station and working for Jones on a new project on which he had barely started. He was no doubt as eager as ever to try something new and with an element of danger, promised that he could, in Jones' words, 'work it in' with his other commitments.

With that, he and Piggott left the room and disappeared from Jones' view for two months. Jones concludes his account with the words: 'I had no idea what I was in for', a resigned comment which he could have applied to many of his encounters with his maverick subordinate over many years. Jones calls what followed, 'the most remarkable of all Ackermann's efforts', which is certainly saying something. Eric was to be out of contact with Jones for most of his two months away, but it is nevertheless recounted in some detail in *Most Secret War*. We also have Dr Dieminger's own account, which he wrote for an issue of the German news magazine *Der Spiegel* in 1983 which he called *The Long March to Lindau* – the title of which we have used for this chapter.

Now Jones may have thought and indeed hoped that Roy Piggott and Eric Ackermann, the one a boffin and the other a rare combination of scientist and man of action, were getting on with things once they had left his office to proceed with the operation. After all, he had just put Eric in charge of the Air Scientific Research Unit (ASRU) and now he had been persuaded to send him off on an enterprise which was at best uncertain and at worst foolhardy and possibly illegal. Furthermore, it did not have much to do with what Eric was supposed to be doing in Germany.

It turned out, however, that they were not moving as fast as Jones had assumed they would be. He writes that he was hearing rumours about their activities and his suspicions that something was up were confirmed when the head of the Radio Division at the National Physical Laboratory, Dr R.L. Smith Rose, was asked by a member of the Radio Security Service if he had any information about a suspected black market gang operating in Germany. The gang was using radio to keep in touch with its members and to plan its criminal operations. Most of the messages were in an unbreakable code and were using RAF frequencies, though not an RAF code. There were a few words in clear and Jones writes that these were: 'Smith Rose', 'cheese machine', and, to his astonishment, 'fifty thousand Reichsmarks'.

Smith Rose was baffled and worried that his name was appearing in such sensitive signals. The explanation was that Eric had sent the messages and was referring to Smith Rose in connection with the ionospheric research project. He had not, however, taken the precaution of copying them to Jones. The cheese machine turned out to be a diffraction grating ruling engine which Eric had found in Hamburg and which he knew would interest Jones. Indeed he was trying to get the machine's builder to come to England to meet him. The small fortune of fifty thousand Reichsmarks was intended to support the work of the ASRU, which was supposed to be Eric's day job back at Obernkirchen.

Shortly after the long-suffering Jones had learnt what the coded messages meant, his WAAF secretary, Flying Officer Margaret Masterman, appeared in his office carrying a standard War Office file with the legend 'Hand of Officer only' on its cover, accompanied by another heading which Jones had probably never seen before. It said: 'Obscene W/T traffic'. Miss Masterman suggested that Jones read it and then, in his words, she fled. Jones, thoroughly exasperated by this time, read it and realized that it was part of the same story about which Eric had been sending his encrypted signals only a few days before.

It seemed that the same gang was operating somewhere in southern Germany and was moving around using the radio signals which had so alarmed Jones. How they got hold of RAF frequencies was not his concern, apart from muddying the waters in which Eric was immersed. It transpired anyway that the signals' contents were not at all obscene, merely insulting, because the incident they describe had, in R.V. Jones' words, 'come when parties to celebrate the success of the expedition had occurred simultaneously, both at the fixed headquarters and at the mobile unit, with a foreseeable result on their operators who, after a minor misunderstanding, engaged in hurling "opprobrious epithets" over the ether, scandalizing the Radio Security Service who thereupon redoubled their efforts to find who was responsible.' In the end the RAF frequencies used to send their signals narrowed the search to find their originator and the trail led inexorably to Eric Ackermann.

Jones goes on to say that the broadminded Miss Masterman had hardly left his office, 'when of all people Ackermann himself appeared. He asked me whether I had been hearing things about him, and I pointed to the file. He said that that was only part of the story, and I had better hear the rest of it.' The 'little job' he had been doing for Appleton was turning out to be a prodigious undertaking. In the first place, it involved a journey of some hundreds of miles from north Germany down into the American Zone of Austria; and he had decided that they ought to have enough fuel to cover the whole of the expedition to Austria and back to base. The total requirement came to seventy 3-ton lorries with their drivers and twenty thousand gallons of petrol.

Eric had managed to get hold of all this by being somewhat economical with the truth. He had persuaded the Command Transport Officer at BAFO Headquarters that Dr Jones had requested it and furthermore, had added to his shopping list five armoured cars and a posse of motorcycle outriders. Eric had also acquired an official document, drafted by a young officer, Pilot Officer Hugh Smith, requesting that British and American forces afford the bearer (himself) all assistance he might require, and to allow him to travel by service or civilian aircraft, rail or road, find him accommodation, and give him permission to carry with him a carte blanche or laissez-passer – what an opportunity for an enterprising officer enjoying what was to be his final fling on the loose and far from interfering higher authority. This is not to imply that Eric regarded the mission as another adventure. With Piggott at his side he now knew that it was a serious matter and that ionospheric research was of vital military importance.

By the time the mission had got on its way, David Box was grappling with keeping his truck in the right place in the enormous convoy and keeping it on the road in the icy conditions. Back at Bad Eilsen, however, a man rather higher up the order of things, Marshal of the Royal Air Force Sir Sholto Douglas, the Military Governor of the British Zone (a job he disliked) and also Commander-in-Chief, British Air Forces of Occupation (Germany) was holding his weekly conference and wanted some transport for a headquarters operation. The Command Transport Officer had to confess that there was none. Flight Lieutenant Ackermann had it all, doing a job which he had claimed was for Dr Jones.

The Commander-in-Chief was a man under some strain and he wrote in his memoirs that he found his command in Germany to be the most difficult had ever undertaken. Now there was this junior officer and not a real one at that, making off with most of his transport. Not only that, but the next item on the conference agenda was the little matter of the obscene signals which the luckless Command Transport Officer had to deal with. He had to admit that the frequencies used had been allocated to Flight Lieutenant Ackermann. Sir Sholto's patience must have been at breaking point and he summoned Eric to his presence.

George Medal or not, this could have been Eric's most dangerous moment and R.V. Jones writes that, 'Ackermann very sensibly decided that it would be better if I had the whole story from him first, and so he had flown over from Germany for the afternoon to tell me.' Eric had clearly thought his problem through and he hoped that the BAFO Chief Intelligence Officer (CIO) would clear the way for him by inviting him to lunch in the Senior Staff Mess, where he might have the chance to meet the Commander-in-Chief socially over a drink, with the carpeting due to start after lunch. This was in itself something of a liberty, as Eric was a junior officer and therefore not normally allowed into this particular mess. He may have wondered if all this would lead to his becoming even more junior.

What happened at the Commander-in-Chief's interview was unexpected. The C.I.O. took Eric into the office for his presumed ordeal and returned twenty minutes later to, as he put it, 'pick up the pieces'. He was amazed to see Flight Lieutenant Ackermann smoking one of the Commander-in-Chief's cigars while the great man was listening closely to his account of his exploits. Sir Sholto seemed rather put out when the C.I.O. appeared, but nevertheless politely brought the proceedings to a close, saying to him: 'This has been very interesting, Ackermann. I can quite see the importance of the work that you are doing and if you don't get enough help in future you just come to me direct.'

Jones rounds off his account of the confrontation that never was with the laconic words: 'So Ackermann survived!' Eric lived to fight another day and carry on with what he was supposed to be doing back in Obernkirchen. This was to be his last off-the-leash foray, and probably his greatest – and still shadowy – contribution to the Royal Air Force and to the security of the United Kingdom and its allies was still to come. His growing reputation in the sphere of signals intelligence was to lead him to further and long-lasting achievements which are described in the following chapters.

Eric's partner in all this, Roy Piggott, did not escape retribution. He was told that what he had done was illegal and as he still held a commission in the RAF he might have to face a Court Martial. Fortunately for the future of ionospheric research, nothing happened and so both miscreants got away with what might have been a very difficult aftermath.

The laboratories which Eric and his airmen so laboriously transferred have remained in Lindau am Harz to this day and now form part of the Max Planck Institute for Solar System Research, formed out of the Fraunhofer Institute in 1955, with Dr Walter Dieminger as its first director until his retirement in 1971.

R.V. Jones had a high regard for Walter Dieminger and visited him in April 1950 as a member of the Physics Section of the British Control Commission for Germany's Scientific Branch. He wrote of the visit: 'We met Dr Dieminger, who is the head of the [Fraunhofer] station and who had just returned from a visit to England… Dr Dieminger, who had played a minor part in the operation of the Beams against

England in 1941, has an attractive personality and is almost certainly the best radio physicist in Germany today.'

It seems that Jones also met Eric during this visit, as he had asked J.W. Lees, his successor at the ADI (Science) at the Air Ministry, if Eric was likely to be at Obernkirchen during the visit. Lees replied, 'Yes, Ackerman will be there and he is expecting you to stay with him and Mrs Ackerman from 31 March to 4 April.'

Scientists were able to overcome the boundaries of nationality and Dr Jones continued to keep in touch with those he had worked with, and against, for the rest of his life. Dr Dieminger was just one of these and the names of these, Eric Ackermann chief among them, occur throughout Jones's book. Dr Dieminger wrote his own account

Der lange Marsch von Leobersdorf nach Lindau

Dr Walter Dieminger's map of the Long March to Lindau which shows that the convoy took the long way round rather than a more direct route.

of those remarkable two months in 1946 and part of the story is reproduced below in the original German. Much of Dr Dieminger's account has already appeared in this chapter in English. It begins with Eric and Roy Piggott meeting Dr Jones:

Dr Walter Dieminger (centre) with his driver, Herr Zwölfer, Dipl. Eng. Greisweid and one of the Fraunhofer Institute's scientists. This photo of a happy and apparently carefree group was taken in 1945 at Ried am Innkreis.

Dr R.V. Jones, who viewed the Long March from a distance with concern and finally surprised relief.

'*Das bemerkenswerteste Unternehmen von Ackermann in diesem Rahmen begann an einem Nachmittag im August 1945, als dieser zusammen mit Edward Appletons Assistant W.R. Piggott in Jones Büro erschien. Sie erklärten, Appleton sei daran interessiert, die Zusammenarbeit in der Ionosphärenforschung zwischen England und Deutschland jetzt nach dem Krieg wieder in Gang zu bringen. Es sei da eine wichtige deutsche Ionosphärenstation unter Leitung von Dr Dieminger, die irgenwohin in die amerikanische Zone von Österreich geflohen sei. Ob Jones Dienstelle Diemingers Aufenthalt feststellen und dafür Sorge tragen könne, dass er mit seinen Mitarbeitern und den ganzen Geräten nach Lindau bei Göttingen gebracht würde, vorausgesetzt, dass Dieminger damit einverstanden sei? Jones stimmte zu und fragte Ackermann, ob er die Aufgabe zusammen mit dem übrigen Programm erledigen könne.*

Post-war Germany and the occupation zones. From '*German Politics*', 1945–1990, by Peter Pulzer. Reproduced by kind permission of the Oxford University Press.

Ackermann bejahte dies. Hätte Jones die verborgenen Fähigkeiten Piggotts gekonnt, ware er wahrschleinlich mit seiner Zusage vorsichter gewesen. Jedenfalls hatte er keine Ahnung davon, in was er hineingeschlittert war.'

Right to left: Professor W.R. Piggott, Frau Dieminger and Dr Walter Dieminger.

There are more references including one to the 'cheese machine' signal:

'eine Graviermaschine für Beugungsgitter in Hamburg, für die sich, wie Ackermann wusste, Jones interessierte und deren Erbaquer zu einen Interview nach England gebracht werden sollte. Die fifty thousand Reichsmark waren ein Teil des Geldes, das Ackermann für seine Dienstelle brauchte.

'Für Ackermann hatte die Sache noch ein Nachspiel. Er müßte sich vor dem Chef des Stabes wegen der Funksprüche verantworten. Doch die Angelegenheit verlief für ihn glimpflich, um nichtzu sagen erfolgreich. Der Chief Intelligence Officer, der Ackermann zu dem Stabschef gebracht hatte, war night wenig erstaunt, als er diesen nach einer halben Stunde nicht etwa am Boden zerstört, sondern, eine dicke Zigarre des Stabschefs rauchend, in angeregtem Gespräch mit diesem vorfand. Noch erstaunter war er, als dieser zu Ackermann, sichtlich ungehalten über die Unterbrechung des Gesprächs, sagte 'Das war außerordentlich interessant, Ackermann. Ich verstehe sehr gut, wie wichtig es ist, was Sie da tun. Wenn Sie Unterstützung bekommen, verstehe sehr gut, kommen Sie direct zu mir.' Ackermann fand in der Folgezeit ein sehr angemessenes Bestätigungsfelt in einer eigenen Dienstelle in der Nähe von Bückeburg. Er war unter anderem maßgebend an dem technischen Aufbau des British Forces Network, der Organisation für die Rundfundversorgung der englischen Besatzungs-soldaten in Deutschland.

'Sein Bericht kann übrigens noch etwas ergänzt – was den unentzifferbaren Code betrifft. Ackermann mag wohl für bestimmte Zwecke einen von Tag zu Tag wechselnden Spezialcode des Foreign Office verwendet haben. Der Großteil des Funkverkehrs erfolgte aber in englischem Klartext. Dem ganzen Unterrnehmen war als Motto die Geschichte von der Rückkehr des Odysseus von Troja nach Ithaka zugrunde gelegt.'

Chapter Eight

The Air Scientific Research Unit

With Lindau now just about in the past, at least as far as Eric Ackermann was concerned, he returned to Obernkirchen to take up where he had off in February. He moved from being a much-travelled officer under the distant and tolerant control of R.V. Jones to a more settled life, remaining in the same place for more than a dozen years. Before the Lindau interval he had been involved in rescuing enemy equipment and disposing of it in whatever way would be most useful to the occupying forces.

Some of the equipment went to Obernkirchen where it was stored for future use, although more often it was just left there and never looked at again. Other items went to the UK and Keith Ackermann recalls his brother arriving home with a cavity magnetron, a small piece of equipment twelve inches by four, with applications in radar technology. Eric probably should not have had it with him, but, as was his way, he bypassed the usual channels to show it to Keith before handing it over to the Air Ministry. He had become quite used to avoiding channels, both usual and unusual.

Another gift he had was that of being in the right place at the right time. In 1946 he managed it once again. He was still only twenty-six and had had an exciting war as well as making a valuable reputation in his own field of electronics. Germany was now the place to be, a blank slate on which to make his own mark. Moreover, he was still working for Jones and was thus assured of both support and interesting, not to say challenging, employment.

In his work as Assistant Director of Intelligence (Science), R.V. Jones was anxious to ensure the retrieval of information and equipment of importance to scientific intelligence and to research programmes in the United Kingdom. The work his few scientists – some of whom had been rapidly converted to temporary RAF officers – had to cope with was steadily increasing. He describes the next step in *Most Secret War*:

'The demands on our services [in immediate post-war Germany] grew; we purchased, at a very favourable exchange rate, chemical balances for the Agricultural Research Council; we supplied German radar components which were generally much better engineered than our own, to both Bernard Lovell and Martin Ryle. This kind of activity became so substantial that I decided to convert our overseas party into a new unit, the Air Scientific Equipment Recovery Unit, with the specific object of bringing back equipment for distribution in Britain. I put Eric Ackermann in command, especially since he was anxious to stay on whilst others such as Hugh Smith, Ken Dobson and Andrew Fell were intending to get back to civil life reasonably shortly.'

The new unit was established at Obernkirchen near Bad Eilsen, the new RAF airfield at Bückeburg, and in the town of Bad Eilsen, HQ British Air Forces of Occupation from 1945 to 1951 and then of 2nd Tactical Air Force until 2nd TAF moved to Moenchengladbach in 1955.

The unit's name tied in neatly with the work of the Air Disarmament Wings (ADWs) and perhaps Jones was ensuring that the equipment which the ADWs were finding was routed to his unit and not just sent off to the UK (or indeed destroyed) without proper investigation. Maybe Eric came across Sidney Goldberg again, whom he had met or heard of in North Africa and again in Belgium and Holland after D-Day.

The world of the ADWs was a relatively small one and two veterans of the desert war would have been sure to seek each other out and talk about old and less complicated times, added to which they both had an active interest in interception and the 'Y' service.

Despite his new responsibilities, Eric Ackermann seldom appears in any of the official documents held at the National Archives. We have already seen this during the war and not much changed later on. The Jones archive at Churchill College is more informative and contains three documents relating to this period. One is a memo Eric sent from one part of the BAFO Headquarters to another in June 1946, asking for equipment for his work at Obernkirchen, shortly after his return from the Lindau mission and his convivial meeting with the Commander-in-Chief. The other two, written in 1950, are about the same equipment. We make no apology for reproducing them in full as they have considerable rarity value. The first reveals how Eric was funded:

From: A.D.I. Science, Air Headquarters Ops., B.A.F.O.
To: Equipment 1d. Air Headquarters Ops. B.A.F.O.

Ref: S51/5

GERMAN OPTICAL EQUIPMENT

With reference to your letter of 18 June 1946, ref: BAFO(O)5111/E and the attached postagram from Air Ministry, ref. E5A/2/20802 of 14 June. It is confirmed that unit holds Special Secret Funds, which are in no way connected with the Air Ministry vote, for use as directed by the D. of I.R., Air Ministry.

It is requested therefore, that you will make the necessary arrangements through the Mil. Gov. at HANNOVER, for us to purchase the equipment from Spindler and Höyer at GÖTTINGEN.

We should be grateful if you will inform us when we can contact the Sales Department of Spindler and Höyer direct in this matter.

Eric G. Ackermann, F/Lt:
Commanding A.D.I. Science

The Air Ministry postagram is not in the file, but the D. of I.R. is R.V. Jones himself, who was appointed to the post two months earlier, on 9 April, at a salary of £1600, rising by £50 annual increments to £1800. The reference to Special Secret Funds reveals the source of Eric's funds. We know from his service record that he was at no time paid by the Air Ministry, but was regarded as a civilian and paid as such.

The firm of Spindler and Höyer still exists and has its UK Headquarters in Milton Keynes in Buckinghamshire. It manufactures a wide range of optical equipment and in Germany it covered the Hamburg and Schleswig-Holstein area from where some of Eric's convoys had set off to deliver those precious cargoes to Obernkirchen.

Eric was careful to send a copy of this memo to Jones, maybe remembering an incident a few months earlier when he was 'somewhere' in Germany on his way to Austria. His job title of Assistant Director of Intelligence (Science) with the British Air Forces of Occupation may seem a bit over the top, but that is exactly what he was, despite still being a flight lieutenant and still without a service number. R.V. Jones had the same job, but at the Air Ministry therefore with vastly more seniority. Nick Ackermann has written that in June 1945 his father was 'given command of the entire British [intercept and scientific intelligence] effort'. His exalted post with BAFO does therefore seem fully justified.

The other letters in the Jones Archive were written in January 1950, but are about a different transaction four years earlier, also in 1946. In the first one, Eric is writing to Dr B.K. Blount, who was the Research Branch Zonal Officer of the Economic Advisor at Göttingen:

'Dear Dr Blount,
    'You will remember that whilst you were here we discussed the matter of the scientific balances I hold for Proff: [sic] Jones. You asked me to let you have full details.
    'The items consist of seven semi-microbalances and one micro-balance made by SARTORIUS/GÖTTGEN [sic]. They were ordered on 24 April 1946 and were delivered to me on 29 November 1946. I hold the bill which I paid and is made out to me at my London address. The Deutsche marks were obtained by Dr Jones. Taking the Deutsche Mark to equal 10 Reichsmark, their value today is about £50, the original bill being RM. 5955.30.
    'I think I can obtain an export permit, and could transport these instruments to the United Kingdom. Would it be possible for you to arrange an import permit or authority, on the grounds that they are required by Universities and Ministries. [Dr Jones would know more about their disposal.]
    'One of the semi-microbalances belongs to me, and I would like to get it to the United Kingdom if possible, possibly we can decide on that nearer the time.

Eric G. Ackermann, F/Lt:
Commanding A.D.I. Science

Dr Blount's response, dated 17 January 1950, is not to Eric but to Dr Jones, even though Jones had by this time left the Civil Service and was Professor of Natural Philosophy at the University of Aberdeen, though still very much in touch with his former colleagues.

> 'Dear Jones,
>
> 'I enclose a copy of a letter which I have had from Ackermann concerning certain balances held by him on your behalf in Germany. When I was out there recently he asked my advice about getting them across to England.
>
> 'This is not a very simple matter, but I am quite willing to take it up with them to see what change I can get out of them. Before doing so, however, I should like to know whether you have any comments to offer, as you have made some plans already about how this should be arranged.'

Jones' reply is not in the file and, as with so much of Eric's service life, we only have half the story. By Göttgen, Eric means Göttingen and a semi-microbalance is a high precision laboratory weighing apparatus which can work to one hundredth of a milligram. The Sartorius company is still in production in Göttingen. These may be the chemical balances to which Jones referred in the earlier extract in this chapter, though the manufacturer is different.

There is another letter in the files from Dr J.A. Lees, Director of the ADSII, to the aforementioned Dr Blount. It is dated 5 May 1951 and refers to something quite different from the other letters shown previously. It is particularly interesting as it mentions not only Eric Ackermann, but also his old friend Derek Garrard and his second in command at Obernkirchen, Flight Lieutenant J. A. F. Morgan. Lees is urging the ADI's listening station in Berlin to start intercepting signals being sent to the type 27 aircraft at the Oranienburg base in the Soviet Zone of Germany. Type 27 is the Ilyushin IL-28, a jet bomber which first flew on 8 July 1948 and on Stalin's orders was displayed at the 1950 May Day parade in Moscow.

It became the Soviet Air Force's standard tactical bomber and was also in service with the Chinese, Polish, Czech and North Korean air forces. Its engines were unlicensed copies of the Rolls-Royce Nene jet engines which the United Kingdom, somewhat naively, and to boost its export trade, had sold to the Soviet Union in the late 1940s. The government chose to believe the Soviet Union's assertion that the aircraft equipped with these engines would only be used for peaceful purposes. Clearly the ADI was interested in the radar equipment in the aircraft and the information provided by the defector seems to have been the solution to a longstanding problem. Eric must have been delighted to receive yet more radar equipment and this time, for a change, from a Soviet aircraft.

At the beginning of his time at Obernkirchen, Eric was concerned with collecting and using the equipment they captured, at least that is what he meant to do, but in reality much of it was left unused for many years. It was only later that he concentrated, under

Letter from Dr J.A. Lees to Dr B.K. Blount with reference to the Russian defector.

Jones' direction, on building up the Obernkirchen station to carry out signals intelligence and later still to extend it widely in the British Zone.

In 1952, the unit duly reflected this with a change of both name and of function when it became No. 646 Signals Unit, a more realistic title now that they had safely stored at Obernkirchen all the equipment they had managed to get hold of. There was another signals unit doing the same work at RAF Uetersen, a former Luftwaffe base near Hamburg, which Eric had been instrumental in setting up in 1950. These two were to form the basis for a network of RAF intercept units in the British Zone, which was to last until 1994 when the so-called 'Cold War dividend' brought about the closure of the last RAF Sigint station in Germany.

Jones himself was directed to: 'proceed on or about 10 August 1946 from the United Kingdom to carry out duties assigned to him at Obernkirchen, Göttingen, Wetzler, Frankfurt-am-Main, Esslingen (in the American Zone in southern Germany) and Amsterdam, and any such other places which may become necessary in the course of his duties. At Obernkirchen he will report to ASRI, BAFO Ops.', in other words to Eric Ackermann himself. This is a nice reversal of roles: the older and senior man ordered to report to someone much junior. They met and it was probably on that visit that Eric put forward his suggestion that Jones might care to build him his laboratories.

As the 1940s progressed, the western Allies were having to face up to the fact that the Soviet Union had opted out of co-operation with them, although this had been recognized as early as 1945 from the Soviets' constant bickering and obstruction and worse, over the running of Berlin. The Berlin blockade and the Airlift from June 1948 to May 1949 confirmed this view. Surveillance of the activities of what was now a potential enemy now needed reinforcing.

Although intelligence from Soviet military sources was already being gathered, it was on a small scale and the Royal Air Force had no ground based signals intercept units in Germany or Austria. Reliance was placed instead on airborne interception, which had some effect, but could not be carried out every minute of every hour of every day. There were also dangerous incidents, such as accidental over-flying of the zonal border, which could explode into major crises. These flights continued well into the 1950s and beyond, and in March 1953 an RAF Lincoln did just this and was shot down by MiG fighters right on the border, with the loss of its entire crew. The Air Ministry claimed that the aircraft was entering the Berlin Air Corridor when it was attacked. Sightseers claimed that the MiGs shot at the crew who had baled out and were parachuting to the ground, and this could explain the unusual injuries they suffered.

It was a very serious incident which promptly brought a vigorous protest to the Soviets, and Winston Churchill, then Prime Minister, referred to it in Parliament.

It produced an apology from the Head of the Soviet Control Commission in Germany, who also proposed a conference of Russian and British representatives to discuss how to avoid similar events happening in the future. No matter which aircraft was involved and why, the incident served as a warning not to trespass over or near Soviet airspace in the Corridor, or the interzonal border, making ground-based surveillance even more important.

Reverting to the late 1940s, the RAF had one Sigint unit, No. 276, on the ground at RAF Habbaniya, near Baghdad and this is where Eric went for just a week in 1948. His arrival and departure are recorded faithfully in the unit's Operations Record Book (AIR 29/1952, which covers the years 1946 to 1950).

1 December 1948.	Flight Lieutenant Ackermann arrived on Temporary Duty from B.A.F.O.
8 December 1948.	Flight Lieutenant Ackermann departed on cessation of Temporary Duty.

There is no other available record of Eric visiting Habbaniya and he must have been completely absorbed in his work in Germany, particularly as the Cold War was moving either towards a hot war, or getting even colder, whichever way one wishes to look at it.

No. 276 Signals Unit was formed on 11 August 1946, at Brazzacco in Italy, taking its number from the defunct 276 Wing in which Eric had served in during the war. It moved to Habbaniya between 1946 and early 1948 (its ORB for 1946–47 is missing, despite the file's cover title). The visit was fleeting, but it foreshadowed the future course of his career, as the Habbaniya unit was to become part of the Ackermann-influenced network of RAF Sigint stations. Signals Intelligence at Habbaniya appears to have been divided into sections. There was the Signals Unit, whose activities were quite obviously secret, and there was also a mysterious outfit sheltering behind the agreeable name of the Palm Grove. This unit was responsible for Elint (Electronic

Intelligence), as distinct from Sigint (Signals Intelligence) and was set apart from the rest of the station and was even more secret.

The units at Habbaniya ceased operations in July 1958 following a coup d'état in Iraq which overthrew the monarchy and installed a military government. An Iraqi colonel arrived at the base on the 15 July and ordered the Station Commander to close down and get out. The request was complied with, although immediate evacuation was not possible and the station lingered on in its death throes until May 1959. Its departure ended the RAF's presence in Habbaniya, which had lasted for twenty-three years. Sigint was transferred to RAF Akrotiri in Cyprus, to continue a listening watch in the Middle East and Mediterranean.

The Army and the Royal Navy were also taking note of what was happening in eastern Europe, and were assuming responsibility for intercepting the opposition's land and naval forces signals. The Navy had two listening stations in Germany, HMS *Royal Albert* and HMS *Royal Charlotte*. These were not seaborne ships, but land bases near Cuxhaven. The Army was spread widely through the Zone, so between them the three services had the opposition comprehensively covered. The reverse was also true of course and indeed there was a kind of comradeship of the air waves between those listening in the west and their eastern counterparts, even to the extent of wishing each other a happy Christmas.

The National Archives has a bulky file (DEFE 40/26) entitled Professor R.V. Jones. Miscellaneous Papers. What might have been a treasure trove of information about Eric Ackermann has turned out to be a disappointment, at least as far as references to Eric are concerned. He is mentioned in just one document, dated 29 June 1948, which gives a good deal of information about Eric and his colleagues as it is a staff chart listing those working for the Air Ministry Deputy Directorate of Intelligence Research (DDIR). Eric is listed in one of the lower levels in the hierarchy – without his RAF rank. Several of Eric's wartime and postwar colleagues are also listed, Howard Cundall, Harold Jordan, J.A.F. Morgan, Ron Farmer and Derek Garrard.

This is Eric at RAF Habbaniya in February 1948. He is the shorter figure in the middle and the only one wearing a tie. On his right is Flt. Lt. Ron Farmer who was to be Best Man at his wedding later that year and still later his second-in-command at RAF Obernkirchen. The other man with his hands shading his face is not identified. They must be off duty as none of them is wearing RAF uniform.

By this time R.V. Jones had returned, though not completely, to academic life in Aberdeen and his post as Assistant Director of Intelligence (Science) had been taken over by Dr J.H. Lees. Jones was still very much involved, however, and his own papers show that he made regular visits to Germany in the late 1940s and early 1950s, sometimes to lecture at German scientific conferences, or to visit wartime colleagues and adversaries, including Dr Dieminger at the Fraunhofer Institute.

The list shows Howard Cundall again, safe and sound after three and a half years as a prisoner-of-war in Germany, now back home and resuming his work as a civilian scientist with the Air Ministry. His first meeting with Eric Ackermann must have been interesting: the ex-PoW reunited with the man who, but for the grace of God and Air Chief Marshal Sir Philip Joubert, might well have been the one captured in 1941.

Harry English confirmed that Cundall had left the RAF by 1948 and was therefore a genuine civilian. Eric meanwhile, was still, by his own choice, in the air force as a hybrid and still, after eight years in the air force, without a service number.

Two others mentioned in the document were to figure large in Eric's immediate future: Ron Farmer has already been mentioned and was best man at his wedding later that year. J.A.F. Morgan (given the wrong third initial on the chart) was Senior Technical Officer at 646 Signals Unit at Obernkirchen from 1955 until 1958. R.V. Jones is listed as an outside consultant working for the Joint Staffs/Joint Technical Intelligence Committee. Eric's position at the very bottom of the chart might seem a bit ungracious after his splendid wartime career and his subsequent activities, but this was the Civil Service and he had to give way to superior beings higher up the order of seniority. He probably did not mind too much: such details were not for him to concern himself with. In any case, this is a Civil Service list and not much attention would have been paid to his RAF achievements and service rank.

Eric was in London again in September 1948 and perhaps meeting his old colleagues. David Lewis recalls their first meeting in an article in the March 2007 issue of the Bad Eilsen *Gazette*:

'In September 1948 I was stationed at the European Signals Centre at RAF Chicksands in Bedfordshire. I was told that I was being posted to the Air Ministry in London. On reporting, I was informed that my posting was to an Air Ministry Unit and, together with two others – Ron Walsh and John Sullivan – was instructed to report to an address in Bryanston Square near Marble Arch, which was a requisitioned block of flats. There we were ushered into a room to meet a person dressed in civvies who introduced himself as Squadron Leader Ackerman [sic]. His first comment was, "Is there any reason why you should not go to Germany?"

'To which, after overcoming our surprise, we all said, "Yes." [Surely this should be 'No! or perhaps No, Sir!]

'We all duly arrived at ASRU Obernkirchen seven days later. At that time, the unit consisted of a Gasthaus [this is the Gasthaus zur Alten Bückeburg in the town itself] where the airmen lived and were fed and a row of huts comprising the technical lab and the signals unit. The number of personnel did not exceed twenty-five, plus an RAF policeman seconded for guardhouse duties, which, to say the least, were basic. There were two small detachments of one or two people in Vienna and Habbaniya (Iraq), although I never went to those places. There was also a German civilian by the name of Rosemeir at Obernkirchen.

'The personnel at that time were the CO, Squadron Leader Ackerman, 2 i/c Flight Lieutenant Farmer, Warrant Officer Wilkins (admin.), Flight Sergeant Napier, Sergeant Ogilvie (transport), and Sergeants Hunt and Kent, followed by myself – a lowly corporal i/c the signals unit. I left in November 1949 and at that time the unit had not materially changed since the date of my arrival.'

In a later conversation, David added some more information. Another man, not named above, who presented himself with David at the Bryanston Square building, said that he really couldn't go just now as he was having trombone lessons. An original excuse, but it didn't work – he went. There were sheds which were workshops and Eric Ackermann worked in one of them with Leading Aircraftman Charlie Brown, who worked with Eric on prototype equipment.

Somewhat confusingly, Eric's organization used two Gasthäuser. The Gasthaus zur Alten Bückeburg was a kilometre from the railway station and on the outskirts of Obernkirchen. It formed an integral part of the RAF station and was where most of its single personnel lived, ate and worked until 1955, when much needed building development took place.

The other was the Gasthaus Walter, fifteen kilometres from the town by road, though about five on foot through the woods, to its home on the 367 metre high Bückeberg. It contained a listening post on its upper floor, with the ground floor housing the dining facilities for staff working on the Decimeter/ Bückeberg Site. The eponymous Gasthaus was owned by the Walter family. Herr Fritz Walter and his son Stephan met David Haysom in 2005 and had their own memories of the end of the war. Fritz Walter's mother was the cook for the hungry workers. Fritz Walter was fifteen in 1945 and he seems to have had the run of the building even after the British arrived. He remembered two small rooms on the first floor which were kept locked. One room had a bed and was used as a rest room, while the other was manned by one or two airmen. Herr Walter recalls how on one occasion he had the opportunity to sneak a look into the rooms, where he saw what appeared to be two receivers, which in his words, looked like 'large black boxes'. The sets were operated by the airmen, who made notes on pads in front of the receivers which David Haysom believes indicates that it was a listening post and the black box was an RCA AR88 receiver.

Security must have been loosely enforced, otherwise a German civilian would not have been allowed anywhere near the business part of the station. The Obernkirchen unit at this period was still experimental rather than operational, so perhaps intruders would not have learnt much about what was going on.

Charlie Olito remembers that in late 1949 he installed a vehicle, probably an RVT (Radio Vehicle Type), for language interception. It was on a concrete pad in a wire fence compound opposite the Gasthaus Walter, at the ASRU decimetre site and Charlie fitted up another language installation in a shed built outside the vehicle compound. These two units were manned by two pilot officers in each unit. The hall in the Gasthaus was full of recovered German and Italian radar and other technical equipment which Eric may have retrieved on his expeditions around the British and other zones of Germany, including, possibly, the Soviet Zone.

On 29 March 1949 Eric was promoted to Squadron Leader, effective from 8 February. These dates do not correspond to those in the *London Gazette,* where the effective date of the promotion is given as 6 July. The *Gazette* announcement includes in all fifteen honorary officers: one group captain, three squadron leaders and eleven flight lieutenants, all but two of whom had a service number in the same small group as Eric's, beginning 1928, so the Air Ministry had presumably decided to regularize the position of all these officers in one go.

Eric's service record has this entry: '2.8.49. Relinquishes Commission (on cessation of duty), Effective from 6.7.49'. This did not mean that his life as an officer was at an end, but that, as he had been promoted to his previous rank of flight lieutenant for his special duty visits to the Middle East, that period was now considered closed and the next in his new rank was about to begin.

From time to time the ASRU, and later 646 Signals Unit, went on detachment to Putlos, a bleak place on the Baltic Coast, used as a tank training ground during the war and later by the British for the same purpose. The RAF Regiment frequently used it for training exercises. John Mitchell, at the time a Corporal Technician from RAF Uetersen, had to build a specially designed vehicle in which the unit's wireless operators would work while detached to Putlos. John, like many others, recalled that Eric was very much 'one of the boys' and popular with his airmen. In November 1952, John was detached to the newly formed RAF Hambühren to make the set room desks in readiness for another signals interception unit with the number 291.

Stan Platts was one of four RAF policemen at Obernkirchen and he remembers two rather different aspects of Eric Ackermann's character. On the one hand, he felt that life at the ASRU was relatively relaxed and that Eric was only concerned with getting the job done and was not interested in the length of the airmen's hair or whether they buttoned up their jackets. Stan was told on arrival that charges would

Appointment to commission (class CC).

As Group Captain:—
    Isaac HODGSON, O.B.E. 20th May 1949.

As Squadron Leaders:—
    Francis Vincent GAUNTLETT (192860). 29th Apr. 1949.
    William Harold WILLIAMS (192862). 30th May 1949.
    Eric George ACKERMANN, G.M. (192868). 6th July 1949.

As Flight Lieutenants:—
    Austin John HOOKER (192853). 5th Apr. 1949.
    Frederick John SHERMAN, C.B.E. (192432). 12th Apr. 1949.
    Eustace Lionel LEADER (192850). 7th May 1949.
    George Frederick WESTERN (192859). 14th May 1949.
    George Francis LYONS (71351). 30th May 1949.
    Rupert HODGES (192864). 13th June 1949.
    John BEDFORD (192867). 25th June 1949.
    Leslie Alfred WENN (192866).
    Charles Andrew COLLARD (192869). 30th June 1949.
    Robert Wilfred FARRANT (71921). 2nd July 1949.
    Desmond Kenny RYAN (192865). 4th July 1949.

The *London Gazette* for 2 August 1949, showing Eric's promotion to Squadron Leader.

not be entertained and consequently throughout his time at Obernkirchen there were none and he was not to worry too much about hats and haircuts, which made it a very unusual station. As a footnote, Stan regretted that the guardroom had no cells! There was a police dog, however, to give the police some practical means of enforcement.

The guardroom was a modified Nissen hut, complete with a small flower garden in which the flowers were always losing their fight for existence. There were four policemen in all, and their job was much more to do with security than with enforcing discipline. Nevertheless, they made the best of an umpromising building by painting it white, including the steps.

In 1955 another more elaborate guardroom was built, so different that it must have been architect designed, at least when compared to the off-the-peg mass-produced Nissen huts which were widely used for the airmen's accommodation and utility buildings, though more so in the UK than in Germany. This was part of phase two of the development of RAF Obernkirchen, constructed to accommodate a considerable increase in its personnel and to a high standard.

Despite the alarming reputation usually enjoyed by guardrooms, this one must have been an attractive building, and anyway the RAF Police at Obernkirchen were far from the fearsome gentlemen who terrified airmen at other stations. Guardrooms sometimes displayed an admonitory, though somewhat rhetorical notice: 'Are you a credit to the Royal Air Force?', together with a mirror so that the airman could check that they were. This was not necessary at Obernkirchen.

Discipline was functional and Eric, a pragmatic officer certainly did not want his airmen to waste their and his valuable time dealing with the sort of apparently trivial charges and subsequent punishments which were inflicted on airmen at other stations.

Two photographs taken by Stan Platts (left) and David Lewis, showing the Guard Room, described by David as 'Our total security!'.

In any case, being small, the station was relatively easy to control. Eric did, however, always insist on being asked for his Form 1250 (the RAF identity card to be carried at all times) when entering the unit and that his airmen always had to be properly dressed in uniform. Even those who were civilians on the station, who worked for the German Civil Labour Organization – later the German Service Organization – had their own version of official dress. One day, though, Eric went too far and was reprimanded by the Bückeburg station commander. This was entirely down to the need for security and although he would have been well known to the SPs (Police), he nevertheless felt that they should never let their guard relax.

The second guardroom, architect designed and in a sad state of dereliction when this photograph was taken in 2010.

He was generous as well and one evening he took all the off-duty staff, including Stan Platts, to Bückeburg to see an opera, performed by not just any old opera company, but by La Scala, Milan. He followed that by treating the airmen to a meal afterwards – all of this at no charge to them. Stan summed him up in these words:

'Ackermann was a truly remarkable man to his staff. His only order was not to talk, even to other personnel in Bad Eilsen or Bückeburg. In BE we always said we were stationed at Bückeburg and vice versa.

Stan goes on to say:

'We also had civilians (women), RAF cooks came I think about 1954. They finished about 6 pm, but we could help ourselves during the evening if we wished and food was left available. They even cleaned our rooms for us, although we had to pay one shilling each per week.

'Pay day was just as casual in that we went to Warrant Officer Wilkins' office between 10 am and 4.30 pm to pick up our pay. Not having our own NAAFI, the NAAFI van called once a week for us to get what we needed. And a hairdresser visited the Gasthaus to keep us trimmed.'

On another occasion Stan had to help out his commanding officer. According to Alan Cox, Eric had decided that as it was St. George's Day, there should be a parade. This happened and the airmen paraded and maybe were inspected. Time passed and Eric realized that he had no idea how to get them off the parade square. He appealed to Corporal Platts, who obliged and gave the order: Parade – Halt! Parade – Dismiss! A half turn to the right and the agony was over. Alan, by the way, remembers that in his day, the airmen called themselves 'Ackermann's Air Force'. If Eric knew, as he must have, he would surely have enjoyed the flattery.

Stan also remembers that the dining facilities in those early days were as functional as the discipline. Everyone had their meals in the same building, with senior NCOs at one table, airmen and corporals at another and the two officers (Eric Ackermann and Ron Farmer) and one warrant officer (Wilkins) at a third. Later on matters became more formalized and conventional, at least as far as a unit commanded by Eric Ackermann ever could be, with the officers and senior NCOs having their own Messes and the corporals and airmen theirs.

The two officers, Warrant Officer Wilkins and those flight sergeants and sergeants who were married also lived out, while the rest were accommodated in the Gasthaus zur Alten Bückeburg. At this stage, in the late 1940s and early 1950s the station was very small but growing slowly. David Lewis's figure of twenty-five rose to about forty by 1953, compared with, say, its nearest neighbours, 365 and 291 Signals Unit at Uetersen and Hambühren, each of which had some 300. These two were commanded by squadron leaders, while Eric Ackermann was now rapidly approaching promotion to wing commander and would outrank all the other SU commanders, with only the OC 5 Signals Wing as his equal, despite his station being the smallest in the Sigint network in Germany.

This chapter and the next two chapters include several photographs of RAF Obernkirchen. They are there because they show the kind of station which Eric created and the airmen who served under his command. There are only a few of Eric himself as he always seemed reluctant to have his photograph taken and airmen anywhere did not often take snapshots of their CO. Most of these images from the past come from veterans of the Air Scientific Research Unit (ASRU) and 646 Signals Unit and their co-operation, willingly given, is gratefully acknowledged.

The Gasthaus zur Alten Bückeburg was very much the hub of the station and it fulfilled several important functions. A well as providing messing and sleeping facilities, the lower ranks also slept there, and it was the place where Eric's electronic booty was stored. The complex of buildings comprised the Gasthaus itself, a long wooden

A happy group of fifteen airmen who worked for the ASRU and 646 SU. Left to right: 1. Don Swan, 2. Van Cuylenberg (who played cricket for the Officers' Mess and formed the ASRU cricket team in 1951. He was a machinist who worked with Willi Schaeffer), 3. Don Welch (driver), 4. Stan Platts (RAF Police), 5. Ron Newman, 6. George Paxton, 7. Alan Price, 8. George Briggs, 9. Bill Jackson, 10. Alan Syndercombe, 11. Charlie Olito, 12. Ken Hodgkins, 13. John Pope, 14. Unknown, 15. Charlie Brown (who worked for Eric Ackermann on prototype equipment).

barrack hut which was built by the local building firm of Ackemann & Sohn for the ASRU and a few smaller ancillary buildings. Those who lived there said that their commanding officer ensured a cosy atmosphere for his airmen. They were content, provided their own entertainment, had their own bar and there was little reason to visit the town. It was a happy unit with a CO who ran it with a light touch, eschewing the usual

This is Parker's Circus outside the Gasthaus Walter, with Ron Pugh on the left. The children are those of the quarry workers whose families provided civilized company for the airmen.

military formalities, except when orders from Bad Eilsen or Bückeburg dictated that he should, to mark events of national importance such as the Sovereign's birthday.

There was another unit which arrived in 1946, known as Parker's Circus, named after its Commanding Officer, Flight Lieutenant Parker. It got its nickname because every time it stopped on the way through France, Belgium and Holland and into Germany it would erect eight 75 ft. tubular aerials. The name refers to its being constantly on the move rather than to anything to do with clowns and acrobats. On arriving at Bad Eilsen, it first set up its equipment at a small village near Südhorsten with the name of Aptly, before moving to the Bückeberg. Whether the circus bothered to set up its own aerials there, or rely on the single, much taller one already thoughtfully provided by the Luftwaffe some years before, is not known. Though having dragged its own through north-west Europe, it probably did use them. It appears, however, to have been completely independent of Eric's ASRU, though certainly rubbing shoulders with its personnel from time to time.

Ron Pugh was one of Flight Lieutenant Parker's group and he remembers that they used the most advanced equipment on microwave frequencies with a UHF frequency generator called a magnetron. This would have been the same type which Eric managed to take back to England, much to the surprise of his brother Keith. Ron also has a happy memory of revisiting the Gasthaus many years later and meeting Frau Maria Walter. He asked her if she remembered him. 'Oh yes,' she replied, 'You were the first to give us white flour since 1938.'

The Gasthaus and the wooden hut built by Ackemann & Sohn (spelt very slightly differently so no relation) provided accommodation and a workplace for the airmen, many of whom were working at the Decimetre Site. This was on the top of the Bückeberg Hill, 367 metres (1204 feet) above sea level opposite the Gasthaus Walter. It was exposed to the wind, rain, snow and ice of winter.

Charlie Olito was a radar/radio technician in 1949/50 and he did most of his work in the laboratory and in a small hut next to it, servicing five or six 300-watt radio transmitters operating in the 4–6 MHz band, which he believes were used to transmit to the 646 SU outstations in Berlin, Putlos, Vienna, Habbaniya, the UK and the mobile units when they were out on detachment. John Harris confirms that the transmitters were part of the radio links with GCHQ, Bletchley Park and the RAF bases mentioned above. Charlie also remembers a large hall adjacent to the bar which housed an assortment of decommissioned German and Italian radar equipment, the very material which was delivered from Hamburg and elsewhere in 1945. A local resident, Heinrich Knickrehm, much given as a youth to roaming round the perimeter, remembered that the Gasthaus was surrounded by a high fence. He noticed pieces of military equipment inside, some with desert camouflage.

The other Gasthaus, several miles away, consisted of a main, very elegant building, a much smaller half-timbered house which the airmen called the Cottage, as well as outbuildings and fine gardens.

The British had lost no time in requisitioning the Gasthhaus, as they did with so many other buildings in Obernkirchen, including Eric's own house. The RAF, of course, promptly disfigured it by putting up functional buildings, surrounding it with a security fence, and installing lighting which illuminated the compound twenty-four hours a day. The architecture of the station improved considerably with the ambitious building programme of the mid-1950s. Photographs in this book show that much of what was built then was, if not exactly elegant, much better than some of the hurried constructions of the 1940s.

The quarry's sandstone had been earmarked by Hitler's architect, Albert Speer, for the Nazi's grandiose Germania project in Berlin, which would have remodelled the city to fulfil Hitler's grotesque ideas of what his capital city should look like. The materials were eventually used in Berlin by Sir Norman Foster for the interior walls of the rebuilt Reichstag building in the 1990s.

The Decimetre Site in 1949, showing the mobile communications trucks in the compound opposite the Gasthaus Walter. The fences on the left of the track are strung with barbed wire but those on the right seem to be just ordinary field fences.

A battered print of a photograph taken by Charlie Olito in 1950. It shows tea break at the Decimetre Site. Left to right: Bill Jackson, Larry Wright, Harry English, Willie Rosemeier (a civilian employee from Obernkirchen, and remembered by David Lewis), Norman Hennington, Dennis Slee (GCHQ representative) and Van Cuylenberg.

Two postcards of the Gasthaus zur Alten Bückeburg taken in 1930s.

The Gasthaus in the late 1940s. The man on the right seems to be aiming a gun. This photograph was provided by David Lewis.

The Gasthaus in its declining years, taken by Stan Platts in 2002.

Sgt. Dave Ogilvie's wedding. The Best Man is Sgt. Napier and the interested onlookers are families of the quarry and Gasthaus staff. There is no sign of Eric Ackermann in the photograph although it was usual for the CO to attend airmen's weddings if he was able to.

John Sullivan and two of the maids who worked at the Gasthaus.

Stan Platts sitting on the Guardroom steps.

This is David Lewis, who provided several of the photographs in this book and also his own memories of his first meeting with Eric Ackermann.

Stan Platts (left) and Ted Toghill standing beside an RAF Standard Vanguard vehicle.

This shows the communications aerial behind the quarry building and was taken between 1946 and 1948.

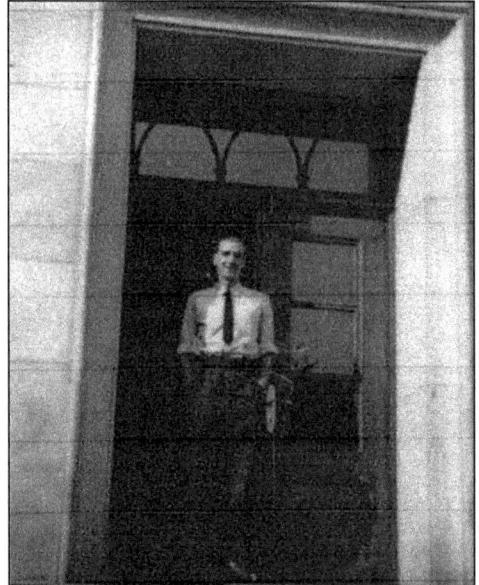

September 1948. Jim Crawshaw at the entrance of the quarry headquarters.

Left to right: George Paxton, Don Swan, George Briggs, Van Cuylenberg, Ron Newman, Don Walsh (at back), Stan Platts, Alan Price.

'Jimmy' Hill and Stan Platts, perhaps preparing to escape over the perimeter fence.

Left to right: Ron Newman, Geoff Allinson (dog handler) and Stan Platts. Stan Platts believes that they were attending a wedding of one of their number at Bückeburg, hence their smart suits.

Left to right: Charlie Olito, Ginger Payne, Stan Platts, George Paxton and Geoff Allinson, also at the Bückeburg wedding.

An elegant dinner party with WO Ted Wilkins, WO Hilditch, Mrs Wilkins, Ron Matheson, Mrs Matheson, René Briggs and George Briggs.

The ASRU football team, 1948/49. Back row: 4th from left Ossie Fenwick, 5th Ken Jones. Front row from left: Ron Walsh, David Lewis, Ken Gaskell, Ron Thomas, John Sullivan. There are only ten of them, so was the eleventh man the photographer? The three eager young spectators lurking at the back are anxious to learn the finer skills of the game.

Second from left: Ron Matheson with Ted Wilkins leaning over the bar. The others cannot be identified.

A mixture of ranks. Back row, third from right: WO Ted Wilkins, next to him Ron Matheson, Charlie Brown (wearing glasses). Seated and straddling the chair: Flight Sergeant Dave Ogilvie, next to him in civvies Dickie Hunt.

The 646 Signals Unit football team in 1951 or 1952. This photograph appeared in RAF News in April 2005, with an appeal from the late Alan Harris for any information about the members of the team. As far as is known, Alan received no replies.

Moderate horseplay in the airmen's bar with Jack Ross, Johnny Peters, Bunny Warren and Stan Platts sitting on Larry Wright's knee. Stan's caption for this is 'In our recreation room and bar built by ourselves'.

Chapter Nine

Life and Work at Obernkirchen

In April 1948, Eric and Dorothy were divorced and three months later, on 17 July 1948, Eric married Gizella Maria Anna von Schmidt, aged twenty-four, whose occupation was given as interpreter and her nationality as Hungarian. The marriage certificate records the couple's residence rather surprisingly as ASRU Air Headquarters, BAFO, Admiral Scharn [sic – Scheer] Strasse, Abernkirchen [sic, again]. His age is shown as twenty-eight. Marianna's father's name is given as Sandon Schmidt (the 'von' is omitted in the register, although it is included in the bride's name) and his occupation as Agriculture Advisor. His name should have been recorded as Sandor. What is surprising about their address is that BAFO seems to mean that it was both his workplace and his home, despite his having the beginnings of a functioning RAF station more or less at the end of his road.

Their marriage was solemnized in the PMUB (Presbyterian, Methodist and United Board) Garrison Church and it may also have been blessed according to Catholic rites. It is unlikely that Eric's Catholic wife and her family would have allowed her own church to have no part in the ceremony. The Roman Catholic priest would have been unable to conduct the full marriage service in his church as Eric was a divorced man. Nevertheless, Frau Hobohm, who worked for the family, held strongly to the view that they were married in a Roman Catholic Church, but she probably meant that the marriage was blessed in the Catholic Church after the PMUB service, in deference to the bride's wishes.

In a conversation with David Haysom, Harry English, who was a Flight Sergeant Radar Fitter at ASRU in 1950–53, recalled that Eric may have been a Plymouth Brother and that even if he was not, he was well versed in Bible studies and may have been a Methodist or a member of one of the other non-conformist churches. Certainly his family background confirms this.

In due course, Eric and Marianna had two children, Peter David Alexander, born on 29 September 1952 and Nicholas John George, born on 19 April 1957, both at the Rinteln Military Hospital, which was conveniently near their home in Obernkirchen. The old family name of George continues for a further generation with Nicholas. Rudolph, however, has completely disappeared.

Marianna Ackermann's nationality sometimes confused the airmen, some believing that she was German or Austrian. She did give German lessons to at least one airman, Malcolm Stewart and probably others both at Obernkirchen and later on at Scharfoldendorf. Sometimes the situation was reversed with airmen giving English lessons to local people.

As she would have been at least tri-lingual: German, Hungarian and English, she was a useful person to have around and it is not surprising that BAFO appointed her as an interpreter in the fragile days after the end of the war. Jobs of any kind with the occupying forces were much sought after and provided security in a very insecure time. Marianna was now the wife of an RAF officer with a responsible job and considerable prestige, and, for good measure, a large house with staff to help run it. She must have long reflected on her good fortune.

Marianna and Eric both had unusual ancestries and hers was exceptionally complicated because of the part of Europe she came from. Her family originated in Hungary and on the family tree compiled by Brian Ackermann there is a mixture of German and Hungarian names. Until 1918 Hungary was the smaller part of the Dual Monarchy which formed the Austro-Hungarian Empire. She herself was born in Kula Puszta in Hungary and among her relatives was a cousin, Theo

This is the official photograph of Eric and Marianna's wedding as they emerge from the PMUB Church at RAF Bückeburg. The Best Man, Ron Farmer is standing behind the bridegroom. The other officer is not identified.

von Besnard, who, according to the information on the family tree, was shot by the British at Uelzen, near Hamburg, in 1945, though no reason is given.

This is Marianna as a young woman, probably taken before or during the war in Hungary.

Another relative was a colonel, Paul Kaczirek, who died in 1986 in Austria at the age of sixty-nine; yet another was a fighter pilot, Gyula Horvath, who was born in Zsombolya, survived the war and died in 1990, aged seventy-eight. Further back there was another Gyula Horvath, who rose to the rank of general and died in 1966 at the age of eighty-seven. The family's home area of Hungary was one where borders were constantly shifting as different powers invaded, conquered and were then repelled.

The war inflicted appalling hardship on the people of the area and in 1945 the German population fled, or was expelled. During the war some 1300 Germans living in Hungary were forced into the Hungarian or German armies and sent to the Eastern front, where many of them were inevitably captured or killed. The Red Army arrived in October 1944 and many of the inhabitants were deported to death camps established by the Russians in the neighbourhood, many of them remaining there until 1948, when around 2000 prisoners were released.

At the age of twenty-one, Marianna wrote an account of her experiences in the closing days of the war, which are as harrowing as any tale of the plight of refugees fleeing west to get to the advancing Allies, where they would at least be safer than with the Russians advancing in the same direction. This is her stark story of a desperate time:

'Easter fell early in 1945. The chilly March winds were still blowing over the Hungarian plains and with the wind from the east came the sounds of cannons booming. Our capital, Budapest, had fallen on Christmas Eve. We, that is my sister and I, were already in the westernmost corner of our small land. Stories of misdeeds – particularly to young women – by the oncoming Russian troops came long in advance of their actual arrival, and whoever could, fled further and further to the west. The exodus was greater than when Genghis swept [from] the east. Everyone was going on the one highway towards the setting sun. Buses, trucks, military and civilian motor cars of every vintage, bicycles, planes and wagons.

'My sister and I were in the covered back of a lorry going to Vienna, the Austrian capital, some ninety kilometers west of our previous abode. On arrival there we managed to find floor space for the night in the all dark, but still intact, Collegium Hungaricum. After a few restless hours of sleep, we had to think by which means to get further. Money had no bargaining power, the currency of the day was tobacco, food and gold and jewelry. We had some of each, but not knowing our destination or length of stay, had to bargain carefully and of course very secretly, as all the above goods were strictly black market items and forbidden to us by the rulers of the day. However, we managed to get another lift on the back of an open lorry going west.

'On Good Friday, amongst the sounds of the town siren blowing the all-clear, we arrived in a little farming town on the Austro-German border. This was it, as there was no more petrol in the tank and none to be had anywhere in the fast-diminishing Third Reich. We found night quarters in a former youth hostel too weary to think of tomorrow. Nevertheless, morning came only too soon and we had to face it. Everywhere we asked we got the same reply: "Full up, we already sleep in the bath and kitchen." After a lot of walking and asking we found a little room on a farm two miles outside the already overfilled town. Though we were in Austro–Germany, we heard all the thumps of the Balkans. We even met a refugee who left Russia in 1918. He told us, in still broken German, [that] one gets used to being a DP(Displaced Person).

'We existed on the meager [sic] rations we were allowed. Refugees were entitled to less than PoWs, or foreign workers. We met a lot of other DPs and all prayed for the war to end soon. The death of President Roosevelt was announced on the wireless. We wondered whether this would in any way influence the outcome of the war. We worried whether this would stop the Western Allies' advance, wondering whether we would have to move on again with our meager little belongings and how. For want of anything else to do, we went on long kicks [i.e. trips] around, exploring the country, meeting other refugees, hearing their sad stories. One lady came on a covered wagon. When the Stukas came down one bullet killed her husband beside her. She stopped, buried him and carried on. Another had to leave her dead daughter in the rail yard where she was gunned down. The tales of woe and sorrow run endlessly.

'Nevertheless, 5 May came, the war was over. The German Army had surrendered on the [Lüneburg] Heath. We met the first allied troops while out on a kick. They were four Negroes in a jeep. The first we ever saw. Genuinely terrified, we sat down by the side of the road to await our fate.

'One jeep stopped, two fellows jumped out and gave us some Hershey bars and a balloon. We were practically speechless, particularly as our knowledge of English was very scanty in those days.'

This is a story with a happy ending and for the lucky ones it was not all that unusual, but that does not lessen its impact as we read about someone tragically stranded in the wrong part of Europe as the war ground a bitter way to its end. Many of those who reached the western zones looked for work with one of the occupying powers. Marianna was one of these.

Some time after his return from the Lindau expedition, Eric moved out of the Gasthaus zur Alten Bückeburg into the house on Admiral-Scheer-Strasse, where he assembled his domestic staff and to which he brought his new bride. He also had with him from the Gasthaus a former PoW, Herr Rosocha, whose basic knowledge of English was good enough for him to work as Eric's translator. His mother worked for the Ackermann family as a cook until 1958 when the Ackermanns left Obernkirchen. The Rosochas became very attached to the family and missed them greatly when they had gone; they had, after all, been working for them for a dozen years. Herr Rosocha kindly provided many of the photographs of the family in this book and also met David

Haysom many years later, following the publication of two articles in local newspapers, both instigated by David, and which appeared in 2006 and 2007.

Another man who remembered those times was Herr Fritz Walter, whom David also met to talk about Eric and his life and times in Obernkirchen. They met at Herr Walter's home in Steinbergen. Herr Walter was a teenager when Eric arrived in Obernkirchen, but he was able to recall some of the unusual activities conducted at Obernkirchen and show photographs of some of those who had worked on the Bückeberg. Herr Walter's son, Dr Stephan Walter, wrote an article which appeared in the *Schaumburger Zeitung* on 12 January 2006, describing Eric as a phantom. This is an apt description, as he had flitted to and fro during the war and certainly afterwards, on one obscure mission after another.

There was another article in a local newspaper, on 27 October 2007, and this is also about the Walter family, their eponymous Gasthaus and the Jahn Tower, as well as much else about those times. The title in English is: *Beneath this roof the Russians were listened to.*

Resuming now with Herr Rosocha and his interview with David Haysom, who writes that:

'He [Rosocha] was called upon to assist with basic domestic interpreting, to help with local authorities and workers and also in collecting food from depots, and general domestic jobs at the Gasthaus and later at the house. At no time was he involved in the technical side of Eric's activities. After leaving the employ of the Ackermann family to study, Rosocha continued to live in Admiral-Scheer-Strasse, in a flat near to the villa and frequently saw Eric in the street, or when visiting his (Rosocha's) mother. He remembers Eric to be a friendly and helpful

A photograph of three generations of the Walter family outside the Gasthaus Walter: Dr Stephan Walter, his daughter Victoria and his father Fritz Walter.

man, who was easy to get along with and someone who cared for and looked after his staff. In fact, he helped Rosocha obtain his flat and employed his mother as a cook from 1946 until he left Obernkirchen in 1958. Mrs Rosocha had her own room or flat in the Ackermann household and was obviously much appreciated by the family. She remained in contact with Mrs Ackermann by mail after the family returned to the UK and was disappointed that the Ackermanns never revisited Germany. The letters petered out in about 1962.'

The Ackermann's domestic ménage included a cat and a maid, Frau Lautenstroch. There was also a pig. Poultry was also represented by a goose, which was probably going to end up as Christmas dinner for the family and the staff.

David remembers asking Harry English how Eric, as a flight lieutenant, could afford such a big house and a large staff. According to English, Eric claimed that it was because he needed a suitable property and staff to entertain foreign visitors, and also a splendid car. This does not directly answer the question, but the letters in the previous chapter show that Eric and his activities were financed from a secret fund which did not go through RAF accounts. This is not something which he would ever have revealed though maybe some of his colleagues guessed that something like that was going on.

It was, of course, completely legal and not at all underhand, nor particularly unusual in the shadowy world of intelligence gathering. The question Harry English might have asked is, 'What foreign visitors and where did they come from?' We are getting into the area of the Official Secrets Act with this and Eric could never have given answers to these questions, though there are clues in some of the correspondence in the Jones archive.

Frau Hobohm recalled the Ackermann family in another meeting with David Haysom, following the very fruitful newspaper articles mentioned

This is the 'phantom' article referred to elsewhere in the book.

Ein Phantom mit Spezialauftrag: Wer kennt den geheimnisvollen Briten?

Er lebte 13 Jahre in Obernkirchen: Wer war Eric George Ackermann?

above. She worked for the family in the Admiral-Scheer-Strasse house from 1946 to 1948 and again from 1952 to 1958. This is David's account of their conversation:

'She described the Ackermanns as good employers and she enjoyed her work. During the period 1946–48, she recalls a man called Farmer, a tall man of about forty-five, who was often at the house and, although she is not certain of the name, she thinks there was a Mr Hall, whom the staff called Mr Manchester because she vaguely remembers that he had some kind of textile factory in Manchester, or, and more probably, because he wore cord trousers, which at that time in Germany were known as Manchester Hosen.'

The Ackermann's domestic ménage at 27 Admiral-Scheer-Strasse included a cat and a dog, seen here with Frau Rosocha and a maid, possibly Frau Lautenstroch.

Mr Farmer was the Flight Lieutenant Farmer who had been best man at Eric and Marianna's wedding, and was at the ASRU for many years, travelling frequently with Ackermann on trips in Germany. He was also probably Eric's closest friend in the RAF. Mr Hall may have been Flight Lieutenant Hall, who was the unit's Adjutant but he could have been a civilian because of the trousers. She recalls that Mr Hall was always very smartly dressed and was very particular about his clothes, unlike Ackermann himself, who was slovenly dressed and untidy. [Keith Ackermann has added the terse comment: 'Typical!]

Eric's mother and father occasionally visited the villa and several times his brother Keith came with them. Frau Hobohm thought that he was named George. She was probably confusing him, at least as far as the name goes, with Marianna's sister Georgia or Georgi, also known as Georgina or Georgy for short. Georgina had been married several times, her final husband being a colonel in the Austrian army. Georgina was friendly with Ron Farmer. Like her sister, Georgina spoke fluent German and she is remembered as having visited Obernkirchen two or three times. She was eight years older than her sister and was born in Munich during the First World War. She died in 1984.

Frau Hobohm remembers two visitors to the villa between 1946 and 1948 well, because of the unusual circumstances of their arrival and departure. On different occasions they were blindfolded on arrival and were taken to an upper room in the villa where the blindfold was removed. The staff were instructed not to speak to them, but Frau Hobohm did serve them food in the room. One of the visitors once asked where he was and was told 'Obernkirchen'. Understandably, the staff were inquisitive and Frau Hobohm readily admits that she would have been prepared to take the paper out of the waste paper basket to try and find out more about the mysterious blindfolded visitors. Unfortunately, Eric had already removed the contents before she could start cleaning the room. The visitors later departed the villa – again blindfolded. She believes that one of them may have had the name von Zahn.

Peter von Zahn was a highly respected German journalist and had been an officer in the Propaganda Ministry during the war. After the war he was in charge of Nordwestdeutsche Rundfunk, now Norddeutsche Rundfunk, in Hamburg. Eric himself had some part in establishing the then British Forces Broadcasting Service (later British Forces Network [BFN]) in Hamburg in 1945. Unfortunately, Peter von Zahn died in 2001 and no information has been obtained about his reason for visiting Eric's house. One can only guess that it was to do with communications involving radio signals.

She also said that Eric was a keen amateur radio enthusiast (Keith Ackermann remembered that his brother's call sign was DL 2AU), with a transceiver and other equipment which he stored in a separate room in the house. Yet another room was reserved as a photographic dark room. A Frau Lautenstrauch (née Lohmann), since deceased, also worked for the family as a nanny.

Frau Vera Freise-Folle, the younger sister of Fräulein Lohman, was another person who contacted David Haysom. She worked for the Ackermann family from 1955–1958, but has since died. She told David that on at least one occasion her elder sister travelled with the family on holiday to Grossenbrode, in Schleswig-Holstein on the Baltic coast, where they stayed, she believed, at the Gasthaus zur Linde. Grossenbrode is ten kilometres from Putlos, where No. 646 Signals Unit maintained an outstation. Frau Freise-Folle also recalled that a priest was with them sometimes, but she did not know who he was, or where he came from, or even why he was there. Maybe he was an RAF chaplain from Bad Eilsen, or Bückeburg, or a Catholic priest who got to know the family.

It was common for service families to 'employ' airmen as babysitters and Eric and Marianna were no exception. Alan Harris performed this service from time to time and recalled being left a supply of beer and sandwiches with which to while away the evening hours. Memory plays tricks after so many years and Alan believed that there were two children, one of whom was Peter and the other he thought was a baby daughter. It was not Nicholas, who was not born until several years after Alan had left. The little girl was probably the daughter of a neighbouring family placed in his care on those occasions. Babysitting was a fruitful source of income or payment in kind for impoverished airmen and one of the rare occasions when the barriers between officers and other ranks wavered a little, although it does seem that Eric was not very concerned about what he may have felt were unnecessary barriers, particularly in such a unit as his.

John Vickerman was another babysitter and he was probably as close to Eric in his working capacity as any airman. There was a very large fridge in the house and Eric would say to him, 'Take what you fancy'. John says he never dared to. His day job was as a clerk (Progress) in station headquarters. His work included a great deal of typing for his commanding officer, often of highly technical reports and also collating the watch reports from the 646 Signals Unit's intercept stations at Obernkirchen and its two detachments at Gatow and Putlos.

John recalls that Eric was a very clear speaker, a good boss and altogether a 'nice chap'. In the same group of offices was Captain Knott, who had his own office, and Corporal Martin Eggleton, both from

Eric and Peter playing cars either on Peter's birthday or at Christmas.

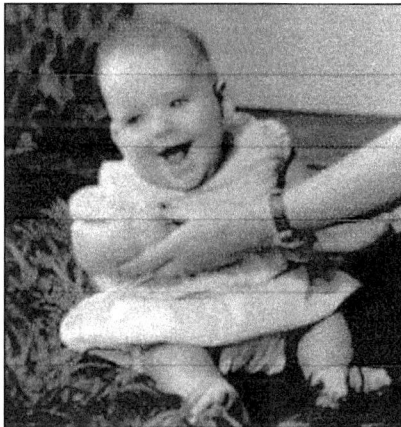

the Royal Signals. John believes that Captain Knott was actually with MI8, the British Signals Intelligence Department. Their task was to receive the signal reports from the signals unit and its detachments at Gatow and Putlos, log them and then scan through them for whatever seemed worthy of referring higher up the intelligence ladder and specifically to GCHQ. John has kindly provided several photographs of the camp at that time and these appear in this book.

Mervyn Williams remembers his superior officer's tendency towards unconventional behaviour. On one occasion, during a parade to mark the Queen's Official Birthday, which Squadron Leader Morgan was taking, Eric drove up and got out of his car to reveal that he was wearing RAF uniform augmented with brown shoes and a red scarf. He called out casually, 'Carry on', and then wandered off to his office, obviously determined to take no part in the formalities. This had nothing to do with his patriotism, or lack of it. He was a

Respectively, the family pig, attended by Frau Rosocha and the gardener, and Nick as a baby, with apologies to Nick for bracketing him with the pig, though they are not difficult to tell apart. The size of the garden can be seen behind the fence.

staunch patriot, but he did not much like the formality of parades very much – rather like the airmen whom he commanded. He seemed to have problems with parades, forgetting his hat on an earlier occasion, and, as we have seen, not knowing how to get the airmen off the parade ground. Such delights were in any case a rarity at Obernkirchen and were reserved for important national commemorations, and the CO, a busy man, can be excused his occasional forgetfulness.

John Vickerman also recalls rumours that Eric carried out certain operations 'in the east' in the late 1940s. 'Certainly he disappeared for days at a time with no explanations on return.' 'In the east' could simply mean Austria, as Eric would hardly have been able to cross the Iron Curtain into East Germany or elsewhere, unless he was going to RAF Gatow in Berlin, which he certainly did from time to time. He was many things, but not a real life character on whom John Le Carré might have based a character in one of his novels.

Charlie Olito confirms the other ranks' regard for their commanding officer, saying that he never acted 'officerish', but as one of the boys, although he had to maintain some distance from them to keep a grip on things, as an officer should. He walked this particular tightrope successfully and was friendly, though not over-familiar, while always supporting them in any trouble as far as he could.

Eric's car at this time was a Packard 120, described as a premier luxury automobile and several steps up the automotive ladder from his little Morris two-seater of the early 1940s. It had a London registration number, FMK 216, and was manufactured in 1940. Eric said that he had bought it secondhand. He made sure the car was looked after. According to Peter Ackermann, his father later had an Opel Kapitän and then a Mercedes. Eric clearly fancied cars which were out of the usual, although this was not uncommon, as officers and senior NCOs often went in for large cars in which they sometimes gave humble airmen a lift. We know that he had extended this courtesy in North Africa (alarming his passengers in the process) and it would have been in character for him to do so in Germany. He was, after all, 'one of the boys' and at Obernkirchen he was the right man in the right place.

Herr Rosocha cleaning and polishing Eric's 120 Packard car, with a lady, possibly Marianna, doing some gardening and another lady watching from the back of the house.

It is hard to imagine Eric fitting in on a much bigger station, with a defined hierarchy around and above him, more ceremonial and more, to him, meaningless rituals in the Officers' Mess, and – dread word – more parades. Dining-in nights were something which, according to his sons, he did not relish. Years later, when he had returned to England, it was partly this which persuaded him to leave the RAF at a time when he had much more to offer, and transfer his expertise and experience to civilian life. He might even have moved one rank further up and become a group captain, with gold braid on his hat, if and when he ever chose to wear it and maybe a nice official car, even more spectacular than those he had already owned.

In Obernkirchen there was a building firm confusingly named Ackemann und Sohn. The firm was given a contract by the British to build a large barrack hut adjacent to the Gasthaus zur Alten Bückeburg. The Gasthaus was where Eric had set up his headquarters. An employee of the firm, Herr Horst Börner, who still lives in Obernkirchen, had been an employee of Ackemann und Sohn and he contacted David Haysom with some helpful information about Eric and the building project he carried out for him.

He remembers that the commandant of the site – Eric, of course – was known to the workers as 'Mister Accy', who, so they were informed, was the nephew of a high-ranking officer in the War Office in London. This was probably a confused reference to R.V. Jones, who was in Obernkirchen in 1946 when the building was going up and he would have taken a keen interest in it.

The construction of this hut and an adjoining Nissen hut, both of which contained offices, a laboratory and workshops for the ASRU, was certainly authorized by R.V. Jones and financed by one of his departments. Herr Börner recalled that the dismantled German and Italian radar equipment strewn around the Gasthaus site was visible from the perimeter fence. There was an RAF policeman at the entrance to the secured area to which only authorized persons had access.

Herr Börner wrote this letter on 12 January 2006, which was passed to David Haysom:

'A few days before Christmas in 1945, I arrived as a PoW at the camp at Sülbeck. The German commandant was a Major Teller.

'At first we were employed felling trees at Bückeburg, above Gasthaus Stieler in Wendthagen. In September 1946 I was assigned to work at the Alt Bückeburg (formerly Gasthaus) for Ackemann and Sons. My workmates at Ackemann and Son were Herren Eherling and Simon. At first, our task was to build a barrack hut with a large room which was to hold a big sand pit. The sand pit was for the reconstruction of battles. The barrack was finished by Christmas. If I remember correctly the frost came early and our next task was to excavate the foundations for a very large Nissen hut. In order to dig into the earth we had to use pneumatic drills. As soon as the hut was finished, metal working equipment was installed. This workshop was under the supervision of the Oberkirchener Herr Rösemeier (Langestrasse). At the Alt Bückeburg site German Würtzburg (radar) equipment was gathered together, most of which was disassembled.

'The British commander was a Mister Accy (Acci?), an officer in the British air force, who was said to be a nephew of a high ranking officer in the War Ministry in

London. The radio station near Walter on the Alt Bückeburg (sic) and the station at Achum, was said to be under his command and that they were in constant contact with London. The headquarters of the British air forces was at Bad Eilsen.

'Mister Accy, I don't know if this was an abbreviation of the name Ackermann, lived in a villa in the Admiral-Scheer-Strasse. The villa was demolished when the new Obernkirchner School was built. There must be documents in the town archives from this period. The villa was requisitioned. Whether my small contribution is of use to Mr Haysom I can't say and you must decide. I ask that you pass this information to Mr Haysom.

Sincerely
Letter signed by Horst Börner

Herr Börner's reference to the Würtzburg [sic – Würzburg] radar equipment is interesting, because way back in 1941 Eric Ackermann was on a flight in a Wellington from RAF Boscombe Down and wrote a report on this very same system. (See Chapter 2 for the details).

Back now to domesticity at Obernkirchen with Mervyn Williams recalling another incident, describing Eric as:

'the 646 Signals CO who was known as Wing Commander Ackermann, allegedly a civilian with the honorary rank. He lived off camp with his wife (a Hungarian lady, I think). Early in 1956 he came to see me, as camp "chippy", saying that he had "shot his mouth off at the Yacht Club." He had boasted that "we" could repair a small badly damaged yacht – it had a couple of big holes in the lower hull area. That weekend, he drove me to the club to see the damage, announcing to the onlookers that it was to be made seaworthy! The following week it was in a shed at 646. He told me to meet him at nine on the Sunday morning to make a start. He was under some illusion that UK carpenters knew something about repairing boats. Fortunately, I found a book with some information in the Bückeburg camp library – with such terms as caulking the joints.

'So, for about six Sundays, he and I patched up the holes, with me trying to give the impression that I knew what I was doing. The caulking was a funny mixture of string, putty and paint, and he kept giving me useful amounts of money each time. At least, with the final coats of paint on, it looked pretty good, but I wondered what would happen when it hit the water. I wasn't invited to the launch, but the CO appeared in the workshop the following Monday morning.

'You should have seen their faces when he explained it went like a dream – "great job, great job." And that was it – never heard any more.'

The yacht club where Eric sailed his yacht was based at the Steinhuder Meer, a short distance away. This is Germany's largest inland lake, with an area of 120 square miles and it is a beautiful place for water sports, yachting and walking. A local delicacy is smoked eel (Rauchaal), caught fresh from the lake.

Another attraction of the area to the historically minded was, and still is, the Dinosaur Park, where the fossilized footprints of dinosaurs are carefully preserved. With Eric's passion for education, it is likely that he took his family there, or at least his elder son Peter. Nicholas, born in 1957, would have been rather too young to appreciate such ancient sites.

As well as babysitting for the CO and mending his boat, the airmen had time for football and the annual pantomime and photographs of some of these have survived, though only rarely featuring the commanding officer himself. When he does appear he almost seems to wish that he was invisible.

Geoff Eastough worked as a draughtsman at Obernkirchen from 1951 to 1953 and his main task was to compile maps and pinpoint targets from co-ordinates given to him by the CO. He also spent some time in Berlin when 646 Signals Unit was situated on the roof of the control tower at RAF Gatow, as well as going on detachment to Graz in Austria.

Geoff remembers that while at Obernkirchen, he found a report which Eric had written about a Junkers 88, which landed, or was forced to land, in Lincolnshire during the war. Apparently, the aircraft was packed full of radar equipment and Eric had been given the task of writing a report on it, which he kept on file and obviously had with him in Obernkirchen. This was the sort of operation to interest Eric and maybe it happened during a brief period when he was on detachment at RAF Stradishall in 1942.

An occasional duty for commanding officers was to act in loco parentis and give the bride away at a wedding in the garrison or station church and probably Eric did it more than once, standing in for the bride's father.

The Steinhudermeer on a summer's day in 2010.

Squadron Leader Ackermann giving the bride away at the wedding of Sgt. George 'Jock' Craig and Dora Winifred Evans on 13 October 1951, at St. Andrew's Garrison Church, Bückeburg.

RAF Obernkirchen was too small to have its own church and there is no record of a chaplain of any denomination visiting from Bückeburg or BAFO/2nd TAF Headquarters, though this is probably because chaplains' visits were not always noted in Operations Record Books. There would certainly have been transport to Bückeburg or Bad Eilsen for those wishing to attend church.

This does highlight the problems which faced small stations. Many of the facilities which were important, particularly for the single men at the station, were just not there, although things did improve in the mid-1950s with the building programme set in hand in 1955. Therefore, they had to rely on the local town or make the best of what they had, and Eric Ackermann was particularly helpful. He gave permission to install a bar and a cinema and generally looked after his staff with great consideration.

Hambühren and Scharfoldendorf were in much the same position, though Hambühren had the facilities of RAF Celle, a few miles away, with churches of different denominations, a proper cinema, Malcolm Club, large NAAFI, well staffed sick quarters and regular transport between the two stations. Scharfoldendorf was much more remote – beautiful but remote – and was a long way from the nearest large RAF station which would offer all those extras denied to those on small stations. Uetersen, Butzweilerhof and Gatow, on the other hand, were self-sufficient and able to provide their signals units with everything they needed.

Christmas was a special occasion for all military personnel and collecting signatures on the menu cards was an important part of

Tony Elliott took this photograph in the summer of 1950 of Mrs. Ogilvie and her new baby on the forecourt of the Bückeburg Schloss with Marianna Ackermann.

The airmen's Christmas dinner 1953, contributed by Alan Harris, who signed the photograph. Eric is the shorter figure in the doorway, just behind Wing Commander F.T. Solis and Sergeant Ron Matheson.

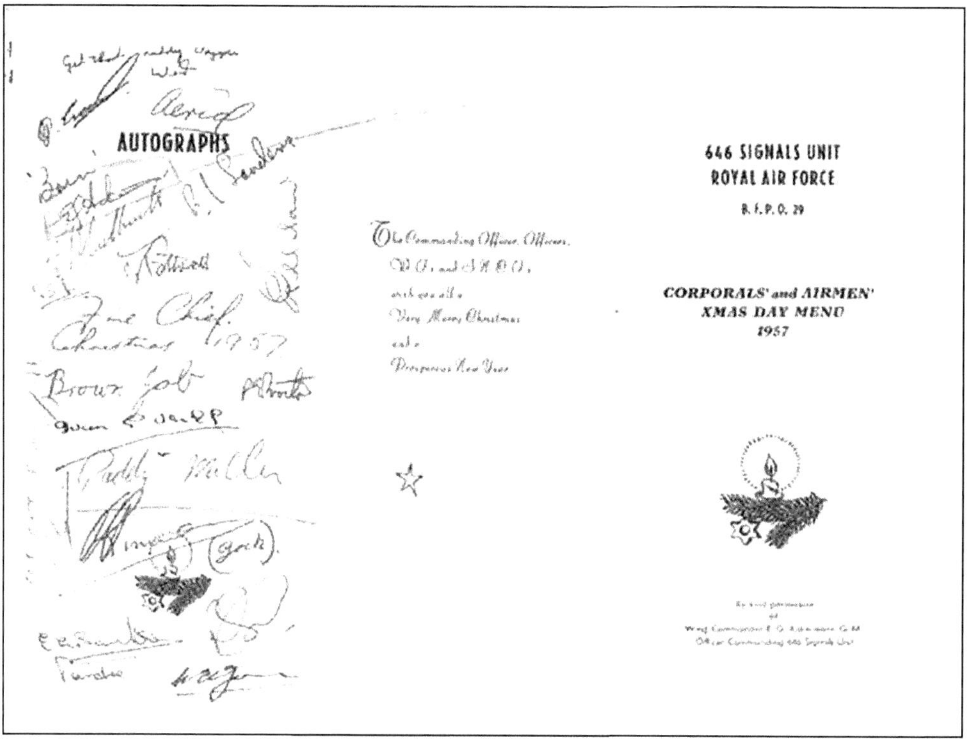

AUTOGRAPHS

646 SIGNALS UNIT
ROYAL AIR FORCE
B. F. P. O. 29

The Commanding Officer, Officers,
W.O. and S.N.C.O.,
wish one and all a
Very Merry Christmas
and a
Prosperous New Year

CORPORALS' and AIRMEN'
XMAS DAY MENU
1957

By kind permission
of
Wing Commander F. G. Adamson G.M.
Officer Commanding 646 Signals Unit

Breakfast

GRAPE FRUIT

CEREALS AND MILK

GRILLED BACON

PORK SAUSAGE

FRIED EGG

FRIED TOMATOES

TOAST AND MARMALADE

HOT ROLLS

BUTTER

TEA AND COFFEE

Dinner

HORS D' OEUVRE

CREME PORTUGAISE

ROAST PORK

ROAST TURKEY

SAGE AND ONION STUFFING

APPLE SAUCE

CHATEAU AND PARSLIED POTATOES

PEAS A LA MENTHE

BRUSSELS SPROUTS

CAULIFLOWER AU GRATIN

VICHI CARROTS

BROWN SAUCE

XMAS PUDDING AND RUM SAUCE

DESSERT · FRUIT · NUTS

BEER · CIGARETTES · MINERALS

Evening Buffet

SLICED COLD HAM AND BEEF

ASSORTED SALADS

CHEESE STRAWS

SAUSAGE ROLLS

FANCY CAKES

XMAS CAKES

HOT MINCE PIE

TRIFLE AND FRUIT

TEA · COFFEE

ROLLS · BUTTER

The cast of Aladdin, the Christmas pantomime in 1953. Left to right: Eric Ackermann, unknown, George Briggs, Mrs Briggs, Ron Matheson, Mrs Matheson, Ken Hodginson, Ron Newman, Bunny Warren, John Gay. Ted Wilkins. Eric Ackermann and Ted Wilkins were not performers but putting in an appearance to show their support. The poster on the wall is Widow Twankey's laundry list which includes 'Pants, Fancy'!

the Christmas ritual. This was the one day of the year when the airmen up to the rank of corporal were served by the officers and senior NCOs from the rank of sergeant upwards. These temporary waiters always seemed to enjoy the task, before going off to their respective Messes to be waited on themselves. It was also the highlight of the airmen's gastronomic year, as the cooks always excelled themselves. For their health's sake, however, the airmen were restricted to beer, and the more varied drinks available to the officers and senior NCOs were not available to them. Boxing Day, however, was an anti-climax, but who can blame the cooks?

All RAF stations (and Army camps and Royal Navy ships) required some unlucky people to be on duty over the very short holiday period, although the Scottish airmen sometimes did volunteer for this, given their preference for Hogmanay. The lucky ones were given two days off and it was back to work on the day after Boxing Day. Stations like Obernkirchen, which were required to maintain a twenty-four hour interception watch, could never be entirely off duty, and indeed, in one instance at least, to the writers' knowledge, there was a series of flights by the opposition air force up and down the Zonal border, though that was on New Year's Eve and not on Christmas Day. It nevertheless served to reinforce the need for constant vigilance.

Although nobody knew it at the time, this was to be the last Christmas at Obernkirchen, not that it made much difference, as the menu was the same everywhere. From Habbaniya to Lossiemouth, from Singapore to Schleswigland, the menu would have been exactly the same as it was for Obernkirchen in 1953. It should be said

The audience watching the performance. Marianna Ackermann is second left on the front row. Flt. Lt. R.A. Ruane is on the extreme right. Eric is not in the picture.

that the unimaginative range of drinks provided for the airmen (it was beer, and only beer) compares poorly with the huge variety available in the Officers' and Sergeants' Messes. To compensate the airmen and because it was Christmas, cigarettes were provided – no health warnings in those days - and as a matter of course they were also issued with coupons which they could redeem and pay for in the NAAFI using British Armed Forces Special Vouchers (BAFSVs), a form of currency which could only be used in forces outlets, including among others the NAAFI, Globe and Astra cinemas and Malcolm Clubs. This was an attempt at a rationing system as each person had a weekly allocation of 140 cigarettes – 20 a day – though the heavy smokers got round this by buying the non-smokers' coupons for whom it was a useful addition to their not over-generous pay. Added to this inducement to indulge, the price of cigarettes was remarkably cheap at 10d (ten pennies) for twenty Woodbines and an exorbitant 1/- (one shilling) for twenty of a better brand.

To conclude this insight into a small part of daily living in the British Zone of Germany, service personnel could exchange their BAFSVs for Deutschmarks at the rate of twelve to the pound in West Germany and forty in West Berlin.

The other Christmas tradition was the pantomime, a genuinely democratic show in which all ranks took part.

The information we have about the life the family led in Obernkirchen indicates something out of the ordinary for a young flight lieutenant, although, as noted earlier in the 1946 postgram to Dr Jones, Eric Ackermann's special position and his access to an equally special source of funding, go a long way to explaining this. Eric's service record goes a little further by revealing that he was paid by the Civil Service and not by the RAF and that other funds at his disposal came the same way: 'Emoluments will remain on a civilian basis wef 6.7.49. Not entitled to RAF pay, allowances or non-effective benefits.'

RAF Obernkirchen's progress from ASRU to Operational Signals Unit is blurred when it comes to writing about it and some of those who served in both remember them as being more or less one and the same. The clearest indication when and why the change took place is the subject of the next chapter.

Chapter Ten

No. 646 Signals Unit and the RAF Signals Intelligence network in Germany

As time passed in the 1940s the western Allies came to realize that the Soviet Union was no longer the ally it had been for most of the war and was now set on a path which seemed bound to lead to confrontation in one form or another. Consequently, the countries behind what Winston Churchill in 1946 called the Iron Curtain needed watching and listening to. By 1948 there was certainly ample evidence to suggest that the wartime alliance had crumbled and that the west was under severe and possibly imminent threat from the east. This was confirmed by the Berlin blockade, which cut off access to the western sectors by land and water from June 1948 to May 1949. There were many other provocative acts by the Soviet Union, including harassing the land routes to the city, even after the lifting of the blockade, and menacing allied aircraft flying down any of the three agreed flight paths.

The British and the Americans began to revert to their wartime practice of monitoring their enemies' military signals traffic. At first this seems to have concentrated more on radar interception than ground-to-air and air-to-air signals traffic, but it was not long before the need for W/T, D/F and R/T interception became apparent, as R.V. Jones reveals in his second book *Reflections on Intelligence*, published in 1989.

'In the post-war maelstrom, signals intelligence had paid little, if any, attention to Russian radar, and almost the only interceptions that were being made came from the unit that I had established in 1946 with Eric Ackermann near Obernkirchen. So good was his work that our American colleagues told me that although this was almost the only British effort in the field, it made it well worthwhile for them to exchange information with us – and they were now flying excellently methodical "Ferret" flights to plot Russian radar.'

He then goes on to express his views about GCHQ's new charter widening its responsibilities and directly affecting Jones himself:

'In the meantime GCHQ had prepared a new charter for itself and this charter included responsibility for intercepting all Russian signals, both communications and radar. Then, armed with this charter for which they had obtained approval, without my predecessor as Director of Scientific Intelligence having the chance to comment, they proposed to take Ackermann and his unit over. I was very much concerned to be presented with the fait accompli, for I was sure that

GCHQ, for all their ability in communications intelligence and cryptography (Comint), had neither the interest (as their record had shown), nor the expertise to study the technical transmission associated with radar and radio-navigation (Elint)… As a quid pro quo for my losing direct control of Ackermann's unit in Germany, an uneasy compromise was reached in which I was to be scientific adviser to GCHQ'.

By the late 1940s, Sigint was being retrieved with specially adapted aircraft flying along the Zonal border, while taking the greatest care not to stray over it. As Richard Aldrich, in his history of GCHQ, published in 2010, puts it, when discussing Sigint operations at that time: 'Although the most important Sigint collected at short-range came through perilous operations by air and sea, the British and Americans also boasted vast armies of land-based listeners crouching over their radio sets in wooden huts, often in inhospitable locations.' Air interception was certainly hazardous and there were accidents, with more than one being due to hostile action. Aircraft continued to be used, even after the ground-based units were in full swing and from time to time some of these 'ground-based listeners' were detached from bases such as RAF Uetersen, to nearby flying stations such as RAF Wunstorf, for intelligence duties on board Hastings and other aircraft.

Professor Aldrich goes on to write that:

'Tactical sigint in peacetime presented a problem, since there was not much for Y service sigint to listen to. Yet on the first day of any future war with Russia – and war, if it came, was expected to come very suddenly – the RAF would be required to reconstitute its vast legions of secret listeners. In the event, the three services kept a large inter-service intercept formation in place, using personnel who were doing National Service. By 1950 a system was in place whereby all those beginning National Service were asked if they would volunteer to learn Russian.' (To which would later be added Czech, Polish, German, Hungarian, Arabic, Farsee and Chinese)

Down on the ground at Obernkirchen, Eric Ackermann was now busy establishing an experimental Sigint unit. This was set up in November 1949 and was given the unusually high number of 1514, which must have been chosen at random and certainly no other signals unit had a number remotely like it. Its relationship with ASRU is unclear, although possibly, while the ASRU was continuing with its research activities, particularly into radar interception, the Signals Unit was given a very precise and different remit. This was to investigate the feasibility of creating a permanent signals intelligence base in north Germany. Obernkirchen's proximity to the BAFO Headquarters at Bad Eilsen and the newly built airfield at RAF Bückeburg as well as the presence there already of the ASRU and of Eric Ackermann, made it the obvious place for this new development. It is not clear how the ASRU and 1514 SU related to each other and presumably the lines drawn between them were vague. Indeed an entry in the BAFO ORB states that on 16 January 1950, two officers were detached to the Research Unit, but later appear as belonging to 1514.

They were Flight Lieutenants J.J.R. (Jim) Crichton and P.S. (Paddy) Engelbach, who were both linguists. Engelbach had qualified as an Interpreter (2nd Class), which is a notch above a linguist. They were detached to the ASRU from one of those multi-initialled organizations much favoured by the military: AMU (SDL MISC)30C on 16 January 1950, and two days later they moved into what the ORB calls hostel accommodation at Kromers Hotel in Steinbergen, a small village about ten kilometres from the Decimetre site.

The two men were very different. Paddy Engelbach was a pilot, a daredevil in the air and a man in a hurry on land. He was born in 1922, and joined the RAF in 1942. After qualifying as a pilot all went well until, on 27 June 1944, he was piloting a Mosquito over northern France when he was shot down by a night fighter. He survived, was captured and spent the rest of the war in Stalag Luft III at Sagan. He therefore brings to three the number of prisoners there whom Eric knew, or would know after the war. The story of the other two is related in Chapter 2. Frank Brigham remembers him showing off his flying prowess by beating up the operations site at Obernkirchen in a Mosquito from a local RAF station (Bückeburg).

Colin Burleigh, a wireless operator at RAF Uetersen, recalls that Engelbach was a short, squat, dark-haired man who needed to keep up his flying hours to retain his wings, and to do this he somehow needed to transfer his skills from Bückeburg to Uetersen, where he took to doing aerobatics in the station's sole Tiger Moth. Such antics would not have been welcomed in the busy skies above RAF Bückeburg, which was the station nearest to Command Headquarters and an important operational flying station. Uetersen had just four light aircraft, with very little flying other than those of its Communications Flight and occasional visits by other aircraft, including those diverted from the usual flight paths during the Berlin Airlift.

In 1946, Engelbach married Helena (Libby) Philby, who was Kim Philby's sister and had worked with her brother in the Middle East in Section V (countermeasures) of the SIS in the 1930s. Eric Ackermann himself had also worked in a similar unit at Worth Matravers back in 1940 to 1942 and the work Mr and Miss Philby were doing was not all that different. According to Frank Haig, who was with 26 Signals Unit at RAF Gatow, Libby was a 'raven haired beauty'. She was also a fluent Russian speaker and a very good pianist. Nigel West, in *At Her Majesty's Secret Service*, writes this about Kim Philby:

'The idea that he (Philby) had been a dedicated Communist since graduating from Cambridge and had been in almost continuous contact with Soviet intelligence officers since 1934, simply did not occur to many of those who had worked with him and his sister in Section V, where he had distinguished himself as an expert on Spain and a very capable analyst of the enemy's wireless traffic.'

The last few words are interesting, as analysing wireless traffic was exactly what Eric Ackermann was now doing in the 1950s. At the time of Libby's marriage to Paddy Engelbach, her brother's spying activities had not been exposed, so there was no question of her being a security risk, despite the fact that as early as 1951 Kim was under suspicion of aiding the defections to the Soviet Union of Guy Burgess and Donald Maclean. Libby's close connection with an RAF officer involved in signals intelligence would otherwise have been investigated and she would certainly have been screened before the marriage was allowed to take place.

Engelbach was promoted to squadron leader in 1951, but was killed in a flying accident on 15 February 1955, when his Venom NF.2 clipped a tree on take-off from RAF Coltishall and crashed just south of Rougham in Norfolk. At the time of his death he had just taken over command of No. 23 Squadron. Widowed at a young age – she was only thirty-one – Libby eventually remarried, but not until 1980. As far as is known she is still alive.

Jim Crichton was very different, a tall, slim man with a 'wizard prang' handlebar moustache, which added to his swashbuckling appearance, he was also rumoured to be an excellent swordsman. Little else is known about him, except for what he was not – aircrew, prisoner of war, or married to a wife from an unusual family. Between the two of them, and with Eric in control, they worked to create the signals unit described in the following pages.

No. 1514 Signals Unit led a short and secretive life and was disbanded on 31 August 1950, to be replaced on the following day by No. 365 Signals Unit at Uetersen. This important event is recorded in the BAFO Operations Record Book in July and August, in the usual unemotional official language of these documents:

FORMATION OF No. 365 SIGNALS UNIT

Authority is given for the formation of No. 365 Signals Unit with effect from 1 September 1950.

1. The Unit, which will be located at RAF Uetersen, will be operationally controlled by Air Ministry DDS(B) and under the administrative control of Headquarters BAFO. Day-to-day administration will be provided by RAF Uetersen.
2. On formation, No. 365 Signals Unit will absorb the personnel and equipment resources of No. 1514 Signals Unit.

MOVE AND DISBANDMENT OF No. 1514 SIGNALS UNIT
1. Consequent upon the formation of No. 365 Signals Unit, No. 1514 Signals unit is to move to RAF Uetersen by 1 September 1950.
2. No. 1514 Signals Unit will be disbanded with effect from 31 August 1950.

It looks from this entry as if 1514 SU was disbanded the day before it moved to Uetersen. It means of course that it had to be at Uetersen on the day 365 SU was formed, so that the change could move seamlessly without any interruption, even though 1514 was an experimental, rather than an operational unit, while 365 was the real thing. The number 365 is an echo of 365 Wireless Unit, which was in being during the Second World War and possibly the number was reused when the Signals Unit was being formed. A parallel pair of units are those with the number 367. The Wireless Unit resurfaced after the war as No. 367 Signals Unit, based in Hong Kong, listening to Chinese signals.

Unusually, even for a highly secret signals unit (apart from the almost invisible 1514), No. 365 did not have its own Operations Record Book (or if it if had, it has not survived), unlike its successors in Germany, 646, 755, 291, 477 and 26. Was there something odd about the number 365, as neither the Wireless Unit nor the Signals Unit has left any individual trace in the form of an ORB in the National Archives? No. 365 SU crops up now and again in RAF Uetersen's ORB, but only to mention sporting successes, its personnel's involvement in station-wide exercises and their occasional confrontation with authority.

Crichton and Engelbach were officially attached to Uetersen for part of July and August, returning to Obernkirchen once the Uetersen unit was running smoothly, but making frequent visits, along with Eric, for several months. As their Commanding Officer, Squadron Leader Ackermann visited Uetersen from time to time to make sure things were going as planned.

It was not at all a foregone conclusion that Uetersen would be the base for the new unit. Two other sites were examined, one at Glückstadt, further up the right bank of the River Elbe. The other was at Glinde, to the east of Hamburg. The British Army already had a signals unit at Glückstadt, No. 1 Special Wireless Regiment, which had arrived in 1946, but was due to move to Birgelen near the Dutch border in 1950. Paddy Engelbach was photographed there at a sports day in 1949 or 1950. He wasn't there just for the sports, but to assess the suitability of the camp for the future RAF signals unit.

The Army and the RAF frequently exchanged Sigint stations with one another for strategic and tactical reasons and although Glückstadt was the first, it was by no means the last.

Uetersen's location was ironically one of the factors which led to its closure in July 1955. Situated on the east side of the River Elbe, and without any defences, the station

An athletics meeting at the Glückstadt base of No. 1 Special Wireless Regiment. Flt. Lt. Paddy Engelbach is the solitary figure in shorts, standing a few feet to the right of the spectacular offficer in striped blazer and white flannels.

would have been vulnerable in the event of an attack. At several points during the RAF's tenure of the station, there was at least one, and frequently more than one, RAF Regiment squadron there to provide some sort of security, but the last of these had left in 1952. Another reason for its closure was to be the steady reduction in the number of RAF stations in the east of the British Zone during the mid-1950s.

RAF Uetersen was a fully functioning, splendidly equipped station, which was captured by the RAF Regiment on 3 May 1945 with everything intact – hot water, kitchens, barrack blocks, in fact a real find for the occupying force, which at that time was more used to finding barracks and Luftwaffe stations which had suffered severe bomb damage. Uetersen was one of the first Luftwaffe stations to be built after the First World War and work started in 1935, an early indication that the German Government was intent on flagrantly ignoring at least one of the provisions of the Treaty of Versailles. The RAF stayed there for ten years, but meanwhile, 365 SU began its thirty month tenure as a pioneer in its field.

With Squadron Leader J.E. (Joe) Lewis in command, Eric could now concentrate on developing the ASRU and moving towards the creation of his own signals unit to be given the number 646. From this point, until the 1990s, the Royal Air Force listened to the Warsaw Pact air traffic signals with its wireless operators and linguists keeping watch twenty-four hours a day, every day of every year, while the Army and the Royal Navy were taking care of land and sea signals. By the time the end came, the sole survivor of Eric Ackermann's legacy in Germany was No. 26 Signals Unit at Gatow, in Berlin. All the others, including No. 5 Signals Wing, had been disbanded at various times in the 1950s and 1960s.

Uetersen was a few miles from Fühlsbuttel airport in Hamburg and was included in the regular freight route from RAF Abingdon, which called at the station (and others in Germany) every day. The intercept records were flown out daily from the signals units in Germany to GCHQ in Cheltenham.

Reverting now to developments at a higher level, there was by the end of the 1940s increasing co-operation between the Americans and the British, with the latter frequently making the running. Richard Aldrich again:

'During the early 1950s, target intelligence officers in London and Washington had been busy exchanging sensitive data on "the mission of blunting the Russian atomic offensive". This meant planning early counter-force attacks against Soviet nuclear forces, especially bombers, in the hope of destroying them on the ground in Eastern Europe before they could be used in a future war. GCHQ had given particular attention to this matter because of the vulnerability of Britain, and the Americans were impressed by the progress London had made on it. GCHQ and the RAF's secret units had amassed a significant amount of evaluated intelligence, particularly in the special intelligence field, which would be of the greatest value if war broke out. '

The main gate into RAF Uetersen in 1950, the year when 365 Signals Unit was established there.

Back at Obernkirchen, on and off duty Eric had time to appreciate the benefits of living and working there, not just for its idyllic position nestling against the hills and the attractions of the little town itself and of Bad Eilsen and Bückeburg, but also for its military attributes. Obernkirchen is a pleasant small town in gentle rolling countryside, with the beautiful Steinhuder Meer not far away and the city of Hanover within a short driving distance. After his hectic life up to the late 1940s it must have seemed something of a rest cure. It was also an ideal location for a communications site and a listening post, with the range of hills running from Obernkirchen to Bad Nenndorf and reaching the Bückeberg (not to be confused with the town which is Bückeburg), 367 metres above sea level. Its many footpaths, wooded areas and magnificent views of the Auetal valley made it a popular place for weekend excursions. A couple of hours wandering in the woods, followed by delicious Kaffee und Küchen at Gasthaus Walter at the top of the hill, was a favourite pastime and a pleasant way to have a little exercise. On all counts, therefore, Eric and his family were fortunate and they seem to have made the very best of their time there. Indeed Eric was to remember it as the best time of his life.

Around this time the ASRU was employing civilian telegraphists who were detached to the unit from their base at Cheadle in Staffordshire, though they were employed by GCHQ. Frank Brigham was one of these and was working for 1514 Signals Unit. There were twenty people in Frank's group. He remembers his unit's distinctive uniform, which marked them out as oddities in the eyes of conventional RAF authority, probably more so than if they had worn ordinary civilian clothing. Frank himself was an honorary sergeant, living at first in the Sergeants' Mess at Bad Eilsen and then at Uetersen, where he continued his work until RAF wireless

The Jahn Tower in the woods above RAF Obernkirchen, built by Ackemann & Sohn in 1946.

operators arrived in the summer of 1950. He recalls that his CO made them wear this uniform – with its conspicuous and mysterious shoulder flashes – at all times and this puzzled the RAF police.

Despite this insistence on some sort of uniform, Charlie Olito, who served with ASRU at Obernkirchen for three years, said that he saw Eric in uniform on only three occasions. Curiously, this is at odds with Dorothy Ackermann's recollection of him at Worth Matravers in 1941 and 1942 as wearing a uniform all of the time. Then of course he was not in charge. At Obernkirchen he most certainly was, even though his interpretation as to what constituted full uniform was sometimes not what one would expect of a wing commander. His airmen have remembered occasions when his attire was peculiar, if not downright eccentric.

Frank Brigham bridges the gap between the experimental 1514 SU and the operational 365 and saw how the preparatory work at Obernkirchen was put into real-life practice a few miles away on the far side of the River Elbe. What followed lasted in Germany until 1994, when the so-called Cold War dividend brought to an end RAF ground surveillance of the eastern bloc. In the intervening few years signals units were established and then gradually closed at the following stations:

No. 365 Signals Unit at RAF Uetersen, 1950–1953.
No. 755 Signals Unit at RAF Uetersen, 1953–1955.
No. 646 Signals Unit at RAF Obernkirchen, 1952–1958.
No. 291 Signals Unit at Hambühren, Lower Saxony, 1953–1955.
No. 5 Signals Wing at Uetersen, 1954.
No. 5 Signals Wing at RAF Hambühren, Lower Saxony, 1954–1955.
No. 755 Signals Unit at RAF Hambühren, Lower Saxony, 1955–1957.
No. 477 Signals Unit at RAF Butzweilerhof, Cologne, 1954–1967.
No. 291 Signals Unit at RAF Scharfoldendorf in Lower Saxony, 1955–1958.
No. 5 Signals Wing at RAF Scharfoldendorf in Lower Saxony, 1955–1958.
No. 5 Signals Wing at RAF Butzweilerhof, Cologne, 1958–1965.
No. 646 Signals Unit at RAF Scharfoldendorf in Lower Saxony, 1958–1964.
No. 26 Signals Unit at RAF Gatow, Berlin, 1966 – 1994.

Some of these units kept their number when they were transferred (755 and 291 and 5 Signals Wing), whereas others (26, 365 and 477 and the short-lived 1514), were only ever at the station where they were first established. No. 5 Signals Wing was the co-ordinating unit with authority over the signals units and was established at Uetersen in 1954, but it does not seem to have had much to do directly with 646 at Obernkirchen. This may be because its Commanding Officer was always a Wing Commander, the rank which Eric Ackermann had reached by that time.

Added to this list of units, Eric also had influence, if not actual authority, over units in Cyprus and Iraq, as well as the numerous signals detachments spread throughout Germany and until 1955, Austria, from Putlos on the Baltic, to Graz in the south of Austria. There was another detachment at RAF Schwechat, ten miles south-east of Vienna, which hosted Sigint units from the permanent stations in West Germany from time to time. The network had outstations and field detachments, which were sometimes small huts out in the fields, and in the case of Dannenberg, on the west bank of the Elbe, within shouting distance of East Germany on the east bank. Hambühren had a small D/F hut in a field some distance from the station itself and there were also mobile signals detachments which travelled south to the American Zone and set up their RVTs at Furth im Wald in Bavaria, close to the Czech border.

Hambühren was in the deep countryside, four miles from Celle, surrounded by woodland and Displaced Persons' Camps. In the 1950s it was almost an ideally remote place for the clandestine activities of the signals unit, apart from the very obvious presence of its aerials alongside the road to Celle. It had a murky past, of which the airmen who served there in the 1950s were unaware. It was built in 1940 for the Luftwaffe and housed a huge munitions factory making anti-aircraft shells and also aircraft parts for the Focke-Wolf 190 fighter aircraft. It was an important place with the official name of Lufthauptmunitionsanstalt 1/XI, or main air munitions establishment no. 11. The workforce came largely from the occupied countries as forced labour and for just six months, from August 1944 to February 1945, there was a sub-camp from Belsen, which had the cruelly idyllic name of Waldeslust (woodland joy). The inmates were 400 Polish Jewish women, who were so ill-treated that the Commandant, one Karl Heinrich Reddehase, sent from Belsen to establish the camp, was tried by the British as a war criminal and hanged in 1946.

In 1945 the camp, as sturdily built as any Luftwaffe base of its period, was taken over by the Royal Electrical and Mechanical Engineers as a vehicle and tank repair workshop until 1950. After an interval the RAF arrived in November 1952 to find a station needing a great deal of work to make it suitable for its new function. The giveaway aerial farm was erected and the set room, airmen's accommodation, cookhouse, officers' and sergeants' mess, and all the other buildings required to make it work for an entirely new purpose, had to be built from scratch, or renovated through the winter of 1952/53. It opened for business in February 1953 and welcomed the arrival of its first group of wireless operators and linguists, mainly from Uetersen.

Further building work took place in 1955, including a sports field and gymnasium and a second accommodation block, making RAF Hambühren a very agreeable place to be, with the airmen's accommodation far more comfortable than those draughty wooden huts back in the UK. It was also cosily small, so that it was possible to get to know more people on this station than at the larger camps. Like Obernkirchen, discipline was functional and unnecessary and trivial charges were frowned upon. It relied on its nearest large station, RAF Celle, just four miles away, for most of its support services. Celle was a 'proper' station, with its jet fighters, Meteors, Venoms and Vampires, flying overhead to remind the airmen at Hambühren of the other and more visible side of the RAF. Celle had a large NAAFI and a Malcolm Club, and most importantly it was the place from whence came the cash brought to Hambühren for the fortnightly pay parade.

The camp was in two unequal halves, divided by a public road. On one side were the two accommodation blocks and the guardroom and on the other the operations, administrative and recreational buildings, as well as a sports field. Occasionally, vehicles of the Soviet Military Mission (SOXMIS) would drive up and down the road taking photographs, including the prominent aerial farm alongside the road. These incidents were always logged and reported to 2nd TAF HQ, although on one occasion the German civilian gate guard urged the CO to let him shoot at the vehicle with his machine pistol. Mindful of the possibility of setting off World War Three, the CO refused. The SOXMIS counterpart in East Germany, BRIXMIS, was being equally tiresome (or active, depending on your point of view) on the other side of the border to both the Russians and the East Germans.

No. 755 Signals Unit was not to last, much to the regret of its airmen who enjoyed its fairly relaxed atmosphere. It was disbanded in November 1957 and the RAF departed. There was then a seamless transfer to the Luftwaffe and No. 71

The Queen's Birthday parade in June 1957 at RAF Hambühren. Being such a small camp of around 300 personnel it was never possible to put more than a third on parade at any one time. The others were on duty as day or shift workers or on rest days, leave or off sick.

This photograph appeared in the Cellesche Zeitung on 10 April 1992, two years before the closure of what had been RAF Hambühren, and at that time was the home of Fernmelderregiment 71 (Telecommunications Regiment) of the Luftwaffe.

Fernmelderregiment arrived to take over the RAF's intercept role. It stayed for a long time – thirty-seven years – and finally moved to Gatow in Berlin in 1994, where it replaced No. 26 Signals Unit of the RAF. The camp was demolished in 2000 and a housing development built on the site. Its roads were named Die Alte Kaserne, Morseweg and Auf Die Wache, commemorating the intercept units which were there for forty years. It is a matter of regret that some soft-hearted former RAF policemen, who had served at Hambühren, were unable to prevent their beautiful Swiss-chalet

Local traffic passing along the road between the two parts of RAF Hambühren.

A slight accident at Hambühren as a civilian truck has come off the road and broken through the fence at the back of Station Headquarters.

type guardroom from demolition. They had the idea that it could be converted into a holiday villa to provide an income for them in their well-earned retirement,.

By the end of 1957 there were four Sigint units left: 477 SU at Butzweilerhof, 646 still hanging on at Obernkirchen, and 291 SU together with HQ 5 Signals Wing at Scharfoldendorf, as well as various detachments scattered round West Germany and at RAF Gatow in the British Sector of Berlin.

RAF Hambühren's big brother at Celle closed only a month later, at the end of December 1957, and its fate was not dissimilar, as the Luftwaffe took it over in its entirety and have used it as a helicopter base ever since. The former RAF stations at Celle and Uetersen – now Luftwaffe bases – are the sole survivors as operational air force stations from all the others in the British Zone which housed signals intelligence units. By now there were no other RAF flying stations in the vicinity. Wunstorf, Fassberg, Schleswigland, Lübeck, and several others, were closed or transferred to the Luftwaffe or the new German Army as the RAF began concentrating its operations on bases much further west.

RAF Hambühren was very compact, with an operations block, aerial farm, recreational buildings and administrative buildings. The road ran between the accommodation blocks and the guardroom on one side of the road and the operational part on the other. In 1985, the station was officially twinned with the town of Hambühren and it regularly held open days for the inhabitants to come into the camp and have a good look round.

A strange paradox was that in the 1950s, when the Royal Air Force was there, the gate guard was a German civilian in the uniform of the German Service Organization. He carried out a perfunctory check of visitors whom he did not recognize, but otherwise left the airmen alone. After the British left, and as time passed, the danger from the east

The small white dot on the edge of a field in the distance is RAF Hambühren's D/F hut which was manned twenty-four hours a day. It was a delightful spot in the summer but less so in the freezing winter months. SAC Barry Trevethan took this photo from the window of his room in one of the barrack blocks in the summer of 1957.

No. 365 Signals Unit used the hilltop site of RAF Scharfoldendorf for detachments from RAF Uetersen in the early 1950s, before the station became a Signals intelligence unit in its right from 1955 to 1964. SAC Ted Garner took this photograph in the summer of 1953. It shows an RVT perched on probably the highest point of the camp. The vehicle has the number plate TAF/365. The border with East Germany was not far away and the site provided excellent interception.

receded, security became more obvious, with secured gates and signs prohibiting photography and threatening severe punishment to offenders, including the possibility of being shot.

Butzweilerhof was one of those large stations with the range of facilities which smaller stations lacked. It was also very mixed, housing as well as an array of RAF units, some British and Belgian Army contingents. The Signals Unit was on its own at the side of the camp, with a security fence dividing the two and entry required a sight of the RAF identity card, Form 1250.

No. 646 SU frequently used a site at Putlos to send detachments. This was a bleak place on the Baltic, thirty-five miles from Kiel, on the eastern side of the Schleswig Holstein peninsula. It was a sizeable place of some permanence, employing around 130 officers and airmen. It had previously been used for tank training by the German Panzer Divisions during the Second World War and later by the RAF Regiment for their own energetic form of ground combat training, which they sometimes had to inflict on 'ordinary' airmen – Penguins, as the Regiment called them, in response to their own nickname of Rockapes. Putlos was used for some years as an outstation for the RAF Sigint units, as it was much nearer the opposition's western borders and therefore easier for interception. Eric Ackermann visited it from time to time on his version of a tour of inspection. It was a very bleak place in winter.

Gatow was the odd one out. It was on the western edge of the British Sector of Berlin, so far to the west that its perimeter fence was right on the border with the German

The main gate at RAF Butzweilerhof in 1958 where No. 477 Signals Unit began life in January 1954. The unit stayed there until disbandment in 1967 and was the longest-lived signals interception unit in West Germany, though 26 SU in Berlin outlasted it by 27 years.

The shore on the Baltic near RAF Putlos, where the RAF Sigint operations had one of its outstations.

Democratic Republic (GDR) and therefore of particular interest to Soviet and GDR aircraft. This certainly made it the most vulnerable station in the Sigint organization, but also the one best situated for its work. Gatow's Sigint work began in 1951, when on 13 March, a small contingent of linguists (RT/DF Op.1) and wireless operators (W. Ops. [A]) arrived on detachment from 365 Signals Unit at Uetersen. It was given the name of the Special Signals Unit and special it certainly was, given its front line location. As time went on it grew in numbers and eventually, on 1 September 1966, it achieved the status of a fully-fledged signals unit, becoming No. 26 Signals Unit. It lasted until May 1994, when the RAF left Gatow and the longest lasting of all of the units which began with the ASRU way back in 1948, closed down.

It was not only the RAF which had its listening stations in Germany. The Army, through the Royal Signals and No. 1 Special Wireless Regiment, established, as Geoffrey Elliot, in *Secret Classrooms* puts it; 'as far as possible from any attack from the east. Birgelen, fifty kilometres north of Aachen, close to the Dutch border at Roermond, was selected and the Regiment moved into the new "Mercury" barracks, proud that in the transfer process it had not lost one day of "operational cover", i.e. intercept work.' From 1951 to 1952, the Royal Signals maintained another listening station at Langeleben, 900 feet up in the hills between Helmstedt and Braunschweig and close to the zonal border.

The Royal Navy's linguists and wireless operators arrived at a shore-based establishment near Cuxhaven, which was named HMS *Royal Albert,* with which is always associated HMS *Royal Charlotte.* The Navy linguists were called Coders and they have been immortalized in Jack Rosenthal's 1992 TV play *Bye, Bye Baby,* which was set in or on-board the *Royal Albert.* Rosenthal himself was a Coder who trained at a Joint Services School for Linguists. It has been confirmed by other Navy Coders that the film gives a true representation of the setrooms where the interception work took place.

While all this was going on in the secret world of signals intelligence, at Obernkirchen, with some of the above units already in being, and the rest due within a year or two, Eric Ackermann was by now working on converting the ASRU to his own Signals Unit, which was given the number 646.

The National Archives documents catalogue has three entries for the new unit. One describes the complex business of its crest, which is given in a later chapter; the other two are its Operations Record Books (National Archives file AIR 29/2501 and 2502), covering the years from 1952 to 1964. The first and second files have been examined, but the third, covering 1956–64, was destroyed when it was damaged by water while being stored in a basement of the Ministry of Defence. It was one of many files awaiting decontamination from the asbestos which had been used in the construction of the store room.

The 1952–55 file gives some information, though not as much as had been hoped. Each month's entry is signed in person by the CO, Squadron Leader, and from 1954, Wing Commander, E.G. Ackermann. The first twenty-eight months, from September 1952 to December 1954, are conflated into a single report, setting out the details of the unit's formation, function (although this particular aspect is still withheld) and establishment. As the unit was very important to Eric Ackermann at this stage in his life, the entry for those months is worth transcribing in full, exactly as it appeared in the original.

No. 646 Signals Unit, Obernkirchen (National Archives file AIR 29/2502)

EARLY HISTORY

1. In September 1952, the designation No. 646 Signals Unit was given to a Signals Unit of the Royal Air Force which had already been in operation for many years. The original unit, A.D.I. Science Overseas Party, was formed during the war and served overseas continuously from 1942. In 1945 it reformed and made its peacetime headquarters at OBERNKIRCHEN, a small German town, five miles from BUCKEBURG and three miles from BAD EILSEN, the post-war location of Headquarters, 2nd Tactical Air Force.

2. Although an RAF unit, the operational control from 1945 to 1952 was in the hands of the Director Scientific Intelligence, Ministry of Defence. The airmen were maintained on the strength of Air Ministry Unit and local administration was the responsibility of Headquarters 2nd Tactical Air Force. The establishment of the unit during the immediate post-war years increased steadily from six to thirty airmen, plus two officers. Of the officers, one was on the staff of D.S.I., Ministry of Defence, as a Senior Scientific Officer [*this was Eric Ackermann*], but in order to command a Royal Air Force unit was also a Squadron Leader in the Royal Air Force with a Class C.C. Commission.

In 1952, two major changes were made in the status of the unit; operational control was transferred from the Directorate of Scientific Intelligence and the unit became a fully affiliated unit of the Second Tactical Air Force; at the same time its name was changed to No. 646 Signals Unit.

FUNCTION. [Paragraphs 3, 4 and 5 have been removed from the file]

TRAINING

6. No. 646 Signals Unit is the only unit of its kind with the Royal Air Force. None of the specialist trades covered by the Royal Air Force trade structure are completely suitable for the work of the unit and thus complete training has to be carried out by 646 Signals Unit. For this purpose the unit has produced its own course, theoretical and practical, and sets its own examinations. Each year, Air Ministry calls for a few selected men from No. 646 Signals Unit to undertake similar, but very limited operations in other parts of the world.

In 1950, GCHQ received a large increase on its budget and began to move from London to two new sites in Cheltenham. It was allocated three hundred new posts and in Richard Aldrich's words 'was going from strength to strength'. With new premises and many more staff, there was a corresponding strengthening of Sigint units in Germany. Obernkirchen benefited from this and the following three years saw its staffing establishment grow to four officers (a squadron leader, a flight lieutenant and two flying officers) and 133 other ranks (two warrant officers, four flight sergeants, twelve sergeants, twenty-five corporals and ninety airmen). There was another officer, Eric Ackermann himself, who was never on the official establishment, but described, not very flatteringly, as supernumerary, because he was paid out of these mysterious

This is what the original actually looked like in the unit's O.R.B., R.A.F. Form 540. It is a copy of the last paragraph of the above transcript, complete with Eric's signature.

secret funds. He makes the number of officers up to five and the total to 138. By 1955 the numbers had gone up even further, to 185. Buildings were provided for technical development, administration and accommodation, and a charter approved. During the same period the unit became self-administered, but non self-accounting.

From January 1955, the ORB reports appear in full for each month and for the only time we have a full account of Eric's and the station's activities for a whole year. In January, for example, in addition to the unit being at Obernkirchen, it had No. 1 Detachment at Berlin and No. 6 Detachment at Putlos, while No. 4 Detachment was being prepared for operations in the summer camp at Gnas, near Graz, in Austria. The same report says that Wing Commander Eric Ackermann was Commanding Officer, Flight Lieutenant R.J.J. Hall was Technical Adjutant and Flying Officer A.L. Winn was Liaison officer with Headquarters 5 Wing at Royal Air Force, HAMBURIN [sic, i.e. Hambühren] near Celle. The RAF authorities had as much difficulty spelling Hambühren as they did with Eric's surname, though they did achieve more variety with the former.

Only the most senior ranks are named in the ORB, and not all of those. Neither the squadron leader (due to arrive in March 1955) nor one of the flying officers are there and those below warrant officer rank languish in anonymity.

Flight Lieutenant R.S.S. Hall, Technical Adjutant
Flying Officer A.L. Winn, Liaison Officer with HQ 5 Signals Wing
Warrant Officer P. Genge, Unit Signals WO.
Warrant Officer J.S. Craven, Administrative WO.

There was also a civilian, Mr R. Hunt, who was filling the vacancy of Assistant Experimental Officer in the laboratories. Flight Lieutenant Hall was probably the man whom Eric's domestic staff called Mr Manchester when he visited the house in civilian clothes, because of the corduroy trousers he wore.

The unit then moved on to other things and during January work continued to 're-equip and standardize the equipment for use by No. 4 Detachment for operations in the summer at Gnas, Graz, Austria'.

A new officer arrived in February, Flight Lieutenant R.M. White, who was posted from Headquarters Maintenance Command to the new post of Unit Adjutant, as distinct from the Technical Adjutant, Flight Lieutenant Hall, who was off to Austria in March, for three weeks on attachment to RAF Schwechat in Vienna for 'operational duties'.

Another new officer arrived in March, Squadron Leader J.A.F. Morgan, previously seen on the staff list of the Deputy Directorate of Intelligence Research, working in the Russia and Satellites section of the Assistant Directorate of Intelligence (Technical). He and Eric are on the same list, but Eric is in the ADI (Science). Morgan was at Obernkirchen to fill the new post of Senior Technical Officer.

Eric's involvement with the Americans, which continued into civilian life when he and his family emigrated in the late 1960s and right up to his death, is confirmed in

February. In March he attended a four day Anglo/American Conference at the Air Ministry and Government Communications Headquarters. March 1955 was a busy month for visiting VIPs. Air Vice-Marshal W.M.L. Macdonald, Assistant Chief of the Air Staff (Intelligence), visited No. 1 Signals Detachment in Berlin on the 4 March and Air Marshal Sir Thomas Pike (Deputy Chief of the Air Staff) arrived a week later on the 11 March. On 29 March, Air Vice-Marshal L. Dalton-Morris (Assistant Chief of the Air Staff) visited the same detachment. It is likely that Eric was in attendance as the most senior officer in the various signals units then scattered about the British Zone.

An intriguing document was received at the unit on 12 April. It was a copy of the unit's charter, which came from the Air Ministry, DD of S(B), reference Sigs.13/523, Copy 5, dated 21 March 1955. A sight of this would be invaluable, but has not been found. The rest of April seems to have been spent on preparing for, and taking part in, the move of No. 4 Detachment to the summer camp near Graz in Austria, a journey of 550 miles. The Convoy Commander was Flight Lieutenant Lou Barry, late of Stalag Luft III, and a well-known and popular officer who had served at Uetersen and Hambühren and now found himself at Obernkirchen. He was a Hungarian linguist, at last able to use his skills in a country right next door to Hungary and possibly converse with Marianna in her native language.

On 21 April, a corporal serving with the unit was tried by General Court Martial and 'was sentenced to be reduced to the ranks, to be imprisoned for nine months, and to be discharged with ignominy from Her Majesty's Services'. Eric intervened with the Commander-in-Chief 2nd TAF and the nine months imprisonment was remitted, though the other sentences were confirmed. The ORB reports that; 'The Commanding Officer of No. 646 Signals Unit had previously supported a petition against the sentence.' There is no information about the man's crime but it must have been serious. Also in April and lasting for twenty-three days, there were detailed preparations for the move of No.4 Detachment to the summer camp at Graz. The record states that:

'Convoy practices were completed and a strong reserve of Class "B" drivers was available. A mobile kitchen, able to tow its own power plant, had been fitted out in the unit workshops. Thus first-class meals were available while on the move. Vehicle loadings were so arranged that all personnel had a mattress and sufficient space to lay it. This made it possible to form the convoy as a self-contained unit, with no necessity to leave the direct route. Petrol was uplifted on petrol coupons from Shell Filling Stations en route, and sufficient diesel and oil were carried to complete the journey.

'Flight Lieutenant L. Barry, on loan from No 5 Wing, was Officer i/c Convoy, which consisted of two components, Advanced and Main. The advanced component consisted of the mobile cookhouse and trailer, a 3 tonner for POL, and a water trailer. The main component was comprised of thirteen prime movers and two trailers. The Advance component moved ahead of the Main component and was able to prepare meals and replenish the POL stock before the Main component arrived at planned halts.'

The convoy left Obernkirchen on 20 April for its three day journey, travelling via Bulzbach (i.e. Butzbach, a typing error in the original document), where it stopped for the night, to Rosenheim, just on the German side of the Austrian border near Salzburg. It had already travelled 550 miles and still had to get to Graz, a long way further on in the south of Austria.

Almost the only news from the detachment which reached the Operations Record Book, was that in May, a corporal with the detachment was driving a Volkswagen Kombi from Gnas to Graz and was involved in an accident with a civilian motorcyclist who received fatal injuries. This stirred up local feeling against the detachment but 'normal friendly relations were soon restored'. The corporal, however, was dealt with severely. The Obernkirchen Adjutant, Flight Lieutenant White, 'proceeded on temporary duty to No. 4 detachment at Graz and Royal Air Force Schwechat, Vienna, in connection with Detachment administration and the forthcoming District Court Martial'. Sadly, for him at least, the corporal was reduced to the rank of senior aircraftman and sentenced to detention for fifty-six days.

Hundreds of miles away in Obernkirchen, several of its personnel and vehicles were taking part in Exercise Carte Blanche. This was a ten day 'war' between British and American forces, with some participation from other NATO countries. Eric did not take a direct part in this, though he probably would have liked to, and the two mobile units from 646 SU were commanded by his deputy, Squadron leader Morgan, who was at Headquarters 2nd TAF, operating from the Chief Intelligence Officer's office.

Although Morgan was at Bad Eilsen, the two mobile units of 646 SU were miles away, at Hannelf, south of Cologne on the Rhine, and Krannenberg in the Ahr Valley, the exercise was deemed to be 'extremely successful and much of value was learned.' On return, Flight Sergeant Marfleet was promoted to Acting Warrant Officer. Despite his sojourn at Krannenburg, his official post was as NCO i/c No. 6 Detachment at Putlos.

Carte Blanche, a worrying name if you were a civilian, implying pillage on a grand scale, was the name given to a NATO exercise simulating an attack against the Warsaw Pact Forces, involving the detonation of 335 mainly tactical nuclear devices. About 1.5 million casualties were expected immediately and a further 3.5 million wounded in the first two days of war. There was no attempt to estimate the number likely to die from radiation poisoning. This was a serious and alarming operation, though only an exercise, after which Helmut Schmidt, the future German Chancellor, said that these tactical weapons 'will not defend Europe, but destroy it'.

In July, Eric records that he was promoted from Temporary Principal Scientific Officer to Acting Principal Scientific Officer in the Civil Service, a small promotion but a promotion nevertheless. (He received full status in due course, shedding the Acting from his Civil Service title). Then, on 7 July, he chaired an Anglo-American conference at 646 Signals Unit, the first to be held at Obernkirchen. This was attended by a Lieutenant Colonel of the USAFE (United States Air Forces in Europe) and other American representatives. It was yet another sign that Eric was a man of importance in signals intelligence circles and someone to be watched for the future.

In August the unit has its annual AOC's inspection, although the AOC himself, Air Marshal Sir Harry Broadhurst, did not come, even though his headquarters was only just down the road at Bad Eilsen. He sent instead his Air Officer i/c Administration, Air Vice-Marshal W.P.G. Pretty, who, having inspected RAF Bückeburg, spared an hour for Obernkirchen. Not all that much to see, one suspects, even though AVM Pretty had himself been involved in signals intelligence during and after the war and his name appears in some of the same records as Eric's in the closing months of the war. He was later to become Commander-in-Chief Signals Command with the rank of Air Marshal and a knighthood.

On 29 August there was another increase in the unit's establishment, up by 35 per cent in just eight months, to 186, comprising four officers, two warrant officers, two flight sergeants, eighteen sergeants, thirty-two corporals and 128 aircraftmen. As before, Eric Ackermann was 'additional to the regular establishment.' The number of airmen went up by 42 per cent, officers remained the same, and NCOs. rose by 31 per cent. This was for the second time in the year, the result of the enormous increase in intelligence funding noted earlier in this chapter.

On 22 August, the ORB compiling officer, Flight Lieutenant White, who was now doing this duty instead of the CO, reported on:

'a meeting at HQ 2nd TAF to discuss the future position of No. 5 Signals Wing and No. 646 Signals Unit Detachments in Berlin. Squadron Leader J. Every (AI 3(a)) was in [the] chair and both Commanders, i.e. of the Wing and of the Signals Unit [646 SU], were present. It was agreed that the present set of rooms in the control tower at Gatow were unsatisfactory for the following reasons:

'Insufficient space was available and any future expansion in the existing building was impossible. Operational traffic was increasing and showed no signs of levelling out.

'Should at any time Gatow Airfield be either given over to civilian use as an airfield, or should an Air Lift develop, the present set rooms would be untenable, from both the radio interference and security viewpoints.

'It was agreed that Hanbury Block, an isolated, unused barrack block, if suitably modified, could satisfactorily house both unit detachments. Plans were submitted and 646 Signals Unit immediately commenced work on production of the additional electronic equipment required.'

Eric then went to RAF Gatow after the 2nd TAF H.Q. conference, and the views of that meeting were presented and agreed. David Haysom has described it in his *'History of the Signals Units'*:

'At a meeting held at Gatow in August 1955, concern was expressed that in the event of another operation "Plainfare" (Berlin Airlift), the Signals Units might be required to vacate their accommodation in the control tower. This disruption would occur at a time when the services of the detachments would be most valuable. The OC 646 SU [Ackermann], the Wing Senior Intelligence Officer and the Senior Technical Officer attended the meeting. Hanbury Block (Building No. 15) was recommended as being the most likely to provide suitable accommodation for the signals units.

'At meetings on the 1 and 2 September 1955, attended by representatives of HQ 2nd TAF, No. 5 Wing, No. 291 SU, No. 646 SU, HQ No. 90 Group and No. 5357 AC Wing Detachment, members agreed that accommodation in the control tower was inadequate and that Hanbury Block was technically suitable. The necessary works services were discussed in detail, as was the technical installation. The Station Commander was advised of the decisions and concurred.'

This may not be central to the story, except that Eric, as a Wing Commander, and the OC 5 Signals Wing, another Wing Commander, were at both meetings, whereas the Squadron Leader COs of 477 SU (W.D. Reid) and 755 SU (W. Edwards) were not. Eric was senior to them both, and not just in rank but in status as well and his job was significantly different to theirs. Or maybe it was just that what happened in Berlin was of no concern to them.

On 1 September the Adjutant, Flight Lieutenant Hall, was posted to RAF Geilenkirchen, but notwithstanding his departure, the CO was off again to attend a joint Anglo-American 'Elint Planning' conference in London, with a representative from GCHQ in the chair. It was followed immediately with a visit to the USA and was at least the third conference involving the Americans which he attended in the first ten months of 1955 and another link with the country which was to provide his future employment. This is what he wrote about it:

'… proceeded to the United Kingdom and then to the United States to study advancement of "Elint" electronic equipment.

'The visit was of considerable value in that N.L.R. Washington have improved in many ways the receiver AN/APR.9, which forms the backbone of No. 646 Signals Unit intercept capability.'

The report goes on to say that, 'While in Washington Wing Commander E.G. Ackerman [sic] gave lectures on intercept problems and results to the Military Electric Group, Air Force Office of Intelligence and a specialist of the National Defence Council.' At the same time, preparations were being made for the withdrawal of the unit's detachment at Graz in Austria. The end of the four power occupation of that country was approaching and would take effect on 25 October 1955 when the troops of the four powers, the United States, the USSR, the United Kingdom and

France, departed. The ORB says of the Obernkirchen detachment's final parting from Austria:

'The Summer Camp at GRAZ was disbanded, the main convoy left on the 6 [September] and reached OBERNKIRCHEN on the 9th. As a result of the Peace Treaty with Austria whereby the occupying powers – Allied and Soviet – were to leave the country before October 1955, it will be necessary to arrange for a Summer Camp elsewhere next year.'

No. 4 Detachment had hardly arrived back at Obernkirchen before it was off again, this time to Scharfoldendorf. One of the reasons was the need to keep the detachment in being as a team and used to working together. By this time a full-time signals unit, No. 291, was already there, having moved from RAF Hambühren in 1955 and the 646 SU detachment also had to work with an Army unit. This was No. 12 Wireless Regiment, Royal Signals, and an Army officer, Captain W. Handy, took over command of the combined detachment.

Eric returned from the UK and the USA on 2 November and his new Adjutant, Flight Lieutenant R.M. White, 'proceeded on temporary duty' to HQ, 2nd TAF, now at Moenchengladbach, for Exercise All Aboard. Despite its name, this had nothing to do with the Royal Navy, but was a paper exercise lasting just twenty-four hours to test the planning staff at HQ and the participating RAF stations, which was in fact all of them. Throughout the twenty-four hours 'No actual signals were despatched or movements made by units'.

It is hardly surprising that several of the airmen who have contributed their memories of the station have said that while Eric was a thoroughly agreeable man and a good CO, they did not see him very often, nor get to know him at all well. He was hardly ever there, at least according to the one complete record we have for just one year, 1955. To end the year, he was back again in the UK for the London Communications Security Agency (LCSA) Conference, held to discuss Exercise Crab and 'a small element of No. 646 Signals Unit will participate. Exercise Crab will take place in the United Kingdom next year'.

The LCSA was created in 1953 to protect British cyphers by separating Sigint and communications security. Richard Aldrich describes it in his book on GCHQ as 'effectively Britain's fourth secret service, the technical security equivalent of MI5. Its main task was to develop new and very secure cypher machines to produce better codes in the hope of thwarting the Soviet Sigint services'.

Eric was back from the conference on 17 December and he summarized the year in the last part of his December report. In it he outlined the building programme at Obernkirchen which had started in April and provided greatly improved facilities of all kinds for officers and airmen. The work would provide: a combined kitchen for officers, sergeants and airmen, the officers mess, sergeants mess and quarters, the airmen's barrack block, guardroom and armoury, dog kennels, transmitter house, MT

A pleasant scene on the sloping site of RAF Obernkirchen taken by Malcolm Stewart. It is looking towards the main gate to the right at the bottom of the hill and across the plain below. The low white building on the right is the officers' quarters and the two-storey block on the left housed the airmen.

This photograph taken in 1958 shows the view up the hill and is more or less the opposite to the downhill view in the other picture.

bays, sports hall and two tennis courts. This ambitious programme was scheduled to be completed by September 1955, but by the end of the year none of the buildings was ready, though 'some would be completed early in the new year.' All this was not because the Ministry of Defence suddenly felt a surge of generosity, but came about following pressure from GCHQ in the early 1950s.

His final sentence for the year notes that detachments had operated at Berlin, Putlos, Graz, Schwechat and Scharfoldendorf. Some seventy-five airmen were employed on direct operations tasks, six on analysis, six on servicing and four on research and

This photograph by John Vickerman was taken in 1958.

A view of the camp from somewhere near the bottom corner of the glass works site. It was also the view from John Vickerman's window, top right in the big white barrack block. Below that are the wooden admin and operations blocks, then the long white MT building.

The Officers' and Sergeants' sleeping block taken in 2002 and disfigured by graffiti.

The airmen's sleeping quarters with SHQ to the right.

Station Headquarters, now hidden in the woods.

The airmen's bar and entertainment room in the Gasthaus zur Alten Bückeburg in 2002 in a derelict state, with Jack Fennelly and Charlie Olito surveying it in dismay. It was an example of Eric Ackermann's concern for his airmen's welfare as it was on his initiative that it was provided.

The Gymnasium.

The MT Section.

development projects. 'The year showed a marked increase in intercept activity with several new types of equipment under investigation.'

RAF Hambühren also benefitted in the same year when a substantial building programme was put in hand, though with only two years left before the RAF was to leave in November 1957, the Luftwaffe unit which took its place was to inherit a handsome legacy.

The story, at least as far as calling on an ORB for information, ends there. The files on the next nine years of 646's life were destroyed in what presumably was accidental damage, caused when files stored in an asbestos-lined room were being cleaned.

Eric and his family were to remain at Obernkirchen for a further three years while great changes were taking place in the structure of RAF Signals Intelligence in Germany. His own role in this is uncertain, but he must have been involved. Clues about this are, first, his rank. He was a Wing Commander, whereas the Commanding Officers of the other Signals Units were Squadron Leaders and the only other officer of his rank was the CO of No. 5 Signals Wing. Then there is his growing involvement with the Americans and his constant visits to the USA and to London for meetings and conferences on the future development of signals intelligence. The whole structure

The back of the Gasthaus Walter.

A sad end. This is what was left by 2010.

The back of the Gasthaus zur Alten Bückeburg, which can be seen as it was in its heyday in another photograph on these pages.

Part of the camp as it is now.

of the Sigint network was being radically altered, and although to the airmen on the ground it must have seemed chaotic and pointless (as the doings of those above them generally did), there clearly was a policy and a grand plan. Eric was the most experienced commander in his field, having been in Germany far longer than any of his peers or near peers and he could hardly have been ignored.

The first phase of this rearrangement took place in July 1955, when No. 755 Signals Unit at Uetersen, the successor unit to Eric's first operational creation, was transferred to RAF Hambühren. RAF Uetersen, left totally bereft after the departure of the only unit it had left by that time, closed down. In the same month, Headquarters No. 5 Signals Wing and No. 291 Signals Unit moved from Hambühren to Scharfoldendorf, and the latter station became the RAF's fifth operational Sigint unit in Germany.

To sum up all this frantic activity, the RAF's Sigint network in Germany now consisted of 646 Signals Unit at Obernkirchen, 477 at Butzweilerhof (which had been formed in January 1954), 755 at Hambühren, 291 and 5 Signals Wing at Scharfoldendorf. All of these, with the exception of 477 SU, far to the west near Cologne, were located towards the east of the British Zone and Uetersen was evacuated because it was vulnerable should the Warsaw Pact forces invade.

Phases two and three were to follow, as throughout the eastern part of the Zone, RAF stations were being closed and handed over to the Luftwaffe or the British Army, or just demolished. Two years after the completion of phase one, 755 SU at Hambühren was given notice to cease operations on 24/25 October 1957, with the station itself to shut down a month later. Most of Hambühren's operational personnel were posted to 477 SU at Butzweilerhof near Cologne and they travelled over three days in convoys, on the long journey down the autobahn, stopping for a break at a curious service station known as the Windmill. It was run by the YMCA and the name came from, fairly obviously, a windmill on the site.

Those not on this convoy went to Gatow and Scharfoldendorf, or were repatriated to the UK, including the Commanding Officer, Squadron Leader W. Edwards, who was posted to RAF Watton, where Eric himself was to go two years later. Operational personnel travelled in three groups, advance, main and rear, in convoys on the long journey down the autobahn and the move was managed without breaking operational coverage. Hambühren's functions were transferred to the incoming German unit, the Feldmelderregiment 71, which stayed there until the so-called Cold War Dividend ended its existence there in 1994 and for the first time since 1939, Hambühren was without a military presence of any kind. It got over its disappointment and is now a flourishing town of 10,000 people.

Chapter Eleven

Farewell to Obernkirchen

No. 646 Signals Unit did not escape this period of frantic change and in August 1958 it moved to Scharfoldendorf, replacing 291 Signals Unit, which went to Butzweilerhof and merged with 477 SU and in the process losing its own identity and number. The move of 291 had been in the air at Butzweilerhof for some weeks and as a 477 Wireless Operator wrote on 31 July, to a recently demobbed friend: 'the lads from on top of the hill are mostly here now'. In fact, as the 2nd Tactical Air Force official record states, the move was not completed until 12 August. The order which set things moving went as follows:

> 'The administrative element of Royal Air Force Scharfoldendorf currently established as part of No. 291 Signals Unit, will, on amalgamation, be taken over by No. 646 Signals Unit, arrangements and at a time to be notified by Headquarters, 2nd Tactical Air Force. The station will be administered by No. 646 Signals Unit, Royal Air Force Obernkirchen, after the move of Headquarters No. 5 Signals Wing, Scharfoldendorf, for the physical transfer of that Headquarters personnel and equipment.
>
> 'This to take place from 0600 hours on 12 August 1958, when "all operational tasks at No. 291 Signals Unit, Scharfoldendorf under the control of a re-established No. 5 Signals Wing" at Butzweilerhof will have been completed.
>
> 'Control by 291 Signals Unit will cease at 0600 hours on 12 August 1958 and will be exercised by No. 5 Signals Wing, Butzweilerhof, on 12 August 1958, at a time to be notified when transfer of landlines has been completed. This is being effected by Headquarters, No. 5 Signals Wing, Scharfoldendorf.'

The following day, 13 August, the station was handed over to the Officer i/c Advance Party, No. 646 Signals Unit, and so:

> 'On completion of the move No. 291 Signals Unit, Royal Air Force Scharfoldendorf, will come under the command of No. 646 Signals Unit. The existing establishment of No. 291 Signals Unit will move on 13 August 1958. Personnel not transferred to Butzweilerhof will be retained at Scharfoldendorf and placed under the control of No. 646 signals unit pending action by Command Drafting Officer, 2nd Tactical Air Force.'

This deadpan language hides the disruption the move caused to the serving personnel and their families. The previous year, when RAF Hambühren was closed and just a few people moved to Scharfoldendorf, there were vigorous complaints from the families because the married quarters were not ready for them and the prospect of being seventy miles apart for a short while was not to be tolerated. The rebellion was inevitably quashed with the comment that 'soldiers (and airmen) had to go where they were ordered'. Maybe the weather on the hill had something to do with it. A 755 Signals Unit airman, who was posted there in November 1957 from Hambühren, but who only stayed there for a week before being repatriated, recalled that he never saw the site as a whole, as it was perpetually fogbound.

Disruption and bad weather notwithstanding, the Ackermann family enjoyed their time at Scharfoldendorf, and Peter recalled his own delight in his notes on life in Germany, which are set down in Chapter 14. The family lived in a building called the Guest House, which is the address given in Eric's service record for his next-of-kin, who is of course Mrs M.A. Ackermann.

Without the Operations Record Book for 1956–64, we are deprived of important information on Eric Ackermann's last years in Germany and of his signals unit's twilight period. It is therefore ironic that probably the most significant record so far discovered was in an army file, which reveals that RAF Scharfoldendorf was further strengthened in October 1958 with the arrival of an Army unit, No. 30 Wireless Squadron, Royal Corps of Signals, until then, based at Minden. It brought with it five officers and eighty other ranks. The following year, on 1 September 1959:

'the designation of the Squadron was changed to 226 Signals Squadron (Wireless). The location continues to be with the RAF and is now established on a co-location basis, complete investigation on all domestic aspects having now been achieved. Operationally, considerable progress has been made both in the establishment of location and equipment.'

Of Eric himself there is, as usual, little information. We do know one trivial fact, which is that he had a brush with Squadron Leader J.A.G. Morgan when Eric called a parade and 'made it abundantly clear to all present that he had been the CO of 646 for the past thirteen years and was still the CO of the unit'. Maybe Morgan felt aggrieved, because as the next ranking officer to Eric at Obernkirchen, he was in charge during Eric's frequent absences and he let his resentment get the better of him. He and Eric did not get on and Morgan must have said something mildly insubordinate. Morgan was a Russian Interpreter First Class and later, as Wing Commander, was the head of the Russian school at RAF Tangmere in 1961/62.

Eric had another ten months in Germany and at Scharfoldendorf before handing over command of 646 SU to Wing Commander Dunlop, in June 1959. He was posted to 192 Squadron at RAF Watton in Norfolk, a station which housed the Central Signals Establishment and therefore very suitable for Eric to see out his final months in the RAF.

Sad as it must have been to leave a country where he had lived for the previous fifteen years, he probably did not mind too much missing the visit of the Commander-in-Chief, 2nd Tactical Air Force, Air Marshal Sir Humphrey Edwardes-Jones, on 7 July. No. 226 Signals Squadron had the honour of taking part in the ceremonial parade

Two views of the solid buildings and attractive landscape of RAF Scharfoldendorf, taken by Malcolm Stewart. Before 291 Signals Unit and 5 Signals Wing arrived in 1955 it had been the BAFO and 2nd Tactical Air Force Rest Centre, noted for its skiing in the winter. The large building on the left was known as the Schloss. During the Second World War it had been a Luftwaffe Gliding School and this was continued by the RAF in later years. The site is still much as it was then and now houses the German Civil Service College.

and the subsequent inspection as an entity in itself. Whether the airmen of 646 were involved, we do not know. They probably were not too upset if they weren't.

The unit stayed on without him for a further five years before disbanding in March 1964, although its operational functions had already been passed to 5 Signals Wing two months before he left.

David Haysom recalls that on his own arrival at RAF Gatow in 1962,

'No. 646 SU was in operation from a strange structure on the top of Hanbury block. They worked independently and were known vaguely as 646, but were very much a part of the 5 Signals Wing (Detachment). Later they moved with us to Hangar 4, where a special Siemens tower was built for their equipment – mainly parabola antennas. They worked from offices at one end of the hangar, whereas we had our set rooms at the other end. There was little contact and as far as I can recall the name 646 was gradually dropped. When we moved to the Hill (Teufelsberg) in about 1969, they remained at Hangar 4. We then had virtually no more to do with them.'

No. 646 SU seems to have been hard to kill off and it lasted in one form or another for twelve years in West Germany and even longer in Berlin. David also writes that at the time when he was in Berlin, those working for 646 SU were radar operators who had done some form of conversion training. They did a tour with 646 SU and then returned to their proper trade in the real RAF. This looks as if it had some sort of role change when on detachment in Berlin and then gradually, and virtually unnoticed, it withered into extinction.

Much the same in the winter, with the Schloss giving it a fairy-tale appearance. Also taken by Malcolm Stewart and reproduced with his kind permission.

Chapter Twelve

The 646 Signals Unit badge

In 1955 Eric decided that 646 Signals Unit needed its own crest and he applied, via Headquarters 2nd Tactical Air Force to the Air Ministry for approval. Whether this was prompted by the spate of building at his station, by the growing number of signals intelligence stations in Germany, or just because he thought he would have a go, can only be guessed at. Success would give 646 SU the first such crest among all the RAF's Sigint stations, although 5 Signals Wing, subsequently 26 Signals Unit, received the same honour a few years later, having overcome a similar problem.

This was normally a straightforward matter, but in this case its unconventional Commanding Officer wanted a German motto. The regulations laid down certain conditions which even in this case should have caused no problems. There was quite a fuss, however, reminiscent of the correspondence about Eric's George Medal commendation twelve years earlier. The details, recorded in National Archives file AIR 2/13092, are worth quoting because the whole affair took a long time, and involved a government minister, several senior officers at the Air Ministry, including two air commodores, as well as Clarenceux King of Arms at the College of Arms and the German Embassy, not to mention a wing commander and some squadron leaders at the Air Ministry and 2nd Tactical Air Force Headquarters.

The first letter in the file is dated 19 March 1956 and is from 2nd TAF Headquarters to the Under-Secretary of State, Air Ministry. It uses the RAF's formal official form of address which always presaged something serious requiring the attention of high authority, which this one certainly received. The apparently obsequious wording was the convention when used from a subordinate officer to one of significantly higher rank, or in this case, a much higher civilian.

Sir,

Unit Badge, No.646 Signals Unit, Royal Air Force

I have the honour to request confirmation that No. 646 Signals Unit, Royal Air Force, Obernkirchen, is eligible for a Unit Badge under the terms of Air Ministry Order A.231/53, para.3.

I have the honour to be,

Sir,

Your obedient Servant,

(H.E. Angell),

Wing Commander,

For Commander-in-Chief,

2nd TACTICAL AIR FORCE

Four days later, on 23 March, a loose minute was attached to the AirMinistry file from Squadron Leader J. Ellison, saying that No. 646 Signals Unit did indeed conform to the requirements of the Air Ministry Order.

The Commander-in-Chief, 2nd TAF, or rather the above-mentioned Wing Commander Angell, who dealt with such matters, then received a letter dated 9 April from the office of the Director of Personal Services at the Air Ministry, written by one R. Stevenson, with a copy to Clarenceux King of Arms at the College of Arms, stating:

Sir,

Unit Badge – 646 Signals Unit

I am directed to refer to your letter 2TAF/C/3014/1/P dated 19 March 1956, and to confirm that No. 646 Signals Unit is eligible for a badge.

There now seems to have been a long delay, although that may simply be because some documents have been lost. Anyway, the next document in the file is dated 15 August, five months later. It is a letter from Clarenceux King of Arms, Sir John Heaton-Armstrong himself, to a man at the Air Ministry whom he addresses simply as 'Ashton', who is actually Squadron Leader H.A. Ashton, DFC, and therefore a man with a distinguished service record:

'Dear Ashton,

'With regard to my letter of 25 May to Air Commodore Hobler about No. 646 Signals Unit having a German motto, I enclose herewith for your information and return a letter from Wing Commander Ackermann dated the 20 July explaining why they want to have a German motto.

'As I mentioned before, the enquiry I made from the German Embassy was answered by the Press Secretary, who thought it remarkable that an RAF Unit wanted to adopt a German motto!

'Apart from certain exceptions, there are no proprietary rights in mottos, but if it were my choice I should prefer one in my own language.

'I should be interested to know what Air Ministry feel about this point now that Wing Commander Ackermann has given his reasons for preferring a German motto.'

The path of research is strewn with difficulties and frustrations and the absence of Wing Commander Ackermann's letter from the file is a good example. It would be fascinating to know his own reasons for wanting the German motto, given that there was so much opposition to it. This would have been the most crucial document in the whole debate. A request to the College of Arms for a sight of the letter produced the apologetic reply that it had been lost.

Then came a minute dated 5 September from Squadron Leader Ashton to the Director of Personal Services (A):

'May I ask you to read Encls. 5A and 5B [these were not included in the Archives file].

'It appears that the unit, in its present form, has served only in Germany, but nevertheless I do not like the idea of a German Motto and suggest the selection of a White Horse on the badge, representing St. George and Hanover, is sufficient to show the German connections.

'However, my views for not liking the German Motto are purely personal and you may feel it's time they were changed and brought up to date.'

There is then a handwritten note on Ashton's minute from Air Commodore D. Finlay, (DPA(A)), which says rather curtly, and showing signs of exasperation: 'If they want a German motto – let them have it.' One can understand the Air Commodore's point of view as a man who saw the Germans as a former and ruthless enemy whose language should not, in his view, defile an RAF symbol.

It is worth pausing at this point to try and justify the amount of time spent on getting to the stage when Eric's request could be approved. The granting of unit badges was not lightly undertaken. Squadron badges would have been fairly straightforward, but others, particularly strange units such as 646 SU, did need looking into. How long had it been in existence, where had it served, did have a long-term future? These questions seemed to have been answered satisfactorily and the one which caused a real problem was the motto in German and one can understand the initial reluctance to approve something so revolutionary. The war had been over for only ten years and the wounds were still raw, but Air Commodore Finlay's 'Let them have it' seems to have clinched the matter and on 10 September Ashton wrote to Sir John Heaton-Armstrong, passing on verbatim the

Air Commodore's briskly expressed view. Sir John acknowledged the letter on the 14 September, prefacing it with a warmer greeting, 'My dear Ashton.' Now at last we reach the crux of the matter, which is the actual design of the badge and its motto, namely:

NO. 646 SIGNALS UNIT, ROYAL AIR FORCE

This Unit wishes to adopt as its Badge the white horse of Hanover in which district the Unit is based.
The portcullis is symbolic of an obstacle.
The motto is:

KEIN HINDERNIS ZU HOCH
May be translated as: No obstacle too high

Squadron Leader Ashton then wrote to the Commander-in-Chief, 2nd TAF, Air Marshal the Earl of Bandon, on behalf of the Director of Personal Services (A) on 24 January 1957, as follows:

'Sir,

Unit Badge – No. 646 Signals Unit

'I am directed to forward herewith the original painting of the badge for the above unit, approved by Her Majesty the Queen.
    'It is requested that this badge may be presented on a suitable ceremonial occasion.'

Flight Lieutenant J.A. Gill acknowledged the letter on 9 February 1957 on behalf of the Earl, and that, as far as the surviving correspondence is concerned, concluded the matter, some eleven months after it was first raised with 2nd TAF Headquarters.

The Earl, incidentally, inherited an Irish peerage, he being the elder of twins. He was affectionately known in Germany as 'The Abandoned Earl', a play on his title rather than a slur on his character. Needless to say he was also called Paddy Bandon. He had a long and distinguished career in the RAF and his last appointment was as Commander, Allies Forces Central Europe.

Unfortunately, there is no documentary or photographic evidence of what Ashton

No. 646 Signals Unit badge.

called 'a suitable ceremonial occasion' ever having taken place. The care taken by some senior officers over what might seem a trivial matter is important. Unit badges were not issued lightly, but had to be fully justified and the problem of the motto had not cropped up before. With its approval, however, a precedent had been set and in 1961 No. 5 Signals Wing made its own application, which, for rather different reasons, occupied the authorities at the Air Ministry and the College of Arms for five years, from 1961 to 1966. It was eventually granted, with a German motto: *Immer Wachsam* (Always Watchful), but the whole process had taken so long that by the time approval was granted, 5 Signals Wing was no more and had been replaced by No. 26 Signals Unit. That did not affect the original decision, so all that had to be done was to repaint the title on the badge.

How unfortunate it was, therefore, that 646 SU did not have a long life, lasting just seven years longer before disbanding in 1964. How many shields with the crest were made? Are they displayed anywhere? Do the accessories which often accompany the crests, such as blazer and lapel badges, car window stickers and so on, exist? Given the persistence with which Eric fought his battle and the care taken to approve the crest by the Air Ministry and the College of Arms, all these questions should be answered in the affirmative.

Not only had Eric Ackermann unwittingly created a precedent with the motto, but also with the badge itself, because none of the other signals units in his sphere of influence ever had its own badge, except for No. 26, which was different in that it was originally granted to a superior unit, the Wing HQ. Nevertheless, if any of the Air Ministry officers who were still around had done battle twelve years earlier over his George Medal award, they might have felt that this particular honorary officer was still causing the writing of many memos to achieve something out of the ordinary.

Chapter Thirteen

Farewell to Germany

It had been seventeen years since Eric last had a settled home in Britain, way back in 1942, when he left Swanage and the TRE. Now he was back with the rank of Wing Commander and a new job and on the verge of a complete change of personal, though not professional, direction. He was posted to RAF Watton in Norfolk to serve with No. 51 Squadron, which he had last met in its previous life as 192 Squadron in North Africa in 1943. Watton was a 'proper' RAF station with a 2000 yard runway and seriously large aeroplanes, such as the de Havilland Comet and the English Electric Canberra. It was also the home of the Central Signals Establishment, providing an environment very familiar to Eric.

He should have felt at home there, apart from its being a large flying station and not a small, remote and very secret unit somewhere in the back of beyond in Germany. Watton was the hub of Sigint and Elint development and accommodated a range of civil airliners converted to being, as Richard Aldrich puts it, 'airborne Sigint platforms'. These were not that dissimilar, at least in their basic purpose, from the Wellingtons and Ansons Eric had been flying from Boscombe Down in 1940 to 1942, apart from their size and greater sophistication.

Numbers 192 and 51 Squadrons – the latter took over from the former on 21 August 1958 – were both formed as part of the Royal Flying Corps in the First World War, they disbanded in 1919 and were re-formed in, respectively, 1943 and 1937. No. 51 had the distinction of dropping leaflets on Germany on the very first night of the Second World War. By early 1940 it was dropping bombs, and, with an interval from 1940 to 1942, when it was attacking U-boats in the Bay of Biscay, continued in that role in 1943. No. 192 Squadron's motto would have served perfectly well for Eric: 'Dare to Discover'.

To move on to the Cold War period, they were both employed in intelligence flights, 192 on Electronic Signals Intelligence (ELINT) and 51 on Signals Intelligence (SIGINT). It was 51 Squadron which Eric joined when he arrived at Watton in 1959. Nick Ackermann remembers seeing the Canberras in the air over their house near Watton when he was five years old.

Life was about to change, however, for Eric left the air force in 1960 after a career lasting twenty years, and was once again plain Mister. His honorary commission was never converted into a real one despite his long service. In 1962 his former squadron was transferred to RAF Wyton, but Eric seems to have had no part in this. He appears for the last time in the *London Gazette* on 2 February 1960, under the heading, 'Commission relinquished (class CC). Wing Commander (on cessation of duty): E.G. Ackermann, GM (192868) 28 September 1959'.

He was still involved with RAF Watton as a civilian and the National Archives file AIR 29/3540, RAF Watton, ORB 1961–1965, records that Mr E.G. Ackermann (Electronic Warfare Support Wing) was present at a meeting held there on 21 September 1961 to discuss the redeployment of units from Watton, mainly to Wyton. The minutes do not record that he spoke.

The world of RAF signals intelligence was a small one and the Operations Record Book for the Central Signals Establishment at RAF Watton in the early 1960s reads very much like a reunion of old friends. Eric would have known them all. Wing Commanders W.E. Satterthwaite (Scats, to the airmen who served with him and the man who signed the order for the transfer of 291 SU to Butzweilerhof), W. 'Eddie' Edwards and A.H. Dormer, all former signals unit COs in Germany, visited the unit during that period, as did his old colleague J.A.F. Morgan. Although Eric was a real civilian again by that time, he would have felt among his own kind on his infrequent post-RAF visits.

In 1961, he and one J.D. Storer, wrote an article in the November issue of *Electronic Engineering* entitled, *A Master Film Unit*. The abstract of the article reads:

> 'The Timing unit based on 1kc crystal oscillator from which a variety of pulse trains and sine waves outputs are derived. A once per second pulse output is used to drive a Dekatron clock which is interrogated each minute and produces a six digit output in Morse code indicating the day of the month and the time in hours and minutes, e.g.: 17, 11.30. This output in turn may be used to modulate the continuous pulse trains and sine wave outputs thus imprinting them with real time information.'

The article runs to eight pages in an A4 publication, with several drawings of circuits, which the writers of this narrative have to admit is beyond them! It is interesting that the two authors of the article are shown as E.G. Ackermann, GM, and J.D. Storer, AMIEE, AMBrit.IR. Storer was a senior officer at GCHQ whom Eric would have met on his visits to England from Germany. Eric had no advanced professional qualifications, while Storer certainly did, but he must have been held in high regard by the engineering profession to have had this paper published in such a prestigious journal. The same situation has been observed in the Civil Service Lists for the early 1960s, when again Eric had the GM and had the same Civil Service grade as his colleagues with a hatful of academic qualifications.

The family left Norfolk in 1965 and Eric finally severed his connection with the RAF on his appointment as Head of the Military Satellite Communications Group at the Ministry of Defence Signals Research and Development Establishment (SRDE). This was situated near Bournemouth and not very far from Worth Matravers, where, a quarter of a century earlier, Eric had begun his career. The family lived at a house called Sandygate, on Elphinstone Road, in the small town of Highcliffe, then in Hampshire and now in Dorset. Not only was he back close to where his career had begun twenty-five years earlier, but also the SRDE was later merged with the organization which was the descendant of the Telecommunications Research Establishment.

The SRDE was conspicuous by its large white Radome (a contraction of Radar Dome), the essential part of which was a dish 40 feet in diameter, making it a conspicuous landmark on the cliff tops near Bournemouth. The Radome's purpose was to track British and foreign satellites and to test the first British Skynet military communications system. It was built in 1965, coincidentally the year of Eric's arrival. As a research institution the SRDE had no manufacturing capability itself and so Marconi Space and Defence Systems Ltd., based at Bournemouth Airport, was contracted to manufacture the Skynet equipment.

Eric had a large staff at the SRDE and his prime responsibility was to develop Skynet in conjunction with his counterparts in the United States, using US Initial Defense Communication Satellites. Work on the project began in 1966 and Eric's particular contribution, apart from managing his staff and directing their research workload, was to develop and engineer three 40 foot antenna terminals for deployment in the UK, Cyprus and Singapore, as well as four 20 foot mobile terminals for the British Army. As if this was not enough to occupy him, he also assisted in the design of a Naval shipborne terminal in Scotland, several of which were put into use by the US Navy and in this he was working with the American Defense Communications Agency – a collaboration that was, like other contacts made over the years, also to affect his future.

Eric visited America in October 1966, almost certainly to go to the California office of Marconi and to visit an old friend and colleague, Jim Sears. Jim was a senior scientist with the CIA and was working for the Agency in Los Angeles. He was at one time Head of the Physics Department at Evansville College in Indiana, so he was very much a man on Eric's wavelength. He knew the Ackermann family so well that he was known as Uncle Jim. As we have seen before, Jim greatly admired Eric. Eric would surely have wished to help him when Jim was so ill.

This is the second such tribute we have found to Eric's ability to combine these two essential qualities. Sadly, Eric found Sears to be ill with a lung disease, which though not malignant, threatened him with a life expectancy of eighteen months to ten years, providing he led a quiet life, something which Sears found impossible to do, although he was now nearing retirement. He did not wish to retire, and despite his poor health asked Eric for help in finding employment. He wrote that he would be happy to work

Eric and Marianna relaxing with their dog in the garden of their house in Elphingstone Road, Highcliffe, in 1966.

Eric's Second World War campaign medals and his George Medal, photographed by Nick Ackermann. They are, left to right: The George Medal, the 1939–45 Star, the Air Crew Europe Star, the Africa Star, the Italy Star, the Defence Medal and the 1939–45 War Medal. Two of the medals have clasps: the Air Crew Europe Star clasp denotes operations over France and the Africa Star is for service in Northern Africa between 23 October 1942 and 12 May 1943.

part-time 'at very little cost to your operation', but added a condition which would have been impossible to fulfil. He would have to work in a more congenial climate than an English winter, such as 'Cyprus, Kuwait, Islands off India, Perth, Australia'. He ends: 'Keep me in mind please'.

Eric wrote to R.V. Jones in October 1966, just after his return home from California and referred to his visit to Jim Sears: 'Jim knows of my work in the field of Comms Satellites (Military) and of my latest venture into orbit control and station keeping'. He also wrote about Sears' hope that he, Eric, could use his influence to find him work. He was clearly very sympathetic to Sears' situation, writing to Jones that, 'I can think of several UK areas where his experience might be of value and feel that I must do something. I am therefore writing to you as the only person I know who might be able to find him some suitable part-time work. If you think I could do anything I would be very willing to do so. Alternatively I could visit you in Aberdeen or London'.

Jones replied on 18 November, commenting that he was pleased that the Ackermanns were enjoying life in Highcliffe, as Eric had written saying that, 'we are happier here than at any time since Germany'. Jones says that, 'it was certainly a very pleasant place in 1917'.

With so much going on at the SRDE and with Eric holding a responsible job there, he then made a surprising decision when in 1967 he accepted a posting to the British Embassy in Washington, which was to provide an opportunity to further his career and to work in the country which he had visited so many times. He and his family were to remain in America for the rest of their lives. Before he left the SRDE he was presented with a finely-crafted model of the Radome with its antenna reflector inside and with this in his luggage off they all went on the *Queen Elizabeth* across the Atlantic, on one of her last voyages before she was decommissioned and ended up as a floating hotel in Hong Kong harbour, until it mysteriously caught fire in 1973 and ended up being partially scrapped.

Chapter Fourteen

Migration to Maryland

Originally Eric's appointment in Washington was for three years, but at his own request it was extended to five, giving the family the chance of a more settled existence than they had had since leaving Germany nine years before. Their first house was at 8303 Thoreau Drive in Bethesda, Maryland, within easy reach of the Embassy. They moved house several more times to addresses with those impressive house numbers that are common in the United States: 7306 Pyle Road, and 6701 Pawtucket Road (both in Bethesda) are just two examples. His wish to stay in Washington for more than three years was prompted partly out of consideration for his sons' education. As he himself did not go to university, he felt that Peter and Nick should be given every opportunity to have the best education he could provide for them. This is what he did and both boys had a university education in America.

Nick Ackermann remembers visiting his father's office at the embassy once or twice. It was several floors up and it faced towards the US Naval Observatory next door, which is also the official residence of the US Vice President. Nicks says that:

> 'I would usually spend my time in the embassy's marvellous library (once, when I was about eleven, I got locked in when closing time arrived and the staff didn't know I was there, but Dad duly retrieved me). Occasionally, in summer we got to use the swimming pool at the Ambassador's residence, the water in which was opaque and green, which made it great fun (in my opinion) as people couldn't tell where you were when you swam underwater. My favourite thing about the embassy was the camp weekend, which would occur once in the spring and once in the fall, when embassy staff and families would spend a weekend living in wooden cabins in Prince William Forest Park, about twenty miles outside Washington to the south.'

Eric was now heavily involved with satellite communications, and particularly the Skynet project, though this suffered a setback when the first attempt to launch the Skynet satellite on an American booster in 1969 failed and it was not until 1974 that a successful launch was eventually made. Despite the delay, this was to pave the way both for the rapid expansion of this complex (and expensive) system and for the further development of Eric's own career for the rest of his working life. It is possible that he also contributed to an Institution of Electrical Engineers meeting on Skynet on 20 April 1970, the proceedings of which were published as IEE Conference Publication, No. 63, although by that time he was living in America.

The five years went by and Eric either did not want, or was not granted, a further contract. He solved the problem of the time limit on his contract by leaving the British Civil Service after more than thirty years. His son Peter believes he left the embassy because at the end of his current contract he would have been posted back to the United Kingdom where he did not want to go. He got another job quickly with the Marconi Corporation, for which he had worked back in England in the years immediately before leaving for the States. He was able to continue his work on the Skynet, the full name of which was the Skynet Defence Communications Satellite Project.

Eric's old friend, Derek Garrard, was in America in July 1974 and he met Eric and Marianna. He wrote that Eric was enjoying his work with Marconi, but Marianna was suffering what he calls a sugar imbalance, which was causing her great distress. He had also passed on news of Howard Cundall's death in the yachting accident that summer. Eric and Howard were colleagues all those years before with the TRE, when they were both scientists and held honorary commissions, though Howard's wartime experiences were very different from Eric's.

The Ackermann family was now living in their fourth house since arriving six years earlier, at Quintana Court, also in Bethesda. They had not been there long before Marconi announced, in February 1975, that it was forced to reduce its staff in America and so Eric had to look elsewhere. He quickly secured a position with the Communications Satellite Corporation (COMSAT) at their laboratories in Clarksburg, Maryland, about thirty miles to the north and well outside the Washington metropolis. Two years later, Eric saw the opportunity presented by COMSAT's rural location to buy a farmhouse, with a useful acreage of land, a few miles east of the town of Emmitsburg in northern Maryland. They kept sheep and did some arable farming, so even as the years advanced, Eric's restless energy was not deserting him. This was to be the family's last move and after much wandering they were able to settle down and embark on a modest form of agriculture as a contrast with Eric's demanding work with COMSAT.

COMSAT was, and still is, a global telecommunications company, based in Maryland, and with branches in central and south America and in Turkey, specializing in satellite communication services. The company was created by the Communications Satellite Act of 1962 and began operations that year with its headquarters in Washington D.C. and a board of six people appointed by President John F. Kennedy. Eric worked there until his formal retirement in April 1984, at the age of sixty-four, by which time his elder son Peter was also working for the company, which he had joined before he was twenty years old. Peter's career was to mirror his father's to a high degree, while Eric was very like Jim Sears in that retirement was not a word he liked and so he carried on working on special projects for COMSAT until his health began to fail the following year and he finally had to give it up late in 1985.

Leaving England did not mean that Eric and his family lost touch with his friend, boss and mentor, R.V. Jones. Jones and his wife visited them in March 1973 and also saw Eric in Los Angeles the same year, accompanied by Jim Sears, to whom both Eric and Jones refer in correspondence later on. Dr Jones was back in America again in April 1982, visiting Electronic Security Command at the Kelly Air Force Base, San Antonio, to give a lecture at a meeting of the Southern Region of the Association of Old Crows, which itself was based at Fort Worth. It is likely that Eric was there too, as he had visited the base during his service in Germany for conferences on intelligence gathering and was himself an Old Crow.

Marianna having an uncomfortable lift in the garden at Quintana Court.

Eric kept in regular touch with R.V. Jones and in a letter he wrote to him in January 1983, he says that since 1980 he had been 'a member of a small team studying remote sensing of the earth's atmosphere from space. As the only engineer on the team I find myself in entirely new technology. In a world of pixels, linear arrays, etc.' He then says that he is supposed to retire in two years, but then comes the magic word 'if' COMSAT were to say, 'of course you'll stay on as a consultant.' The letter is also nostalgic. 'We often talk about the years of Ried in [sic] Innkreis, Fraunhofer and, of course, Roy Piggott. We remember the years of 46–48 and, with gratitude, all you did to help us.'

Nick Ackermann has noted in his diary, eleven references to Jones between 1973 and 1997 and most of these were to do with letters from Jones or visits made to the United States and in particular to see Eric and he remembers that every Christmas there was a card from Reg and Vera Jones.

Eric had become a member of the Association of Old Crows, which, despite its title, is a very serious and influential organization, conveniently located, as far as Eric himself was concerned, not too far away in Alexandria, Virginia. It is a non-profit tax-exempt international professional organization, with seventy-seven chapters specializing in electronic and tactical information operations, and related topics. The Association was formed in 1964 to support the policies of the United States and its Allies in achieving an 'adequate defense capability with the minimum essential electronic warfare resources to operate effectively against any adversary.' The name 'Old Crows' emerged from the first use of electronic warfare in the Second World War to disrupt enemy communications. Allied equipment and operations were known by the codeword 'Raven'. Common jargon changed the name to 'Crows' and those engaged in the profession became known as Old Crows. Virtually all its 18,000 members have security clearances of SECRET or higher. It is now involved in everything concerning electronic warfare and information-gathering techniques. It is therefore no surprise that Eric was a member.

He experienced one of his greatest moments as an Old Crow when R.V. Jones visited Washington in 1984, to be inducted into the Association's Electronic Warfare Hall of Fame at a banquet to be held in his honour at the Washington Hilton on 23 May. It was a glittering occasion, with a guest list which included the Director of the Central intelligence Agency (William Casey), the Director of the National Security Agency (Lieutenant General Lincoln Faurer, USAF), the Secretary of the Navy, the Assistant Secretary of Defense, the British Defence Attaché, and a British Colonel from the Defence Intelligence Service at the Ministry of Defence. And Mr and Mrs E.G. Ackermann. Margaret Thatcher, at that time Prime Minister, was courteously informed of the occasion though it was not expected that she would be able to attend. The full text of Dr Jones' acceptance speech, held in his archive at Churchill College, runs thus:

'I was the mouthpiece through which the Intelligence story emerged into the circles of high command. First I think of the many who worked quietly away, and who only came to notice when something for which they were responsible went wrong. Among these, I think of the intercept operators tirelessly taking down innumerable, and for them, meaningless, Enigma signals without ever being told of the vital results of their work – of the cryptographers at Bletchley, of photographic reconnaissance pilots spending lonely hours high over Germany or hectic low flying minutes involving split-second judgement against radar stations and their defending guns – "dicing" we called this – and dicing with death it certainly was.

'My list of agencies on which I depended was not complete, for a completely new one came into existence in the First World War. The need to listen to enemy radar at close quarters led to special observers being sent on investigation flights, and they set examples of great courage. Harold Jordan (who was awarded an immediate Distinguished Service Order for outstanding gallantry, when his aircraft was attacked eleven times by a German nightfighter whose radar transmission he was investigating) and Eric Ackermann (who is with us tonight and who was awarded the George Medal for more than ninety flights, including many over the Kammhuber Line) being outstanding among the British observers.'

Whether it was Eric's presence there that prompted Jones to refer to him, and, according to Jones, to ask him to stand, it is nevertheless a generous tribute and surely an honour to have been singled out, with Squadron Leader Harold Jordan, from the scores of talented people with whom the honorand had worked. Jordan's mission, which Dr Jones describes, was immediately prior to the Bruneval Raid of February 1942 and Eric had himself flown to France the day before. They would certainly have known each other well, both at Boscombe Down and subsequently when both of them worked for the Deputy Directorate of Intelligence (Science) at the Air Ministry.

This drawing by Nick Ackermann shows the house on 17110 Bollinger School Road in Emmitsburg, where Eric and Marianna lived from July 1977 until his death in April 1986. Nick has also provided all the colour photographs in this chapter.

By now Eric's health was failing and he died on Sunday, 27 April 1986, at the age of sixty-six. He had been suffering from lung cancer. Peter Ackermann believes that he knew about his condition for almost a year prior to his death, but did not wish to alarm his family. He was still living at the address from which he had written to Jones three years earlier in Emmitsburg. His retirement to which, as Nick remembers, he had looked forward, 'raising sheep, chickens and hay', was all too short. His funeral took place on 30 April at St. Joseph's Roman Catholic Church,

Eric and Marianna, taken in the late 1970s or early 1980s.

Eric and his elder son Peter on the farm at Emmitsburg.

Emmitsburg. The local newspaper, the *Frederick News-Post*, carried brief reports, but there does not seem to have been a full obituary. The notices of his death and funeral are in the accepted conventional form.

> Commander E.G. Ackermann, 66, of Bellinger [sic: Bollinger] School Road, Emmitsburg, died Sunday, 27 April 1986 at the Gettysburg Hospital, Gettysburg, Pa. He was the husband of Gizelle Marianne Ackermann. Born 6 October 1919, in Cowes, IOW, Hampshire, England, he was the son of the late Rudolph and Dorothy Webb Ackermann. Mr Ackermann was a member of St. Joseph's Roman Catholic Church Emmitsburg and a member of the Association of Old Crows. He served in the Royal Air Force in the Second World War.

Four years later, on 15 February 1990, R.V. Jones wrote to Peter Ackermann:

> 'Thank you very much for your letter of 28 January with its memories of your father. He was a brave man – at the time when I wrote the citation for his George Medal he had made more than ninety flights, many of them into the thick of the German night fighter defences. I think that he qualified for nearly all, if not all, of the campaign medals issued to British citizens, and he even landed at Anzio (or Salerno).
>
> 'I was very glad that when in 1984 I was elected into the Electronic Warfare Hall of Fame, he was able to be present, and I was delighted to call on him to stand up while I told the audience something of his own part in electronic warfare. I know that he was very moved. He was one of those who made the world tick, sometimes two of three times as fast as it had ticked previously. And he was largely responsible for our holding the respect of the Americans in electronic warfare in the post-war years.'

Soon after Eric's death, Marianna moved to Germantown, Maryland. She survived her husband by eight years and died on 20 May 1994, at the Montgomery General Hospital in Olney, Maryland. She was 70-years-old. Her funeral took place three days later, with a Mass of Christian Burial at St. Joseph's Roman Catholic Church, Emmitsburg. Her two sons were among the bearers. She was laid to rest by her husband's side in the Emmitsburg cemetery.

A decade after Eric's death, the *Frederick News-Post* carried a report in its issue of 12 November 1996, of a tribute and a ceremony carried out at the graveside:

> 'Born on Cowes, Isle of Wight on Oct. 16 [sic] 1919, Royal Air Force retired Mr Ackermann died in 1986. The stone adds a message God Bless and is signed by your sons Peter and Nicholas. Decorating the graves of the Brits was done as a courtesy to our allies, said Mr Humerick, adding that nobody else is going to be doing it.'

R. V. Jones, for so many years both Eric's friend and the man who way back in 1940 had launched him on his career, continued to receive honours and in October 1993 he became the first recipient of the R.V. Jones Intelligence Award. The ceremony was held at the CIA headquarters and although Eric Ackermann's name was not mentioned in the lengthy summary of Jones' life and achievements which his proposer, D.C.I. Woolsey gave, it covers almost every aspect of the work which Eric himself was engaged in, and one could almost substitute Eric's name for Dr Jones' in many places.

Eric wrote very few reports or research papers. One of those, mentioned earlier in Chapter 13, appeared in the summer 1961 issue of *Electronic Engineering*, entitled *A master timing unit*, written with J.D. Storer. This journal is a highly prestigious publication and Eric's professional reputation was now firmly established.

In 1979, he collaborated with others in publishing the results of his research in the COMSAT Technical Reviews series of research papers. It was a substantial fifty-three page report and is on a very similar subject as his work with J.D. Storer:

'*Small earth terminals at 12.14 GHz*, by J. Kaiser, L. Veenstra, E. Ackermann, and F. Seidel.

Again the abstract of the paper is too long to reproduce here, but in essence it concerns experiments with a Communications Technology Satellite given the name of HERMES. One of the experiments was on remote interpretation between a United Nations conference in Buenos Aires and the UN headquarters in New York. Another experiment explored the feasibility of synchronizing two precision master clocks via satellite.

The only other paper we have discovered was in the Italian journal *Alta Frequenza*, when in 1979 he was joint author of a short report, the full reference of which is:

'*Preliminary results of propagation measurements in the eastern U.S. using the SIRIO satellite.*

'Authors: R.E. Marshall, S.O. Lane, S.M. Babula, P. Santaga, E.G. Ackermann.

'Affiliation: Virginia Polytechnic Institute and State University, Va. The research was sponsored by the International Telecommunication Satellite Organization.

'The abstract says: "In this paper there are briefly described the equipment to receive SIRIO SHF signals, used by Virginia Polytechnic Institute and State University in Blacksburg, Virginia, together with COMSAT Labs, under INSTELSAT Research and Development sponsorship. Some preliminary results are given."'

Chapter Fifteen

The Family Man

Eric's younger son Nick has remembered his father in these words:

'By the time I first formed any awareness of what my father was doing when he wasn't at home, he was already a Wing Commander at RAF Watton. [Nick was born in 1957, the year before the family left Germany.] Although Dad was no longer living in Germany when I got to know him, I think part of his heart always remained there. He and Mum routinely employed a sprinkling of German words in our domestic life. It's easy to imagine that he formed an attachment to Germany not unlike the one famously formed by T.E. Lawrence to Arabia.'

He goes on to say that although he knew that his father's work was concerned with signals, questions as to what he actually did brought the vague answer 'Scientist'. He remembers too that Eric, 'made no secret of his contempt for people who leaked official secrets'. He did talk about the science of signals and was, 'always ready to explain electronic theory, and I clearly remember him teaching me the workings of a cathode ray tube when I was about eight. Other kids talked with their dads about rugby scores or cricket matches, while we talked about the conversion from watts to horsepower to foot-pounds-per-second, or Boltzmann's constant, or how many volts of potential difference are required to break down an inch of dry air.' Eric's heroes were not sports or film stars, but men of science like Barnes Wallis, Guglielmo Marconi, Nikola Tesla (a pioneer of wireless communication), Robert Goddard (builder of the world's first liquid-fuelled rocket), Werner von Braun (closely involved in the V1 and V2 and later the American manned space program) and of course Winston Churchill, not a man of science himself, but someone who understood its value. R.V. Jones could justifiably be added to the list.

Nick remembers that Eric, '…continually stressed to us the importance of scholastic achievement, diligent study and hard work as the route to a successful and fulfilling life. When we would embark together on some task that needed to be done, he would invariably say "Right. We've got a job of WORK to do!" He deplored people who shirked their duty, or were given to idleness, branding them 'layabouts'. The worst thing you could do was to turn into a layabout. On the other hand, he often praised people who had, in his words, 'pulled themselves up by their own bootstraps'. Eric was always doing something, building a workshop, a brick wall, a shed, a fence, and even a boat, something which he had already done while at Obernkirchen in the 1950s. He would not have understood the attraction of lounging in an easy chair watching television.

Eric took his sons to the cinema, mainly to see historical films, such as *Young Winston* and *Gordon of Khartoum*, or the all action *The Blue Max*. For lighter relief he enjoyed Gilbert and Sullivan and took the family to see a number of their comic operas. Christmas and birthday presents were often something scientific like a chemistry set, microscope, or transparent models of car engines, or human anatomy.

He encouraged active recreation, cycling and walking, though not apparently, sport, in which Eric never showed much interest.

Nick reckons by present-day standards, his father, 'might have been viewed as a disciplinarian, but in comparison to the strict upbringing he experienced, he showed us great tolerance and generosity. It's my belief that a large part of the reason that he went to such lengths to secure and retain an American posting, was his conviction that the American school system would feed and encourage our educational progress more than the system then in effect in the UK'.

Another reason for the attraction of America stemmed from his post-war visits there while he was in Germany and indeed from meeting Americans during the war. 'It was an American GI who taught my mother her first words in English: "Goddam Limey!", or possibly, as she would never have taken God's name in vain, just "Damn Limey!" The gist of both versions is much the same!' Eric and Marianna were keen on American country and western music and took every opportunity to immerse themselves in American culture and travel widely in their adopted country, taking their sons with them.

The Ackermanns were a religious family and went to church every week. Nick writes: 'I believe Dad had it strongly enforced on him when he was young, but in our

Eric in 1979, aged 60.

Marianna.

family I sensed that my mother was the main source of religious will. It's almost as if they had agreed that he would indoctrinate us with science while my mother took the lead role in religious/spiritual motivation'. Certainly Eric's own parents were deeply religious and had the same sense of duty and hard work which he inherited and passed on to his own children.

Peter, being five years older than Nick, has clearer memories of his early childhood in Germany. He recalls that his father had two boats, a motor cruiser and a large sailing boat, probably the one on which Mervyn Williams had done so much work some years earlier. His recollections give a good idea of the life of a child of a service family in Germany in the 1950s. They also tell us a great deal about Eric's devotion to his family. He was strict but fair and made sure his sons followed his own precept of hard work and then constructive play, though leavened with plenty of enjoyable activities. Peter has provided this collage of his memories:

'Remembering the big house at Obernkirchen, the garden, chasing a goose and asking the cook for the big knife to kill it. I had to use my pedal car to pin the poor bird up against a wire fence while I went for reinforcements (the cook).

'Of Dad giving me the pedal car. An American jeep, but painted in RAF colours, complete with RAF roundel on the bonnet.

'The accident to his father's big Opel Kapitan and the later arrival of his next car, a big blue Mercedes. [Peter does not mention the Packard which Eric must have got rid of some time earlier.]

'Recalling an RAF car and driver taking me to school and then at school my favourite teacher, a young woman who had a Mercedes Benz convertible sports car.

'Seeing him at the end of the dining room table in uniform. Being quiet and fearful of him.

'Vague memories of riding in the lead RAF snowplough when Dad took pity on the local villagers and authorized the ploughing of the main roads by the RAF ploughs.'

Peter also remembers Scharfoldendorf:

'riding my bicycle through the camp and past the motor pool with all the smells of diesel fuel and paint on the trucks. Then on towards the fields and forest to where the sheep grazed and the shepherds were tending to them. Talking with the shepherds.

'Climbing down through the back garden with my mother and further down the steep hills to the valley below. Remembering the smell of the forest and seeing the big outcropping of rocks.'

The boys' education was always very important to Eric, and Peter remembers something he used to say to his sons: 'Until I see you with a wet towel wrapped around your forehead, you're not working hard enough'. Eric's disappointment when he failed his 11-plus was entirely predictable. 'For Dad this was virtually my death sentence.' Maybe Peter's failure brought back the pain of his own similar experience more than twenty years earlier. This disaster occurred when the family was back in England and were living in Hampshire, Eric having left the RAF by that time and moved house twice as well, with the consequent inevitable disruption to Peter's education.

More happily, Eric had a beautiful custom-built house at Watton. His father built the garage, workshop and greenhouse, and also made some of their own furniture, using glue which he made himself in a pot which had to be plugged into AC to make it liquid. One day Eric took his son to work with him and he remembered the sound of the electronics humming away, and he let him climb into one of the Lincoln aircraft at the base. Eric was also a keen gardener, making rose gardens for Marianna and cultivating his vegetable garden and showing Peter how to dig a trench with care and precision.

Down at Highcliffe in Hampshire, Peter went to Gore Road Secondary Modern School and he felt that this was an embarrassment to his father. His eldest son was not going to Grammar School and Peter 'always had the strong impression that I never did, nor could I ever hope to win his acceptance or recognition. That I would never measure up'. Nevertheless, his father did approve of Peter joining the Sea Cadets, believing that he would eventually join the Royal Navy, provided that he went in as what Peter calls, 'an enlisted sailor and not as an officer, i.e. strictly second class'.

There were family holidays to Devonshire and to the Isle of Wight, where Peter and Nick's uncle and aunt were living. They also went each year to the south of France in the Mercedes, towing their caravan, as well as to Paris and once to Linz in Austria to see Marianna's sister Georgina and her husband Paul.

In 1967, the family was uprooted again and Peter had to leave the Sea Cadets with great reluctance as he was doing well and had been steadily promoted (reaching Able Seaman 3rd class, three levels up from his starting point). He also had to leave behind the new boat which he and Eric had built together. America was very different, but as this is Eric's story and not really that of his sons, the details can be omitted. Eric himself was now working for the British Embassy in Washington DC, but the job did not appeal to him all that much and his motive seems mainly to have been to get his sons a better education than he felt they could have in Britain.

Eric brought up his sons very much in the manner of his time and made sure that they got a good start in life, even if it meant moving them to another country. They certainly had a more varied childhood than most children would ever experience and the loss of their father, while still only middle-aged, affected them greatly.

Chapter Sixteen

A Full and Useful Life

Eric Ackermann died while still only in late middle age and before he could enjoy much time in retirement. Not, as it seems from his frantically active life, that he would have been content to sit by the fire in his slippers. The best tribute to his astonishing career was paid in R.V. Jones' letter to Peter in January 1990, quoted in the dedication to this book. He came from a relatively humble background and appears to have had no more than a routine technical education at Southall Technical College, but by demonstrating his abilities and also through his persuasive personality, was taken onto the staff of the Telecommunications Research Establishment. He attracted the attention of another man who 'made the world tick', Dr Reginald V. Jones.

The decision to grant him an honorary commission in the Royal Air Force was an early turning point in his life, but not even he could have foreseen that he would stay in the air force for more than twenty years, and achieve four promotions to finish as a Wing Commander. After some controversy, he was awarded the George Medal, one of the highest awards for courage available to a civilian, for that is what, to the purists at the War Office and the Air Ministry, he always was. The controversy was not about his qualifications for a medal, but about the category of medal, and after considerable toing and froing at a high level, the GM it was.

Then came two of his most extraordinary exploits, Blizna in 1944 and Ried in 1946. The first ended abruptly, at least as far as Eric was concerned, but the second was a resounding success and one which brought a commendation from the Commander-in-Chief himself.

Eric was not even halfway through his RAF career by the end of the war and he stayed in the RAF for another fifteen years, having been instrumental in setting up the RAF's ground based signals intelligence network in Germany and Austria, before returning to the United Kingdom in 1959 to conclude his time in uniform. He was then 42-years-old and after a few years in England he emigrated with his family to the United States to continue his career, further developing communications systems until retirement and premature death at the age of sixty-six. Despite living in America for nearly twenty years he retained his British citizenship and apparently never sought naturalization as an American citizen.

Eric Ackermann is an unknown hero, an RAF officer of whom most people seem never to have heard, and who is scarcely known, even within the air force itself. Not a fighter pilot nor a member of a bomber aircrew, and with his more conventional service years being spent in charge of an obscure unit in a remote part of Germany, almost everything he did was in the shadows, which by its very nature precluded publicity.

So secret was it that even today some of the key records which would surely provide more vital information about him remain closed for reasons of national security. His achievements were substantial, recognized by the continued support of Reginald Jones and above all by the award of the George Medal. Maybe this book and the following event will go some way towards giving him the acknowledgement he richly deserves.

This is not quite the end of the story, because on 6 October 2012, on what would have been Eric Ackermann's ninety-third birthday, the Disabled American Veterans (DAV), Stonewall Jackson Chapter #9, Winchester, Virginia, held a memorial tribute to him at his graveside in St. Joseph's Cemetery in Emmitsburg.

It came about through the initiative of Mr Chance Bazzano, Commander of the Winchester Chapter and a long-time friend of the Ackermann family. With the wholehearted support of Peter and Nick, Eric's sons, and Judith, Peter's wife, Chance went ahead with the arrangements. The ceremony took place in the company of Eric's family, friends and former colleagues, Wing Commander Al Morrow from the British Embassy in Washington DC, representatives of the DAV, the American Legion and the Veterans of Foreign Wars. The Mayor of Emmitsburg, Mr Don Briggs, represented the town where Eric spent his final years, and Peter Jackson, co-author of this book, was also present.

This was a military ceremony, with an Honor Guard firing a 21-gun salute, and a bugler playing TAPS. The Chaplain of the Winchester Chapter, Mr Tom Coyle, led the party in readings and prayers, and Wing Commander Morrow paid tribute to a fellow officer. Other tributes were paid by Nick Ackermann, remembering his brave and inspirational father, the Mayor of Emmitsburg, and Peter Jackson, who recalled the story of researching Eric's life and finding out more and more about an extraordinary man. Peter, Eric's elder son, could not be there – he is currently serving his country as a scientist on an American air base in Thailand.

So, more than twenty-six years after Eric's death, a proper tribute was paid at last, due entirely to the efforts of his family and the loyalty and staunch friendship of Chance Bazzano and his fellow veterans.

The DAV Virginia symbol and motto. Its members organized the ceremony on 6 October 2012 to pay tribute to Eric Ackermann in St. Joseph's Cemetery, Emmitsburg, Maryland.

The official party: left to right: Wing Commander Alan Morrow, Mrs Zena Bazzano, Mr John Smith (DAV Chapter Adjutant), Commander Chance Bazzano, Mr Ernie Sanders (Officer of the Day), Mr Peter Jackson, Mr Tom Coyle (Chapter Chaplain).

The official party with Mrs Judith Ackermann and Mr Nicholas Ackermann standing in front of the table.

Nick Ackermann paying tribute to his father.

Mr Peter Jackson address the audience.

Wing Commander Alan Morrow.

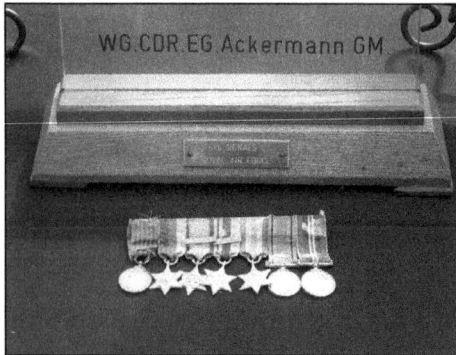

Eric Ackermann's medals and his desk plate from RAF Obernkirchen.

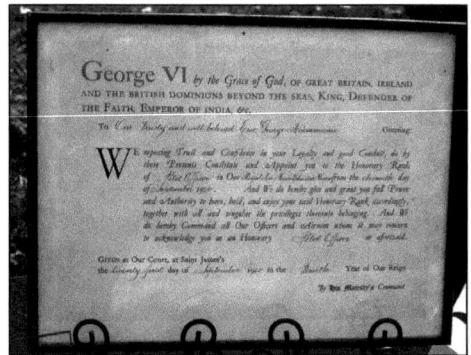

The document granting Eric Ackermann an honorary commission in the Royal Air Force.

Eric and Marianna's graves in the military section of St. Joseph's Cemetery.

A Royal British Legion poppy cross placed at Eric's grave.

The Honor Guard fires the salute.

Bibliography

Primary sources
Imperial War Museum archives
Liddell Hart Military Archive, King's College, London
National Archives, Kew, London
Purbeck Radar Museum Trust
R.V. Jones Archive at Churchill College, Cambridge
Reminiscences of those who knew Eric Ackermann in the United Kingdom, Germany and
the United States of America

Libraries consulted
Bodleian Library, Oxford
British Library
Churchill College, Cambridge
Oxfordshire County Library
Royal Air Museum, Hendon

Printed sources
Aid, Matthew and Wiebes, Cees, editors, *Secrets of signals intelligence during the Cold War and beyond*. Frank Cass. 2001.
Aldrich, J. *The hidden hand: Britain, America and the Cold War: secret intelligence*. John Murray. 2001.
Aldrich, Richard. *GCHQ: the uncensored story of Britain's most secret intelligence agency*. Harper. 2010.
Booker, Squadron Leader Stanley. *Life in the shadows*. Proceedings of the Royal Air Force Historical Society, No. 29, 2003, pp. 62–75.
Brettingham, Laurie. *Royal Air Force beam bombers: 80 (Signals) Wing*. Midland. 1997.
Clayton, Aileen. *The enemy is listening*. Hutchinson. 1980.
Cumming, David. *Beam benders: the secret war of 109 Squadron*. Sutton. 1998.
De Groot, Gerald. *The bomb: a life*. Cape. 2004.
Elliott, Geoffrey. *Secret classrooms: an untold story of the Cold War*. St. Ermin's Press. 2002.
Foot, M.R.D. and Langley, J.M. *M.I.9: escape and evasion: the story of M.I.9*. Bodley Head. 1979.
Goldberg, Sidney. *The other story of the RAF 'Y service*. Proceedings of the Royal Air Force Historical Society, No. 12, 1994, pp. 31–36.
Haysom, David. *The story of the secret signals unit*. Privately published. 2001.
Hinsley, F.H. *British intelligence in the Second World War: its influence on strategy and operations*. HMSO. 3 vols. 1979–1990.

Jackson, Peter. *Hambühren, Lower Saxony: a military history 1939–1999*. Privately published. 2001.

Jackson, Peter: *Royal Air Force Uetersen: the story of an unusual station*. Privately published. 2005.

Jefferson, S. *Radar at Worth Matravers and Swanage*. 15pp. Purbeck Radar Museum Trust. 1990.

Jefford, Wing Commander C.G. *RAF squadrons*. 2nd ed. Airlife. 2001.

Johnson, Brian. *The secret war*. BBC. 1978.

Jones, R.V. *The intelligence war and the Royal Air Force*. Proceedings of the Royal Air Force Historical Society, No. 1, 1987, pp. 8–25.

Jones, R.V. *Most secret war: British scientific intelligence 1939–1945*. Hamish Hamilton. 1978.

Jones, R.V. *Reflections on intelligence*. Heinemann. 1989.

Latham, Colin and Stobbs, Ann. *Pioneers of radar*. Sutton. 1999.

Millar, George. *The Bruneval Raid: stealing Hitler's radar*. Cassell. 2002.

Penley, Jonathan and Penley, Dr W.H. *Secret war in Purbeck*. Purbeck Radar Museum Trust. 2009.

Penley, Dr W.H. and Batt, R.G. *Dorset's radar days: the British radar story, 1935–1942*. Purbeck Radar Museum Trust. 1994. 42pp.

Penley, Dr W.H. *The early days of radar in the UK*: notes dated 11 October 1993 for a talk to local organizations about the R and D work done in Purbeck for the RAF from May 1940 to May 1942.

Price, A. *Instruments of darkness: the history of electronic warfare, 1939–1945*. Greenhill. 2005.

Richards, Denis and Sanders, Hilary St. George. *Royal Air Force, 1939–1945*. 3 vols. HMSO. 1974.

Rowe, A.P. *Our story of radar*, Cambridge University Press. 1948.

Taylor, Group Captain Bill. *Royal Air Force Germany since 1945*. Midland. 2003.

Wigglesworth, Air Marshal Sir Philip W. *Dissolution of the Luftwaffe: the work of the British Air Forces of Occupation (Germany)*. HMSO. 1947 (republished 1995).

Wood, Derek. *The narrow margin: the Battle of Britain and the rise of air power, 1930–1940*. Pen and Sword. 2003.

Zimmerman, David. *Britain's shield: radar and the defeat of the Luftwaffe*. New ed. Amberley. 2010

Air Force Lists, 1940–1960

Army Lists, 1939–1945.

British Imperial Calendar and Civil Service Lists, 1950–1965.

Internet sources: a brief selection

Ackermann, Karen. The Ackermann genealogical website.

Royal Air Force and other military websites.

Wikipedia.

Index